The Labor Process and Control of Labor

THE LABOR PROCESS AND CONTROL OF LABOR

The Changing Nature of Work Relations in the Late Twentieth Century

Edited by
Berch Berberoglu

PRAEGER
Westport, Connecticut
London

Library of Congress Cataloging-in-Publication Data

The Labor process and control of labor : the changing nature of work relations in the late twentieth century / edited by Berch Berberoglu.

p. cm.

Includes bibliographical references and index.

ISBN 0-275-94459-X (alk. paper)

1. Industrial relations—United States. 2. Industrial sociology—United States. 3. Division of labor. 4. Working class—United States. 5. Industrial relations. 6. Industrial sociology. 7. Working class. I. Berberoglu, Berch.

HD8072.5.L32 1993

331.25—dc20 92-23976

British Library Cataloguing in Publication Data is available.

Library of Congress Catalog Card Number: 92-23976
ISBN: 0-275-94459-X

First published in 1993

Praeger Publishers, 88 Post Road West, Westport, CT 06881
An imprint of Greenwood Publishing Group, Inc.

Printed in the United States of America

The paper used in this book complies with the Permanent Paper Standard issued by the National Information Standards Organization (Z39.48—1984).

10 9 8 7 6 5 4 3 2 1

Contents

Preface vii

Acknowledgments ix

Introduction
Berch Berberoglu xi

1. Class Formation and Class Capacities: A New Approach to the Study of Labor and the Labor Process
Jerry Lembcke 1

2. The Historical Roots of the Division of Labor in the U.S. Auto Industry
David Gartman 21

3. Transformations in Hierarchy and Control of the Labor Process in the Post-Fordist Era: The Case of the U.S. Steel Industry
Harland Prechel 44

4. The Labor Process and Control of Labor in the U.S. Computer Industry
Navid Mohseni 59

5. Gender and Control over the Labor Process: Women's Power as Wage Earners
Marina A. Adler 78

6. Race, Nationality, and the Division of Labor in U.S. Agriculture: Focus on Farm Workers in California
John C. Leggett 97

7. The Labor Force in Transition: The Growth of the Contingent Work Force in the United States
Robert E. Parker 116

8. Transformations in the Labor Process on a World Scale: Women in the New International Division of Labor
Julia D. Fox 137

9. Transnational Capital, the Global Labor Process, and the International Labor Movement
Cyrus Bina and Chuck Davis 152

10. The Labor Process and Class Struggle: Political Responses to the Control and Exploitation of Labor
Walda Katz-Fishman and Jerome Scott 171

Selected Bibliography 183

Index 193

About the Editor and Contributors 201

Preface

As the twentieth century comes to a close at the end of this decade, the prospects for organized labor in the United States look bleak, and no clear path out of labor's crisis and indeed out of the general crisis of capitalism is envisioned by those who occupy the highest levels of the trade union bureaucracy. The continued deterioration of life under capitalism in the United States is now posing a challenge to the U.S. working class to reverse the decline in influence and position of labor in this country in recent decades, and forge ahead with an independent program of action to fulfill the interests and aspirations of workers throughout this nation.

The development of capitalism and the capitalist labor process in the United States in the late nineteenth and throughout the twentieth century has resulted in control over workers to assure the continued exploitation of labor and the generation of ever higher levels of surplus value, which constitutes the very basis of the accumulation of capital under the capitalist system. This process of control and exploitation of labor has developed and matured during the past century in line with the growth and development of capitalism in the United States from its competitive to monopoly stages in all major sectors of industry across the domestic and now the world economy.

An examination of the nature and dynamics of the labor process in various sectors of the U.S. economy—from auto to steel to computers to agriculture to services—would provide us with the necessary insight to an understanding of the nature of work relations at the point of production. Such relations, which are at base a manifestation of larger, capitalist relations of production (i.e., class relations), become evident in their social form as workers confront capital and capitalist management who extract from them an evergrowing amount of profits. It is in this context of the struggle between labor and capital at the point of production that we begin also to see the class nature of this struggle to maintain or to transform the prevailing relations of production—a struggle that in its broader *class* context becomes a *political* struggle, a struggle for state power. The balance of forces in this class struggle beyond point-of-production work relations translates into a struggle for preservation or transformation of the capitalist system itself.

It is for a clear understanding of the labor process and control of labor under capitalist production relations at the point of production—a process that explains the structure of work relations within the context of broader class forces in late twentieth-century capitalism—that this project was conceived and carried out with the collective participation of the contributors of this volume. The ten chapters prepared exclusively for this book thus involved the intellectual labor of a dedicated group of progressive academics and activists who, deeply concerned with the condition of labor and its prospects, have expended much time and effort to expose the inner logic of capitalist production, with the hope that such understanding of the underlying processes at work in our economy and society can be utilized by those on the side of labor to effect positive change toward the ultimate transformation of capitalist society into a social order based on the power of labor.

Acknowledgments

A project of this nature is the result of a truly collective effort involving the diligent work of many dedicated people. I would like to thank, first and foremost, all the contributors to this volume for their participation in this project and for producing excellent original pieces of research and analysis commissioned especially for this book, which I hope will make a valuable contribution to labor studies in the United States. My thanks go to Jerry Lembcke, Robert Parker, Navid Mohseni, and David Gartman for their prompt response and for undertaking the necessary work on the project in a timely manner. I would also like to thank Harland Prechel and Marina Adler for their early contributions to the volume and for their patience during the course of the publication process. Walda Katz-Fishman, Jerome Scott, John Leggett, Julia Fox, Cyrus Bina, and Chuck Davis have all provided important contributions under the stress of time pressures and have given me the necessary editorial freedom in the preparation of their respective essays for this volume.

Over the past two decades, friends and colleagues at the University of Oregon, Central Michigan University, State University of New York at Binghamton, and the University of Nevada, Reno, have played an important role in the formation of my views on society and the labor process as expressed in the overall content and organization of this book. In this context, Larry Reynolds, Blain Stevenson, James Petras, Paul Sweezy, and Albert Szymanski have played a central role in the maturation of these views. Marty Hart-Landsberg, Jim Salt, Karl Kreplin, David Harvey, Lyle Warner, Johnson Makoba, and many others have taken part in discussions on labor and the labor process, as they have on other issues of social importance. I thank all those directly or indirectly involved in this wider process of intellectual development, with my appreciation of their important role.

I would also like to thank Anne Kiefer, my editor at Praeger, for her continued support and confidence in my work; it is truly a great pleasure to work with an editor who makes the publication process a very pleasant experience.

Finally, this book could not have been made possible without the working people themselves, who constitute the subject matter of this study. This work, therefore, is dedicated to the workers of the United States and of other countries around the world.

Introduction

Berch Berberoglu

As we enter the final decade of the twentieth century, the maturing contradictions of late capitalism—which have been developing with great speed throughout this century—are beginning to surface in a variety of forms and are calling into question the process of capital accumulation that has affected the control and exploitation of labor in the United States for nearly 200 years.

It is no secret that U.S. capitalism is now in deep crisis. Although the changes at work in the U.S. economy and society have their roots in earlier decades when the consolidation of U.S. monopoly power began to take hold on a world scale, the transformation of the labor process through automation and high technology on the one hand, and the internationalization of capital and the restructuring of the international division of labor on the other, has effected changes in work relations at the point of production—relations that are a manifestation of broader social relations of production between labor and capital. In the struggle between the two contending class forces that characterize the nature of the production process in capitalist society, the control and exploitation of labor are the dual motive forces of capitalist domination that assure its continued growth and expansion. Although the logic of capitalist development from its earlier competitive to its later monopoly stage has ushered in the twin processes of automation and worldwide expansion, which have brought, simultaneously, the growth of transnational monopolies and decline of the U.S. domestic economy, and thus effected certain transformations in the labor force structure, labor process, and work relations at the point of production in a variety of productive settings, the nature of capitalism is such that to rescue itself from the crisis, capital must further intensify the control and exploitation of labor. This obviously worsens the contradictory process of capital accumulation set into motion by the very forces that have effected the crisis. Therein lies the dialectical nature of the process based on control and exploitation of labor that is the hallmark of the capitalist system.

Under capitalism, the intensification of the exploitative process at the point of production has meant the continuation of the struggle between labor and capital during the course of its development, but the contours of the specific nature and forms of control have varied from one industry or economic sector to another, as well as across national, regional, and international boundaries. Thus, the labor process and forms of labor control have both historical and spatial dimensions. Although, therefore, an analysis of the historical development of basic industries, such as auto and steel, reveals to us the methods and tools of control utilized by management during the course of capitalist development over the past century, an analysis of the labor process today as it develops in the context of the world economy shows us the varied forms of labor control under conditions of worldwide capitalist production that involves the control and exploitation of labor on a world scale. In this sense, the internationalization of capital and its social component, the internationalization of capitalist relations of production, involving the exploitation of wage labor throughout the world, has ushered in a process of control, exploitation, and repression of labor across national boundaries. The labor process under late capitalism must thus be seen within the context of its global dimensions, but it is one that still manifests itself in determinate national settings. Thus, although the development of capitalism through its competitive and monopoly stages results in its expansion from the national to the global level, its contradictions at the higher, late-monopoly stage unfolding on a world scale affect the process of control and exploitation of labor in its own home base in a contradictory way: Expansion abroad translates into contraction at home and, thus, changes the nature and structure of the labor force, the forms of control, and the nature, rate, and intensity of exploitation in different sectors of the economy.

As the class struggle between labor and capital develops and matures, and as the working class becomes increasingly class conscious and acts on behalf of its own class interests, the central imperative of transformation of the capitalist mode more and more demands a careful study of the nature, mechanisms, and processes of control and exploitation of labor in specific industries, sectors, and segments of the economy and work force.

The ten chapters included in this book, which were prepared especially for this volume, address these questions in varied historical, sectoral, spatial, and topical contexts, examining many of the issues central to the changing nature of work relations, the labor process, and control of labor in the United States in the late twentieth century.

The opening chapter by Jerry Lembcke examines a number of critical issues that confront labor and the labor process in the United States. First, providing a critical review of U.S. labor studies over the past two decades, Lembcke argues that although the volume of work on the labor process mounted during the 1970s and 1980s, the crisis of the U.S. working class deepened; the inability of labor studies to inform the strategy of a revitalized working-class movement, Lembcke argues, lies in the theoretical and methodological choices made by labor process scholars. To the fragmentation currently characteristic of dominant approaches in labor studies, Lembcke's chapter counterposes an alternative analysis based on class as a relational phenomenon—a new, class-capacities approach to labor studies that captures the nature and role of labor in the class structure. Adopting such an approach, Lembcke opts for an analysis that understands class capacities as having inter- as well as intraclass dimensions, recognizes the historical and spatial dimensions of class power, and comprehends the dialectical relationship between social relations and class consciousness.

Addressing the tough questions around which post–World War II labor politics revolved, Lembcke then examines some key issues that confront workers in the United States today: plant closings, decline in union membership, drop in living standards, automation and deskilling, level of class consciousness and political organization, and the role of the family, unions, and other mediating forces in the formation and transformation of labor and the labor process. Lembcke's essay thus sets the stage for more detailed class-based analyses of the nature, dynamics, and contradictions of the labor process in different historical, spatial, and organizational settings in twentieth-century capitalist production.

In this spirit, David Gartman next takes up the study of the labor process in the U.S. auto industry, which at the turn of the century set the stage for mass production of goods that gave a boost to capitalist expansion reaching far beyond the auto industry. Gartman examines the historical origins of a fundamental aspect of the mass-production labor process—the minute division of labor. Tracing its origins in the all-important U.S. auto industry, he finds that this was not a neutral technique instituted merely to increase the efficiency of labor. Rather, the fragmentary division of labor introduced by Henry Ford and others in the mass production of automobiles was part of a larger political agenda to shift the control of the labor process away from powerful skilled craft workers and toward managers themselves.

The early craft process of producing automobiles, Gartman explains, left a great deal of discretion in the hands of skilled assemblers and machinists, who used it to struggle against their own exploitation. This powerful resistance prevented managers from increasing the intensity of labor sufficiently to mass produce cars. In order to overcome this class resistance, early auto managers divided the unitary crafts of auto production into a plethora of unskilled fragments. This minute division of labor not only made jobs easier to fill, hence reducing the power of workers in the labor market, but it also reduced the power of workers in the production process by giving managers greater control over the quantity and quality of labor.

The class struggle, however, was not completely eliminated in the auto industry by this transformation of the labor process, Gartman argues. Although the division of labor and subsequent changes, like the moving assembly line, undermined the individual power of craft workers, they ironically increased the collective power of the new industrial labor force. With this new power, auto workers were able to force their employers to recognize their union and bargain collectively. The strength of employers, however, soon confined bargaining to the narrow issues of wages and benefits, leaving the basic structure of the labor process untouched.

Recently, Gartman points out, renewed class struggles and international competition have forced automobile managers to reassess the benefits of the fragmented division of labor; they have instituted new programs of job enlargement and worker participation that give workers more responsibility in the labor process. A close examination of these programs, however, reveals them to constitute no fundamental threat to the balance of power on the industrial battlefield. They are but modest attempts to win greater identification of workers with the firm and greater managerial flexibility in the use of labor. In reality, Gartman concludes, these are but revised tactics to achieve the long-term managerial objective of greater control over labor and the labor process in the U.S. auto industry.

Harland Prechel's chapter on labor control in the steel industry demonstrates how the application of the post-Fordist model further centralized control, and made it possible to eliminate several layers of management and reduce the decision-making authority of lower and middle managers in an American steel corporation. This recent change in the corporation was top management's response to contradictions and inefficiency within the Fordist mode of control that emerged as a crisis of accumulation in the early 1980s.

Prechel points out that there are three dimensions of post-Fordism that contribute to the centralization of control. First, technical controls (e.g., computer systems) make it possible to incorporate production guidelines directly into the manufacturing process. Second, bureaucratic controls are specified in more detail. Whereas more precise rules are established to identify the manager or production worker responsible for a specific cost, premise controls stipulate guidelines governing the decisions made by these organizational members. Third, budgetary controls compare the actual specific manufacturing cost to predetermined costs. If managers fail to follow the rules governing the manufacturing process, the new budgetary/cost controls simultaneously identify the location of the subsequent cost variation and the manager responsible for that cost.

The emergence of post-Fordism has far-reaching implications for the distribution of authority. In addition to extending more precise control over production workers, post-Fordism demands that lower and middle level managers base their decisions on criteria established in decision centers, redefines the traditional responsibilities of lower and middle level managers, and reduces their decision-making autonomy. In contrast to Taylorist and Fordist modes of control, which require extensive managerial hierarchies and the allocation of decision-making authority to lower and middle managers, post-Fordism reduces these managerial hierarchies and simultaneously establishes formal controls that ensure managers adhere to standardized decision-making criteria. These efforts to eliminate costs and thereby increase the rate of accumulation project the corporation toward a higher level of mechanization, standardization, and centralization of authority.

Prechel's analysis is in contrast to arguments that suggest recent changes in the corporation have resulted in the decentralization of decision-making authority based on work teams, cooperative decision making, and participation on the shop floor. Prechel demonstrates that although cooperative decision making has been encouraged in recent corporate restructuring, the definition of an "appropriate decision" is predetermined within the centralized decision-making bodies. Cooperation, therefore, must be understood as the process of establishing a means of coordination and control under the centralized authority of top management, who, when faced with competition, progressively tighten the authority structures and control mechanisms within the work place. Although the layers of management within post-Fordism declined, the authority structures became more formalized and centralized to ensure cooperation. Moreover, these post-Fordist controls placed lower and middle managers at a greater distance from the decision-making centers, while providing the organizational capacity to increase surveillance over them.

Prechel demonstrates that the mode of control in the steel industry is being redefined in such a way that it centralizes control and authority, while decentralizing responsibility for decisions. He concludes that the one-sided presentation of corporate strategies based on work teams, cooperative decision making, and participation on the shop floor masks the basic relation of domination and subordination that necessarily prevails when centralized controls are implemented. Rather than allocating authority, post-Fordist controls result in a significant decline in autonomy of both traditional production workers and lower and middle management.

Navid Mohseni, in his chapter on the labor process in the U.S. computer industry, examines the commodification of creativity under monopoly capitalism and its implications for control of the labor process in this important sector of the capitalist economy. He argues that the early development of computers was the result of the need of government and business to speed up data processing and analysis. Later, however, the contradictions of monopoly capitalism manifested through overaccumulation of capital and the imposition of Taylorism created the conditions for the expansion of the computer industry. This occurred through the commodification of creativity, which has been the source of innovation of new generations of computers.

Mohseni goes on to point out that, being lured by the high returns on their investment that every new generation of computers has yielded, companies expanded their research and development departments hoping to increase their monopoly profits. However, the expansion of R&D departments in large corporations and their reliance on technological rent (or monopoly profits) have created new contradictions in capitalist production that are manifested in the nature of control of the labor process.

Mohseni examines the nature of this control by focusing on both the labor process (at the point of production) and the creative process (the work of the engineers, scientists, and programmers) in the computer industry. He explicates the way in which the creative process and the labor process are connected and complement each other as they both come under increased control by management. Thus, generating its own contradiction, this dual process provides the potential common ground for class solidarity between manual workers and knowledge workers.

Marina Adler's chapter on gender and the labor process explores the position of women in the workplace. She points out that although women make up almost half of the American work force, they continue to be in a disadvantaged position *vis-à-vis* working men. Both occupational segregation and the traditional gender division of labor are perpetuated by the organization of work in modern capitalism.

One consequence of the interaction of capitalist and patriarchal structures, Adler argues, is the fact that women are less likely than men to have control over the labor process. Moreover, in addition to the inequalities arising from the labor process, gender and race divide workers into different jobs and activities. This selection process ranks "gendered" tasks by their importance, resources, and remuneration. Since "women's work" has been historically undervalued, women retain less control over their work environment than men. In empirical terms, this means that women have less supervisory capacity, less decision-making power, and less job autonomy than men. Consequently, women may more likely be alienated than men.

Adler points out that research on gender, occupational segregation, and power reveals that there is a persistent income and authority gap by gender, which is related to the class and occupational structure of society. Women are overrepresented in occupations with lower average incomes than men's. Overall, Adler concludes, although both men and women have relatively little control over the labor process, in terms of organizational decision making, supervisory activities, and autonomy, women have significantly less control at work than men.

Race, nationality, and the division of labor in California agriculture is the topic of the chapter that follows. Here John Leggett focuses on farm workers in California's San Joaquin, Imperial, and Coachella valleys. Providing an intimate history of the diverse national origins of the work force in California agriculture from earlier periods to the present, Leggett examines the division of labor in commercial farming in great detail and describes the multilayered relationship between the growers, the farm labor contractors, the crew chiefs, and the farm workers in the fields.

Given the race and national dimensions of farm labor in U.S. agriculture, historically and today, Leggett insists that one cannot comprehend the division of labor, the labor process, and the superexploitation and control of a segment of the working class lodged in corporate agriculture without a clear understanding of the structural underpinnings of racial and national domination that have persisted in California agriculture ever since the expansion of white settlements, which began in the early nineteenth century. Although the racial and national origins of successive generations of local and immigrant labor have changed over the decades, Leggett concludes, the cruel forms of labor control practiced by a small number of wealthy white growers through their intermediaries on the land have been a constant feature of the lives of farm workers who labor under conditions of modern-day servitude that is the hallmark of the division of labor in U.S. agriculture.

Next, Robert Parker examines a recent development in the U.S. economy and labor force structure—the emergence and growth of the contingent work force. Contingent workers are employees who have a loose affiliation with their employers. As the 1990s began, between one-quarter and one-third of all U.S. workers were a part of the contingent work force. Examples of contingent workers include temporary workers (the fastest growing category), part-time workers, and subcontracting workers (usually employed by business service firms). All of these categories are growing much faster than the U.S. labor force as a whole. Parker points out that although some workers choose a contingent working status (often for family or other personal reasons), a large and growing percentage of these workers are finding contingent positions to be their only option as U.S. corporations continue to restructure their operations to meet challenges presented by international competition and domestic economic crisis.

The contingent work force, whether in the core or peripheral sector of the U.S. economy, is demographically distinctive. Disproportionately, it is composed of the young, the elderly, minorities, and most frequently, women. The transition to an increasingly contingent work force, Parker argues, provides American businesses with greater flexibility and other benefits, but it has a number of negative effects for American workers, including lower wages, reduced health care protection, the loss of pension and retirement benefits, and a general decline in their standard of living. Parker's chapter provides an overview of these and other related developments that affect contingent workers who are now becoming a growing segment of the U.S. labor force.

The international ramifications of the move toward a contingent, low-wage labor force that increases flexibility and profits are examined next by Julia Fox. In her chapter on the new international division of labor, Fox attempts to address the strategic question of why Third World women have been recruited and integrated into the global capital accumulation process. She develops a theoretical framework that incorporates both the international division of labor, as an outgrowth of the exigencies of capital accumulation on a world scale, and a more concrete analysis of work relations at the point of production on a national level. Within this framework, Fox focuses on the labor process in three countries (South Korea, the Philippines, and Mexico) to analyze how the specific conditions of a labor-intensive investment strategy—export processing—require the use of the cheapest and most controlled segments of labor, and hence, at the national level, how four major conditions (patriarchy, bureaucratic control of work, repressive labor policies, and low levels of unionization of women) combine to produce the cheapest and most repressed forms of labor—Third World women.

Fox argues that although the mediation of the political, cultural, social, and organizational dimensions of control make Third World women one of the most exploited segments of the international labor pool, the internal contradictions of this exploitation have created the conditions for more militant forms of resistance in which Filipino, South Korean, and Mexican women are becoming an integral part of the global working-class struggle against transnational capital.

Addressing the political implications of the internationalization of capital and the emerging global labor process, Cyrus Bina and Chuck Davis next raise the level of discussion to the political level, and examine the position and prospects of the international labor movement that is developing in response to the transnationalization of the production process and the expansion of capitalism and capitalist relations of production on a world scale.

Bina and Davis argue that the organized sector of the international labor movement in the advanced capitalist countries has played a traditionally conservative, class-collaborationist role, and failed to confront the challenge posed by the postwar global expansion of U.S. capital and its ramifications for the U.S. domestic economy in the past several decades. In fact, the established conservative trade union bureaucracy led by the AFL-CIO since the 1950s, they argue, has played a reactionary, pro-imperialist and anti-Communist role in advancing the interests of U.S. capital by its consistently supportive posture toward U.S. foreign policy during the cold war years to the present.

Bina and Davis also point out, however, the emergence of new rank-and-file workers' movements that are challenging the entrenched sellout leadership of the current trade union bureaucracy, forging a new unity of workers across national boundaries, and strengthening the bonds of solidarity among workers, which may lay the foundations for the development of a revitalized international labor movement that takes an active role in the class struggle and challenges the power of capital and its political arm, the capitalist state, throughout the world.

Finally, Walda Katz-Fishman and Jerome Scott in the concluding chapter of this volume focus on the relationship among the changing role of labor in capitalist production, the crisis of capitalism, and the political response of the working class to increased control and exploitation of labor. They argue that there has occurred a major change in the labor force structure of the United States over the past several decades, such that traditional machine-based factory production, which constituted the basis of the U.S. manufacturing industry for more than a century, is giving way to computer–automated mass production. This development, coupled with the internationalization of U.S. capital since World War II in search of cheap labor and a more favorable investment climate overseas, has effected a shift toward low-paid service occupations and has led to increased unemployment among a growing segment of the working class—a situation that has become a permanent fixture of contemporary U.S. capitalism. The resulting decline in purchasing power and standard of living of workers who are now consuming less and less of the goods produced in a shrinking market has plunged the U.S. economy into a structural crisis that has ushered in a period of decline and decay, pushing the country to the edge of depression.

Responding to this deteriorating economic situation, U.S. labor has begun to mobilize and take action to reverse the defeat it has suffered under an increased capitalist assault during the past two decades. Documenting this response, Katz-Fishman and Scott survey the various forms of class struggle waged by workers at the point of production and beyond the shop floor, which are manifested in strikes, demonstrations, and other forms of protest and political action.

Together, the ten chapters included in this book make an original and important contribution to the study of labor, the labor process, and work relations in late-twentieth-century capitalism.

1 Class Formation and Class Capacities: A New Approach to the Study of Labor and the Labor Process

Jerry Lembcke

The amount of recent academic work dealing in one way or another with labor history and the labor process is almost as impressive as the length and depth of labor's current crisis. Yet, there is little evidence that the outpouring of work during the last 20 years has produced an analysis capable of changing the course of the labor movement in the United States.

Although students of U.S. labor cannot move forward except by building on the gains made by labor scholars since 1970, neither can we progress without clarity about what remains to be done. In the pages that follow I argue that, although the bulk of the studies done on labor between 1970 and 1990 was carried out by radical historians and political economists, their work was based on assumptions consistent with those of neoclassical economics and pluralist sociology, which dominated the field during the 1950s and 1960s. It is their failure to break with those assumptions, moreover, that has impaired their ability to find a path out of the labor movement's current morass. Now, in the 1990s, the sociology of labor appears to be experiencing a revitalization; in this spirit, I next turn to some recent attempts to create a more dialectical analysis of labor's situation. Of particular importance is the theoretical work focusing on class capacities, and some recent work that explores the relationships between the temporal and spatial dimensions of working class formation. I conclude with some remarks on recent political economic developments affecting labor and the labor movement.

SOCIAL HISTORY AND DEGRADATION OF WORK

In 1970, the editors of *Radical America* heralded the emergence of a new school of historiography.[1] The new trend was characterized by its separation from mainstream "celebrationist" accounts of U.S. history and by its critical posture toward the history of "old left" political practice.

Many of the new radical historians had been or were students of William Appleman Williams at the University of Wisconsin, but it was the British historian E. P. Thompson who had the greatest influence on their development. Thompson's emphasis on the subjective aspects of human history encouraged the framing of historical questions in terms of "shared experiences."[2] The new generation of radical scholars was captivated by the notion that history could be studied as occurring within a cultural context as well as a process that created the symbolic world.

The radicals also mounted a challenge to the mainstream approach of the time, institutionalism. Institutionalism had arisen early in the twentieth century, when the theories of neoclassical economics, rooted as they were in psychological assumptions about human behavior, appeared to be inadequate to deal with the task of understanding monopoly capitalism. Thorstein Veblen and John R. Commons were among those who accorded increased importance to institutions as determinants of political and economic behavior. Commons and his student Selig Perlman took the institutionalist approach into the field of labor history and, until the 1970s, it was the dominant paradigm.[3]

The radicals attacked institutionalism at two levels. The first was the preoccupation of the institutionalists with trade unions as the sole vehicle through which working-class history unfolded and could thus be studied. The followers of Perlman had narrowed the field to the point where the only relationships being studied were the contractual ones, and the only subjects in their accounts were union functionaries, company negotiators, and government arbitrators.[4] The new left scholars rejected these traditional formulations and endeavored to restore workers to a class-conscious part in their own history.

At another level, the attack on institutionalism became a euphemism for criticism of practices identified with certain political tendencies. It was argued that institutions (unions, political parties, etc.) *per se* were prone to conservatism[5] and that the political movements, such as the Communist party, which had emphasized the building of unions and party organizations in their work, had retarded the development of the U.S. working class.[6] In their work, the anti-institutionalists emphasized the place of mass movement, general strikes, spontaneous worker rebellions, and the anarcho-syndicalist traditions in the U.S. working-class experience.[7]

The ability of the social history trend to speak meaningfully to the deepening crisis of the U.S. labor movement of the 1970s was thus limited in several ways. First, its approach compelled questions relevant to the specific historic period when U.S. working-class culture was shaped by the influx of large numbers of immigrants and the heyday periods of anarcho-syndicalist movements, such as the IWW. Second, it had an additive notion of class power based on the "association" of sovereign individuals in the production process. This notion elevated the role of craft and skilled workers in history, and dovetailed with the assumptions of the "degradation of labor" school of political economy.[8] Third, its disdain for certain political traditions sometimes led to contemptuous treatment of important organizations and to sectarian interpretations of critical turning points in U.S. labor history. Moreover, by equating working-class capacity with control of production, the trend toward deskilling, which accompanied the development of monopoly capitalism in the twentieth century, was difficult for social historians to deal with dialectically; the fact that masses of lesser skilled, industrial workers, not the craft and skilled workers, had been at the forefront of the battles of the 1930s was difficult to interpret. All of these traits made it difficult for radical historians to examine effectively the period most relevant to the needs of contemporary labor activists: the period of the CIO, 1935–1956.

In other words, the shift away from an institutional analysis also shifted attention away from a specific historical period when the institutions were clearly the locus of labor history, and it refocused our attention on time periods leading up to the formation of unions and/or the very early years of organized labor—the late nineteenth and early twentieth centuries. Embedded in the *method* of anti-institutionalism then was the political consequence that its adherents were able to avoid confronting head on the anti-communism of the postwar labor establishment and the anti-Communist bias of academic labor historians. In that respect, the new social labor history provided an ideological escape hatch for academics. As the 1980s proceeded and the crisis of the labor movement deepened, labor historians retreated further and further into the nineteenth and eighteenth centuries, endlessly producing case studies having less and less to do with the pressing issues facing the labor movement today.

The shift in focus produced by the anti-institutionalist trend had two other consequences. One was that it elevated the importance of craft and skilled workers, versus twentieth-century industrial workers, as agents of social change under capitalism. Another was that the prominence given to craft and skilled workers by the social historians carried with it implications for our analyses of the objective capacities to make social change. The latter question, about the relative capacity of skilled versus less-skilled workers to make change, was at the center of studies of the labor process done following the publication of Harry Braverman's *Labor and Monopoly Capital.*

Braverman has been credited with reviving the Marxist tradition of labor studies, and establishing the relationship between class relations and the development of technology.[9] His followers produced copious studies attempting to specify the relationships between technological change and job displacement, the labor market, skill level, and world system integration. The empiricism spawned by this "decomposed" research agenda rivals that of the social history trend, whereas its influence on the real world of labor strategy and tactics is equally hard to find.[10]

Contrary to claims that Braverman restored Marxist premises to the study of labor, the deskilling school, like the social history trend, continued within, rather than broke with, the fundamental premises of its predecessors. Braverman wrote at about the same time as the early social historians, when the dominant paradigm in the sociology of labor, based on neoclassical assumptions, was best represented by the work of Seymour Martin Lipset and his associates.[11] In accordance with the methodological empiricism dominant at the time, Lipset et al. defined their variables in ways that were neatly operationalized and quantifiable—occupational characteristics, such as income, skill level, and status, were associated with the voting habits of union members. Workers in lower status skill and income levels were found to be less democratic in behavior. In this manner, Lipset et al. isolated work-related studies from larger historical and political economic contexts, and reduced the unit of analysis to the level of individuals and individual job characteristics.[12]

Most importantly, Lipset et al. inverted the relationship Marx identified between development and working-class capacity.[13] For Lipset et al., workers with the least skill were the least capable of what they considered socially efficacious behavior. These findings, of course, supported their hypothesis that only the middle class was capable of democracy, and they conformed to the prevailing cold war ideology that the proletariat was prone to totalitarianism.

Despite the heavy polemics of radical academics against liberal sociology, much of the radical scholarship of the 1960s and 1970s retained the fundamental premises of liberal pluralism. The unit of analysis continued to be the individual or, as for Braverman, the properties of individual job positions. Working-class power, in these studies, was equated with aggregated individual sovereignty, albeit sovereignty in the work place rather than in a political process. These studies were characterized by a strongly normative bias holding proletarianization or deskilling to be "bad," and attempts at resisting proletarianization to be virtuous. Finally, these studies located the cutting edge of history at the interface between monopoly and competitive forms of production, and elevated the central importance of the labor aristocracy in the historical process. In sociology, the result has been a virtual preoccupation with the "middle class."

There is no gainsaying the fact that the voluminous empirical contributions of historians and political economists working within the respective schools of social history and degradation of work have advanced the field of labor studies enormously. What is also true is that the paradigmatic flaws they inherited from their predecessors were not corrected for, with the result that they continue to impair the field.

A summary of the problems as they presently manifest themselves in the study of labor are, first, that the working class has been more or less written off the agenda. Work done under the rubric of class analysis has largely been concerned with questions of class boundaries and class identities, and for this purpose, the middle class has been of much greater interest than the working class.[14] State-centered theory has similarly displaced workers from its accounts of the New Deal policy in favor of an autonomous stratum of state managers.[15] Finally, there is a neoinstitutionalist stream that avoids the atomism of neoclassical analyses but only by downgrading the role of human agency.[16]

Second, there is in recent work a postmodernist tendency toward "fragmentation, indeterminacy, and intense distrust of all universal or 'totalizing' discourses."[17] Ira Katznelson and Al Zolberg, for example, conclude their edited volume of European and American working-class studies with the observation that the classical Marxist notion of *a* working class under capitalism is mistaken; each national working class has to be understood on its own terms.[18] The class analysis trend, on the other hand, tends to overly dichotomize class capacities and class consciousness, and uses survey research and voting behavior to infer meaning about class properties from the responses of individuals.[19] Also, work degradation studies tend to compartmentalize institutionally the economic aspects of the labor deskilling process from the social institutions through which that process is refracted.[20]

Third, the relationship between the working-class formation and the long-term process of capitalist development is inadequately understood. As I have argued above, the dominant literature holds that the long-term consequence of capitalist development is the erosion of working-class capacity and that the cumulative effect of the class struggle is the progressive *dis*empowerment of the working class. Each successive period of class struggle results in working-class defeat, and each period of history begins with the working class buried deeper in the ruins of the past. The problem in this regard is the basically functionalist bent to the literature that radical scholars of the 1970s and 1980s did not address.[21]

Finally, there are anti-working class and anti-Communist biases running through the field of labor studies. The former has been nearly constant since Lipset et al.'s studies in the 1950s. More recent literature treats workers sympathetically, but its bias causes it to misinterpret important data.[22] Lillian Rubin, for example, sees working-class reluctance to pursue higher education as evidence of victimization, whereas I think it could be read as evidence of a solidary culture.[23] The anti-Communist prejudice of work done during the 1950s and 1960s was never challenged by "New Left" scholars. C. Wright Mills added fuel to the fire when he wrote that "communists' rule within unions they control is dictatorial,"[24] and Stanley Aronowitz, whose work was probably the most influential for a new generation of labor activists, reinforced that bias.[25]

NEW BEGINNINGS FOR THE STUDY OF LABOR AND THE LABOR PROCESS

The task of retheorizing the agenda of our work remains to be done. Retheorizing means, in the first instance, getting the problem out of the atomizing neoclassical discourse common to the social history and work degradation paradigms that undergird much of the recent work in labor studies. It means focusing on *class*, rather than individual workers, as the unit of analysis, and it means we try to understand the contradictory, rather than the normative, implications of the proletarianization process. Retheorizing also means getting clear on what it is that needs to be understood, and that, it seems to me, is class capacities.[26]

Retheorizing in Labor Studies

During the late 1980s, a new trend in labor studies emerged that restored the centrality of the working class in labor struggles and portrayed working-class culture in an affirmative way. This new trend does not shy away from the tough ideological questions around which post–World War II labor politics revolved. Its dialectical approach explores the relationships between social consciousness and social organization, understands class capacities as an inter- as well as intraclass phenomenon, and recognizes the historical and spatial dimensions of class power.[27]

We find these characteristics in several recent studies of labor. Rick Fantasia, for example, utilizing studies of recent strike activity, shows that working-class capacity was *not* destroyed by deskilling, bureaucratization, co-optation, and cultural diversification.[28] Howard Kimeldorf begins his work with the observation that the U.S. working class evinces both class-conscious militancy and business union conservatism, and he uses historical-comparative methods to study under what conditions each of those arises and is reproduced.[29] My own recent study combined case histories of CIO unions with organizational analysis to show that proletarianization enhanced working-class capacity but that the unevenness of that process produced a divided working class.[30]

All three of these studies depart from mainstream approaches by the way they treat working-class culture. Within the pluralist tradition, working-class culture is defined by the *absence* of certain personality traits and values.[31] Lacking these personal attributes, pluralists argue, workers have a low level of political efficacy, the result being low working-class capacity.[32] Because the assumptions of pluralist theory are widely accepted, there have not been many attempts to cast working-class traits and values positively as the basis of a collective culture. Those that do, however, make a case for an affirmative concept of working-class culture that is based on collectivity.[33]

The positive treatment of working-class culture in these recent studies is related to the fresh approach they take to the history of Communists in the U.S. labor movement. The power base of Communists within CIO unions was the mass of unskilled workers brought into the union movement by the organizing efforts of Communists themselves. Pluralist sociology during the McCarthyite climate of the 1950s denigrated Communists and constructed the fiction of an authoritarian working-class personality to explain the link between workers, their Communist leaders (a link that was real), and fascism (a link that was not real).

The political culture of the New Left during the 1960s and 1970s was sufficiently ambivalent about Communists in the labor movement that the pluralist interpretation was either reproduced or avoided altogether. Nonconformity with the cold war code could, in fact, be risky business for academics. When Roger Keeran broke out of that mold and wrote the first scholarly account of the purge of Communists from the United Auto Workers,[34] he lost his job at Cornell. With the exception of Harvey Levenstein, who wrote from an academic position in Canada, there were no other major attempts to challenge the cold war mythologies until the mid-1980s.[35] By then, Zeitlin and Kimeldorf were able to pull together papers from authors who, in the words of labor historian Robert Zieger, who commented on the collection, "appear untroubled by association intellectually with a Popular Front world view."[36] Why the cold war mold for labor studies may have begun to thaw in the midst of the Reagan decade is not clear, but that volume coincided with a renewal of interest in the CIO period.[37]

Dialectical theoretical and methodological approaches to labor studies began to emerge during this period with Erik Olin Wright's distinction between relational and gradational definitions of class, and Claus Offe and Helmut Wiesenthal's demonstration that class capacities are class-specific.[38] Goran Therborn has further specified the notion of class capacities by distinguishing between *petty bourgeois* sources of power and *working-class* sources of power: For the petty bourgeoisie, the source of power is autonomy in the labor process; for the working class, the source of power is its collectivity.[39] Therborn also distinguishes between the *intrinsic capacity* that classes have—the respective power resources available to them—and the *hegemonic capacity* of classes—their ability to deploy their intrinsic capacity against opposing classes. The essence of hegemonic capacity rests on the ability of one class to intervene in the process by which the opposite class generates its own intrinsic capacity. Moreover, Therborn points out, class power is not a zero-sum game, and the power of one class is not necessarily the weakness of its opposite. Rather, the process that increases capitalist class power through capital accumulation simultaneously and contradictorily collectivizes the working class and, thus, empowers it, not in material ways, but in social ways.

The key insight here is that capitalist class success depends on its ability to maintain the accumulation process (and thus continue to generate *its* intrinsic capacity) while blocking the contradictory effects of accumulation by mitigating the collectivization of the working class—that is, to exercise hegemonic capacity.[40] There is an important *spatial* dimension to that process that I think provides one of the missing keys to a fuller understanding of U.S. working-class capacity and labor's current situation. Therborn argues that "the extent to which the public practices of the working class are coextensive with the territorial range of the supreme political power which the class must confront" is a key determinant of which class will hold sway at any historical moment.[41] In other words, there is a sense in which the history of class relations under capitalism can be understood as a series of flanking actions, with the capitalist class first attempting to expand its geographical options and then attempting to block working-class efforts to keep pace.

The class-capacities approach makes a significant methodological break with the dominant approaches to labor studies, because it asks questions at the level of class, *qua* class. It does not reduce analysis of class relations to the level of individuals, and thus, it provides a basis for the criticism of survey research methods in class analysis.[42] It also places labor studies in a time-space matrix that creates possibilities for more dialectical analyses of the labor movement.

TEMPORAL AND SPATIAL DIMENSIONS OF CLASS CAPACITIES

Our attention to the temporal dimension of class capacities has been called by several recent studies. Some authors have noted the tenacity of a working-class culture of collectivity,[43] whereas others suggest that it is even an intergenerational phenomenon.[44]

There are, of course, many impediments to the intergenerational transmission of collective culture,[45] but recent studies also tell us that family and unions play an important role in reproducing working-class culture across generations. The social psychological literature on family and political socialization provides confirmation that, not only are opinions, attitudes, and values on matters such as party identification and social mobility passed from one generation to another,[46] but that, at a deeper level, "what is really transmitted from parents to children is basic personality orientations, some of which . . . have important political consequences."[47]

Unions also play an important role in the transmission of working-class culture. Studying the West Coast longshoremen's community, William Pilcher found, "It is the union and its peculiarly democratic nature that is responsible for the maintenance of the essential features of the longshore subculture. . . . The union serves as the center and focus of the community, welding the longshoremen together into a social group and furnishing them with a very real community of interest. . . . Children are often brought into the hiring hall" where the battles and exploits of the heroic "34 men" are recounted "almost every day."[48]

Family: The Mediator of Workplace Deskilling

The connections between intergenerational transmission of culture and class capacities are made most clearly in the literature that examines the intersections of work place and family life. In his reexamination of the Braverman skill-degradation thesis, Harold Benenson found that the gender specificity of the industrial changes taking place during this period made the working-class family central to the way the changes played out.[49] The "importance of the family economies," he points out, "is that they encompassed in microcosm the skill range of their respective industries. Workplace issues affecting one occupational group had direct bearing on the welfare of family members employed in other job categories. Industrial conflicts, refracted through the family, mobilized working class communities *en bloc*."[50] In point of fact, the vertical distance between unionized, skilled, male workers and nonunion, unskilled, and female workers in the garment, shoe, and mining industries was often bridged by father-daughter family bonds. In industries like meat packing, the grievances of young, female workers, "commanded support among the better-organized, skilled male butchers" when the work place relations were mediated by family ties. In addition, there appeared to have been a transmission of values and organizing skills from one generation to another. Newcomers to the world of industrial work—often daughters of male craft or skilled workers—"learned about organizing from their fathers who already belonged to craft unions and mutual aid societies."[51]

There is also an important spatial dimension to the formation of class capacities that needs to be taken into account. As David Harvey argues, economic development is always regionally specific.[52] Economic periods, and periods when certain kinds of technology and skill levels are dominant, are also regional periods. Thus, using the skill-degradation example, we would expect to find that lower-skilled industrial labor developed not only at a later time than craft-oriented production, but that it also came on line in a different geographic region. Thus, the generation entering the emergent, mass-production, economic sector was typically physically apart from the generation steeped in the experience of an earlier era of economic development. In these instances, the "daughters" (from Benenson's study) employed in the new plants would either have relocated from their family residence, in which case the mediating role of the family would be greatly diminished, or, as was often the case, the new work force would be immigrant workers whose "inherited beliefs" would be consistent with the preindustrial work experience of their families.[53]

An expanded presentation of the relationship between labor-capital migration and collective culture would allow several important correlative points to be developed. One of those involves the distinction between *social* mobility (i.e., the movement of individuals from one class or social strata to another through change of occupation, income, or education) and *geographic* mobility. When family ties keep upwardly mobile professionals in touch with their working-class roots, they retain a greater commitment to the needs and values of that class. In such cases, academically acquired skills of, say, a lawyer or teacher can in fact enhance the capacity of the working-class community. If upward social mobility occurs simultaneously with geographic mobility, on the other hand, the intergenerational ties may be broken. Also, simultaneity is probably more the rule than the exception. It is the opening of new sectors of the economy that creates new occupational strata, thus enabling individuals to change social location in significant numbers, and the opening of new economic sectors typically occurs through the expansion of economic space, which means that *social* mobility presumes spatial relocation.[54]

The skill-degradation argument, in other words, does identify important aspects of class capacity—deskilling *does* diminish the autonomy of individual workers—and the aggregated result of many deskilled workers would seem to be diminished working-class capacity. If we view the U.S. working-class experience in its most comprehensive dimensions, however, we can see that class capacity has not been diminished by skill degradation, *per se*. Rather, skill degradation created the possibility for capital to own and control, in absentia, through its managers. Being able to control in absentia, employers were, and are, able to move assets while maintaining a relatively stable existence for themselves, as a class.[55] Workers, meanwhile, are pulled hither and yon by the increasing rapidity of capital's mobility, and their capacity to produce, much less *re*produce, a collective culture increasingly diminished in the later stages of capitalist development. It was the control of space, in other words, that was as important as the control of skill.

Is there any inherent advantage to one class or another in being geographically mobile? David Montgomery argues that nineteenth-century craftsmen were "honor bound" to walk out of a shop if the traditional rules of employment were broken; indeed early twentieth-century industrial workers resisted harsh employers by quitting and seeking work in another factory.[56] On the other hand, Barry Bluestone and Bennett Harrison, as well as Richard Peet, have argued that *capital's* mobility in the mid to late twentieth century destroyed unions and weakened working-class communities, thereby diminishing working-class power.[57] In fact, both of these arguments may be viewed as correct. Prior to the era of finance capital (roughly the turn of the twentieth century), capital was largely locally owned and insufficiently concentrated to afford the cost of strategical relocations. Moreover, the separation between ownership and management functions was not yet fully realized, so that if capital moved, capital*ists* would also have had to move. Monopolization and the advent of finance capitalism altered these conditions. Absentee ownership and management through a newly created stratum of professional managers and engineers shifted the cost/benefit ratio of geographical mobility to capital.

Unions: The Mediators of Spatial Fragmentation

Just as the effects of deskilling were refracted through the family, the effects of spatial particularization were refracted through union organizations. The craft unions, most of which were affiliated with the American Federation of Labor (AFL), adopted a protectionist posture toward the new developments, and resolutely refused to organize the unskilled immigrant workers or to adapt their forms of organizations to one that followed industrial lines. Moreover, because the AFL was formed in the late nineteenth century when industry was still heavily concentrated in the eastern states, most of its members were located in the East and, as a result, the balance of power within the AFL was skewed toward the eastern states.

In *Capitalist Development and Class Capacities*, I showed that craft unions emerged from the nineteenth century with organizational forms based on business union principles. One of those principles was that control of financial resources for organizing purposes was based on a pecuniary logic—those locals and regions that paid the most had the most say in how and where organizing activities were conducted. Given that the nature of pecuniary organizational forms translated size into power *vis-à-vis* other class segments, it was a historical impossibility for more progressive forms to take root and supplant the pecuniary forms within the same industrial and geographic space. Space unoccupied by previous organizational forms had to be created by the class struggle, and working-class advances could not proceed until that occurred.

In the 1930s, the Congress of Industrial Organizations (CIO) was born out of the AFL craft unions. It represented not so much a destruction of the past as a negation of a sectoral and regionally specific level of organization for one that was more inclusive in both respects. The CIO thus constituted a kind of historical elbow joint between the accumulated capacity of the U.S. working class and the potential that lay in a different sectoral and geographic space.

The potential capacity of the unorganized sector lay, first, in the large numbers of workers there. Second, the more proletarianized conditions of workers in the industrial sector encouraged collective action. Brought into the union movement, these workers stimulated a kind of unionism that went beyond the work place and spoke to the needs of the working class in broader *class* terms. The CIO unions took up issues of national politics, foreign policy, civil rights, environmental control, and the welfare of the unemployed. They also brought more collectivist cultural forms, such as theater and group singing, into union institutions. Theoretically speaking, these more collectivist orientations were expressions of a key contradiction within advanced capitalism: namely, that with proletarianization, individualism would break down, workers would begin to think and act as a class, and in so doing lay the groundwork for a Socialist movement. They represented, in other words, a transition from individualized struggle aimed at preserving precapitalist individual autonomy to collective struggle aimed at class control of economic and social life.

Organizational form was the mechanism linking the *accumulated* capacity of the working class (the AFL unions) and the *potential* for increasing the class's capacity. It was only through organization that the unevenness created by the development process, which capital could endlessly manipulate to its advantage (by fostering competition between fractions of the working class and geographic regions), could be offset or counterbalanced by the unions. The key, in other words, was to mobilize the sectors of the working-class movement that were regionally, sectorally, and politically *over*developed in such a way that those sectors underdeveloped at the time could advance, slingshot fashion, beyond the presently more advanced sectors. This is, in effect, what happened during the growth years of the CIO.

Finally, the link between temporal and spatial dimensions of class formation is made by Stephen Thernstrom, who argues that the *length of time* a group of workers reside *in a particular place* is an essential variable in the formation of class solidarity.[58] This makes immanent sense because, not only does the group have to share a common experience, but the process of reflection through which the group comes to a certain consciousness about its commonalities takes time. Collective identity, in other words, emerges out of a social process that occurs across time. Culture, collective or otherwise, however, is something more than experience. It includes the symbols (language) and an interpretive framework by which the group knows and understands that experience; it is the combination of the "inherited belief" component and the experience itself. The notion of inheritance, moreover, presumes the presence of more than one generation in the process by which a class becomes conscious of itself.

A CLASS CAPACITY PERSPECTIVE ON LABOR'S CURRENT CRISIS

The bridge to full working-class consciousness has seldom been crossed, in part, because, by moving, capital has been able to destroy repeatedly working-class community and, thereby, disrupt the process of long-term, intergenerational class formation. This is the context in which labor's current crisis needs to be understood.

The period of expansion that began with World War II ended in approximately 1970. At that point, corporate managers in basic industry "found themselves confronting an unprecedented profit squeeze" and, in response, they created "an unprecedented wave of total plant shutdowns."[59] The class logic of this sequence is made clear by Richard Peet, who constructed an index of class struggle and ranked all states by this index.[60] He found that capital moved from states and regions that ranked high on the index to locations that ranked low. Similarly, David Jaffee found that "the level of unionization was the best predictor of capital flight, such that in the 1970s corporations tended to move to states without powerful trade unions."[61]

The deindustrialization decade amounted to "a class war on workers"[62] and a war against the communities "where the great worker organizing drives of the 1930s and 1940s were most successful and which also retained their industrial structures virtually intact until recently."[63] It was an exercise of capitalist hegemonic capacity that brought to a close a period of working-class formation that began with the radical working-class movements of the 1930s and continued for approximately 40 years.

The social conflict of the Great Depression formed a political generation with a radical culture and a set of institutions with the potential to transmit that culture to the next generation (e.g., the industrial unions of the CIO, political organizations like the Communist party, and community social centers). The economic stability afforded by unions meant that families were stable, and community institutions, like schools, churches, and social services, made it desirable and feasible for the children of that formative generation to stay in the community. In regions like the Pacific Northwest, where working-class radicalism was widespread among woodworkers and longshoremen during the 1930s, the continuity experienced between the generation of the 1930s and their sons and daughters who still lived in the community was readily apparent well into the 1970s.

The intergenerational links had already begun to weaken, however, from the combined effects of anti-labor legislation during the post–World War II years and the cold war purges of labor leaders, who had broad visions of unionism, that narrowed the scope of union activity in the United States to bargaining for wages, hours, and working conditions. It is the havoc wrought by capital flight and plant closings, however, that all but eliminated the settings in which collective culture might be passed from one generation to another. The union halls that provided the "tribal fires" around which "grizzled warriors" recounted "tales of their exploits"[64] are boarded up, and the voices of the elders are silent. Workers who have stayed in declining regions have generally been pushed to the margins of the economy, whereas those who have moved have broken ties with one or more generations of their families.[65] With some exceptions, children growing up in working-class families have little more exposure to the culture and traditions of their own class' experience than children of other families.

CONCLUSION

The United States is witnessing political-economic devastation seldom seen in its history. Unemployment and underemployment, homelessness, hunger, the declining quality of health and educational systems, and the rise of racism and national chauvinism combine to portend a future ridden with crises. The suffering of large numbers of working people and others who have been economically cast off is increasing, and it has been increasing for at least a decade.

Yet, the prospects of a meaningful, effective response to those conditions by the labor movement and its traditional left-wing allies appear distant. The failure of the Bronx, observed political economist Leo Panitch at a recent conference, is the failure, not of capitalism, but of the Socialist movement to respond effectively. By comparison, ten years into the Great Depression of the 1930s, the U.S. Left was mobilized and playing a central role in the resolution of the crisis. *Class* was central to the analysis and strategic vision of the movement, and the working class was the social base on which that movement was built.

To make a contribution to the building of a movement leading labor out of its present condition, the prevailing approaches in labor studies also have to be rethought. The field has generally followed the trends of the 1970s and 1980s, which devalued the role of the working class and fragmented the method of studying class relations in advanced capitalism. I have argued for an analysis that stays at the level of class, using organizations (family, unions, etc.) as the empirical referents for levels of class capacity. I have also argued for an analysis that understands class capacity as a relational phenomena that has intraclass and interclass dimensions, that is historical, that has spatial dimensions, and that comprehends the dialectical relationship between social relations and class consciousness. Finally, I have pointed to some recent developments in the field that I think offer some new and promising points of departure for our work. It is hoped that such an approach will increase the relevance of labor studies for labor leaders and activists who are trying to revitalize the working-class movement.

NOTES

1. Editors of Radical America, "New Left Historians of the 1960s," *Radical America* (November 1970).

2. E. P. Thompson, *The Making of the English Working Class* (New York: Pantheon Books, 1963).

3. John R. Commons et al., *History of the Labor Movement in the United States* (New York: Macmillan, 1918); Selig Perlman, *A Theory of the Labor Movement* (New York: Macmillan, 1928).

4. Philip Taft, "Attempts to 'Radicalize' the Labor Movement," *Industrial and Labor Relations Review* 1 (July 1948), pp. 580–92; Walter Galenson, "Why the American Labor Movement Is Not Socialist," Reprint No. 168, Institute of Industrial Relations (Berkeley: University of California, 1961).

5. Frances Fox Piven and Richard Cloward, *Poor People's Movements* (New York: Pantheon, 1977).

6. Stanley Aronowitz, *False Promises: The Shaping of American Working Class Consciousness* (New York: McGraw Hill, 1973).

7. Jeremy Brecher, *Strike!* (Greenwich: Fawcet, 1972).

8. Harry Braverman, *Labor and Monopoly Capital: The Degradation of Work in the Twentieth Century* (New York: Monthly Review Press, 1974).

9. Ibid.

10. David Hakken, "Studying New Technology after Braverman: An Anthropological Review." *Anthropology of Work Newsletter*, Vol. 1, No. 1 (1988).

11. Seymour Martin Lipset, Martin Trow, and James Coleman, *Union Democracy* (New York: Anchor, 1956).

12. Ibid.

13. For Marx, the problem was not whether technology deskilled, but rather (and how) the capitalist development process empowered the working class. He argued that this process was a contradictory one: As capitalist development occurred, working-class empowerment increased.

14. *See* Erik Olin Wright, *Classes* (London: Verso, 1985).

15. *See* Theda Skocpol and K. Finegold, "State Capacity and Economic Intervention in the Early New Deal," *Political Science Quarterly* 97 (1982). A notable exception to the dominance of state-centered theory is Rhonda Levine's attempt to "bring class back in" through a study of labor and the New Deal. *See* Rhonda Levine, *Class Struggle and the New Deal: Industrial Labor, Industrial Capital, and the State* (Lawrence, KS: University Press of Kansas, 1988).

16. Larry J. Griffin, M. Wallace, and B. Rubin, "Capitalist Resistance to the Organization of Labor Before the New Deal: Why? How? Success?" *American Sociological Review* 51 (April 1986).

17. David Harvey, *The Condition of Postmodernity: An Inquiry into the Origins of Cultural Change* (Cambridge: Basil Blackwell, 1989), p. 9. Harvey also describes this tendency as a rejection of "meta-narrative" in favor of what Thomas Eagleton calls "laid-back pluralism." I will generally use the term pluralism to describe this tendency, but reductionism, particularism, and *as-*

tructuralism would also apply. In other words, the tendency I am describing refers both to analyses that resort to psychology-based explanations for sociological phenomena (e.g., pluralist explanations derived from neoclassical assumptions) and to analyses that separate dimensions of social reality that can only be fully understood through their relation to each (i.e. structurally or dialectically). What I call a dialectical approach may be called a "synthetic" approach by others. *See* Michael Kazin, "Struggling with the Class Struggle: Marxism and the Search for a Synthesis of U.S. Labor History." *Labor History* 28 (Fall 1987).

18. Ira Katznelson and Al Zolberg (eds.), *Workingclass Formation: Nineteenth-century Patterns in Western Europe and the United States* (Princeton, NJ: Princeton University Press, 1986).

19. Wright, *Classes.*

20. The exchange between Harold Benenson, "The Reorganization of U.S. Manufacturing Industry and Workers' Experience, 1880–1920: A Review of 'Bureaucracy and the Labor Process' by Dan Clawson," *The Insurgent Sociologist*, Vol. XI, No. 3 (Fall 1982) and Dan Clawson, "Reply to Benenson," *The Insurgent Sociologist*, Vol. XI, No. 3 (Fall 1982) on this point should be consulted.

21. Mike Davis, "Why the U.S. Working Class Is Different." *New Left Review* 123 (Sept.–Oct., 1980) is probably the best example of this reasoning. M. Gottdiener, *The Social Production of Urban Space* (Austin: University of Texas Press, 1987) and Michael Storper and R. Walker, *The Capitalist Imperative: Territory, Technology, and Industrial Growth* (New York: Basil Blackwell, 1989) are critical of political economic urban studies, for example, William Tabb and Larry Sawers, *Marxism and the Metropolis: New Perspectives in Urban Political Economy* (New York: Oxford University Press, 1984), for its functionalist quality, and John Willoughby, "Is Global Capitalism in Crisis? A Critique of Postwar Crisis Theories." *Rethinking Marxism*, Vol. 2, No. 2 (Summer 1989) raises the same issue about the social structure of accumulation school, for example, David Gordon, R. Edwards, and M. Reich, *Segmented Work, Divided Workers* (Cambridge: Cambridge University Press, 1982).

22. Richard Sennett and J. Cobb, *The Hidden Injuries of Class* (New York: Knopf, 1972).

23. Lillian Rubin, *Worlds of Pain: Life in the Working Class Family* (New York: Basic Books, 1976).

24. C. Wright Mills, *The New Men of Power* (New York: Harcourt, Brace, 1948), pp. 199–200.

25. Aronowitz, *False Promises*, pp. 13–14.

26. Jerry Lembcke, *Capitalist Development and Class Capacities: Marxist Theory and Union Organization* (Westport, CT: Greenwood Press, 1988).

27. In this context, capitalist class power is based on its accumulation of capital, whereas working-class power is based on the association of workers. *See* Claus Offe and Helmut Wiesenthal, "Two Logics of Collective Action: Theoretical Notes on Social Class and Organizational Form" in Maurice Zeitlin (ed.),

Political Power and Social Theory, Vol. I (Greenwich, CT: JAI Press, 1980), pp. 67–115.

Capacity is used here to mean the capability of the working class to act in its own interests (which is to say, against the interests of the capitalist class) in a way that transforms the basic social relations of capitalism. It refers, in other words, to the *means* available to the working class to liberate itself from its subordination to the capitalist class.

28. Rick Fantasia, *Cultures of Solidarity: Consciousness, Action, and Contemporary American Workers* (Berkeley: University of California Press, 1988).

29. Howard Kimeldorf, *Reds or Rackets? The Making of Radical and Conservative Unions on the Waterfront* (Berkeley: University of California Press, 1988).

30. Lembcke, *Capitalist Development and Class Capacities.*

31. Lipset et al., *Union Democracy*; Bernard Rosen, "The Achievement Syndrome: A Psychocultural Dimension of Social Stratification." *American Sociological Review* 21:2 (April 1956), p. 208.

32. Stanley Renshon, *Psychological Needs and Political Behavior: A Theory of Personality and Political Efficacy* (New York: The Free Press, 1974).

33. *See* Fantasia, *Cultures of Solidarity*; Kimeldorf, *Reds or Rackets?*; Lembcke, *Capitalist Development and Class Capacities*; Richard Oestreicher, "Urban Working Class Political Behavior and Theories of American Electoral Politics, 1870–1940." *Journal of American History*, Vol. 74, No. 4 (March 1988); Joe Trotter, *Black Milwaukee* (Urbana: University of Illinois Press, 1985).

34. Roger Keeran, *The Communist Party and the Auto Workers' Unions* (Bloomington, IN: Indiana University Press, 1980).

35. Harvey Levenstein, *Communism, Anticommunism, and the CIO* (Westport, CT: Greenwood Press, 1981).

36. Maurice Zeitlin and H. Kimeldorf (eds.), *Political Power and Social Theory* (Greenwich, CT: JAI Press, 1984); Robert Zieger, "The Popular Front Rides Again" in Zeitlin and Kimeldorf, Ibid., p. 298.

37. Still, work that pointedly challenges anti-Communist interpretations of the CIO period has been slow in coming. In addition to the work already cited and chapters in Zeitlin and Kimeldorf by James Prickett, Frank Emspak, and Ronald Filippelli, there is Jerry Lembcke and W. Tattam, *One Union in Wood: A Political History of the International Woodworkers of America* (New York: International Publishers, 1984); Kimeldorf, *Reds or Rackets?*; and Judith Stepan-Norris and Maurice Zeitlin, "Why Gets the Bird? Or, How the Communists Won Power and Trust in America's Unions: The Relative Autonomy of Intraclass Political Struggles." *American Sociological Review* 54 (August 1989).

38. Erik Olin Wright, *Class Structure and Income Determination* (London: Verso, 1979); Claus Offe and Helmut Wiesenthal, "Two Logics of Collective Action," in Zeitlin and Kimeldorf, *Political Power and Social Theory.*

39. Goran Therborn, "Why Some Classes Are More Succesful than Others." *New Left Review* 138 (March–April 1983).

40. One way of doing that is for the capitalist class to *displace* collectivizing forms of organization that are intrinsic or indigenous to the working class with organizational forms that are intrinsic to the capitalist class. For example, if the capitalist class can foist on workers the notion that labor union reliance on larger treasuries and high-paid legal experts is more effective than rank-and-file mobilization, the capitalist class will essentially be able to place the class struggle on terms most favorable to it.

41. Therborn, "Why Some Classes Are More Successful than Others," p. 41.

42. Fantasia, *Cultures of Solidarity*, p. 8.

43. *See* David Montgomery, *Workers' Control in America* (Cambridge: Cambridge University Press, 1979); Bruce Nelson, " 'Pentecost' on the Pacific: Maritime Workers and Working Class Consciousness in the 1930s," in Zeitlin and Kimeldorf, *Political Power and Social Theory*; Roy Rosenzweig, *Eight Hours for What We Will: Workers and Leisure in an Industrial Community, 1970–1920* (Cambridge: Cambridge University Press, 1983).

44. Fantasia, *Cultures of Solidarity*; Kimeldorf, *Reds or Rackets?*; and David Bensman and R. Lynch, *Rusted Dreams: Hard Times in a Steel Community* (New York: McGraw-Hill, 1987).

45. Throughout the nineteenth and twentieth centuries, the capitalist class gained increasing control over many of the institutions through which working-class culture might have been conveyed. Jean Anyon, "Ideology and United States History Textbooks" *Harvard Educational Review*, Vol. 49, No. 2 (1979) and Rosenzweig, *Eight Hours for What We Will*.

46. Rosen, "The Achievement Syndrome"; Renshon, *Psychological Needs and Political Behavior*.

47. Renshon, Ibid., p. 174.

48. William Pilcher, *The Portland Longshoremen: A Dispersed Urban Community* (New York: Holt, Rinehart and Winston, 1973), pp. 84, 116.

49. Harold Benenson, "The Community and Family Bases of U.S. Working Class Protest, 1880–1920" in Louis Kriesberg (ed.), *Research in Social Movement, Conflicts and Change* (Greenwich, CT: JAI Press, 1985), p. 112.

50. Ibid., p. 118.

51. Ibid., p. 128.

52. Harvey, *The Condition of Postmodernity: An Inquiry into the Origin of Cultural Change*, pp. 201–213.

53. Herbert G. Gutman, *Work, Culture, and Society in Industrializing America* (New York: Random House, 1977).

54. *See* Michael Stroper and R. Walker, *The Capitalist Imperative: Territory, Technology, and Industrial Growth* (New York: Basil Blackwell, 1989), p. 10.

55. Marvin Dunn, "The Family Office as a Coordinating Mechanism Within the Ruling Class" in *The Insurgent Sociologist* (Fall–Winter, 1980).

56. Montgomery, *Workers' Control in America*.

57. *See* Barry Bluestone and Bennett Harrison, *The Deindustrialization of America: Plant Closings, Community Abandonment and the Dismantling of Basic Industry* (New York: Basic Books, 1982); Richard Peet (ed.), *International Capitalism and Industrial Restructuring* (Boston: Allen & Unwin, 1987).

58. Stephen Thernstrom, "Socialism and Social Mobility," in J. Laslett and S. M. Lipset (eds.), *Failure of Dream? Essays in the History of American Socialism* (Berkeley: University of California Press, 1984).

59. Bluestone and Harrison, *Deindustrialization*, pp. 34–35.

60. Peet, *International Capitalism*, pp. 50–51.

61. David Jaffee, "The Political Economy of Job Loss in the United States, 1970–1980" *Social Problems*, Vol. 33 (1986), cited in Carolyn Perrucci et al., *Plant Closings: International Context and Social Costs* (New York: Aldine De Gruyter, 1988), p. 24.

62. Bluestone and Harrison, *Deindustrialization*, p. 19.

63. Peet, *International Capitalism*, p. 51.

64. Pilcher, *The Portland Longshoremen*, p. 48.

65. Bluestone and Harrison, *Deindustrialization*, pp. 99–104.

2 The Historical Roots of the Division of Labor in the U.S. Auto Industry

David Gartman

In a few short years after Henry Ford revolutionized automobile production with the introduction of mass-production techniques at the beginning of the twentieth century, the tradition of skilled, unitary, intelligent work was decimated and replaced by a regime of minutely divided, monotonous, mindless labor. Adam Smith, the prophet of this monumental development in industry, set the tragic tone of commentary on the division of labor for centuries to come. He recognized its detrimental effects on detail laborers: "The man whose whole life is spent in performing a few simple operations . . . has no occasion to exert his understanding. . . . He generally becomes as stupid and ignorant as it is possible for a human creature to become."[1] Yet he also saw the division of labor as the necessary foundation for the efficient production that increases the wealth of nations: "But in every improved and civilized society, this is the state into which the laboring poor, that is, the great body of the people, must necessarily fall."[2]

Recently, however, the American automobile industry, which helped pioneer the system of minutely divided labor, has experienced a monumental crisis that has shaken the faith of many in the productive efficiency of this industrial mode. Highly competitive automakers across Europe and in Japan have adopted new techniques of industrial organization, like quality control circles and autonomous work groups, that recompose previously divided tasks. U.S. manufacturers have slowly begun similar experiments, the most notable of which is General Motors quality-of-work-life groups. What has motivated this reversal in the direction of the division of labor? Have automobile managers, long noted for their hard-nosed, driving approach to labor, suddenly changed into humanitarian do-gooders, concerned more with people than profits?

In order to begin to answer these questions, we must first know the original motives of the minute division of automotive labor and the conditions under which they were formulated. The present changes can be understood only in the light of the historical formation of this hitherto unquestioned cornerstone of the auto labor process. In what follows, I will concentrate upon the historical roots of the division of labor in the U.S. auto industry, and then offer upon this basis a few observations about the current changes in this aspect of the labor process.

The process of producing commodities within a capitalist society is not a neutral one, shaped solely by technological imperatives, but an instrument of social domination, shaped by the struggle of opposing classes. The division of capitalist society into those who live by the wage and those who live by profits turns the work place into a battleground, with capitalists seeking to extract as much surplus labor as possible from the hide of workers who, not surprisingly, resist this hiding. In order to overcome this worker resistance and exert absolute control over work, capitalists and their managers structure the labor process in such a way that it strips workers of all power. Work is deskilled and degraded so as to remove from it all discretion on the part of workers, who may use it to resist exploitation.

I will seek to demonstrate in the following analysis that the fragmentation of the original automotive crafts into a plethora of minute tasks was motivated by the employers' drive to overcome the resistance of a powerful skilled labor force. Although my analysis of the labor process under capitalism follows the approach earlier initiated by Harry Braverman,[3] it departs from his specific treatment of the division of labor. I will argue that at least in the U.S. automobile industry, the cheapening of wages was not the main motive behind the fragmentation of work. Rather, a complex combination of corporate attempts to increase labor productivity and intensity motivated the division of automotive labor.

THE CRAFT LABOR PROCESS IN THE EARLY AUTO SHOPS

Prior to the beginnings of work fragmentation and rationalization, the shops in which autos were produced were small concerns dominated by skilled craft workers. The main task of the skilled mechanics was the assembly of parts—chassis, body, engine, transmission, wheels, tires—purchased from other industrial firms. Only craft workers of the highest skills could turn the heap of ill-fitting and incompatible parts into a functioning vehicle. Teams of from two to five such workers labored together at stationary positions on the shop floor to build an entire automobile from the ground up. At each assembly station was a workbench, where workers kept their standard tools and performed various necessary operations. The auto parts necessary for assembly were generally kept in a central storeroom, to which the members of the assembly team journeyed back and forth as they saw fit.

The skilled automobile mechanics largely controlled their own work in these early craft shops. Because of their knowledge and skills, the successful completion of the assembly depended entirely on them. They could not be replaced by specialized workers, for as long as the imperfect parts required fitting and adjustment, work could not be divided but had to remain unitary. Workers had necessarily to keep in mind the peculiarities of each part, and adjust subsequent parts and operations accordingly as they proceeded. The skilled and variable nature of assembly work also gave workers control over their own work pace. It was impossible for the capitalist or his foremen to dictate to workers detailed commands of what was to be done and how fast. These uncertain elements remained necessarily in the discretion of the workers. Further, strict supervision was thwarted by the legitimate absence of workers from their stations. Long and leisurely trips to the parts storeroom were used to get out from under the foreman's watchful eye and thus reduce the intensity of labor.

The integration of parts manufacture into growing auto firms did not alter the nature or control of the labor process, for the production of precision auto parts required highly skilled machinists. The machine tools available at this time for cutting metal—lathes, millers, planers, grinders—left much to be desired in the way of accuracy and precision. Only the careful guidance of highly skilled hands could coax precision parts out of these mechanisms. Further, the small volume of production of these early firms prevented the use of specialized machines, and dictated the use of universal or general-purpose machine tools. The latter could be adapted to a wide variety of auto work, but required skilled machinists to so adapt and operate them.

As in the assembly shops, the nature of work in these machine shops prevented its fragmentation and left it largely in the control of skilled workers. The variable nature of the tasks and materials necessarily left great discretion in the hands of machinists. It was they who controlled the details of machine operation in order to ensure accuracy and precision. The capitalists and their managers could not dictate exact tasks and times for their completion. Further, as in the assembly shops, the layout of early machine shops also made for greater worker discretion and control. Machines were generally grouped by the function they performed. If the production of an entire part was assigned to a specific worker, as it often was, he had to move about the shop from machine to machine in order to perform all the necessary operations. Because this gave workers a great amount of discretionary time and movement, supervision was very difficult.

This control of craft workers over the labor process was not particularly problematic for capital as long as automobile production was aimed at a small luxury market. However, early in the industry's history, a few visionaries began to aspire to tap the potentially large American market for cheap transportation through the volume production of simple, low-priced autos. At this point, worker control of the craft process loomed as a major obstacle in the road to the mass-produced car, for the employers found that the "human element" was often recalcitrant and refused to produce in the manner and pace required by capitalist mass production.

The resistance that auto companies aspiring to mass production encountered from skilled workers was *not*, as some have postulated, the *cultural* resistance of a group of workers with preindustrial backgrounds against the strange demands of industrial labor.[4] Those who manned the early auto shops were generally second- and third-generation industrial workers and were perfectly at home in their industrial environment. They had a well-developed sense of industrial time, were largely organized into craft unions, were highly disciplined both individually and collectively, and regarded factory production as natural. Rather, this was the *class* resistance of workers who had developed a sense of class struggle. As David Montgomery has documented in his study of industrial craftsmen of this period, these workers were engaged in a collective and deliberate struggle with their bosses, who were seeking to lower wages and intensify labor in response to the ongoing crisis of competitive capitalism.[5] Under these antagonistic relations of capitalist production, workers' control over production, its pace, and accuracy was one weapon that they used to struggle against their own exploitation. As long as they possessed this power, the mass production of autos was impaired.

Often this class struggle in the early auto shops erupted into overt, organized, conscious struggle, as when union machinists struck Oldsmobile in 1897 and again in 1901 over wages and working conditions. However, such overt struggle was the exception rather than the rule for several reasons. The most important was the smashing of the early craft unions in the auto shops. Seeing unions in general as an obstacle to renewed capital accumulation, American employers launched an aggressive "open shop" campaign in the first few years of the twentieth century. As part of this national campaign, Detroit capitalists formed the Employers' Association of Detroit (EAD) with the avowed purpose of making the city a bastion for the open shop. They very nearly succeeded. Using a variety of methods—lockouts, discharging, and blacklisting union workers, wage-fixing, strike-breaking—the EAD had virtually eliminated the craft unions by 1907.[6]

A second factor weakening collective, conscious struggle in the early auto shops was the tight labor market for skilled auto workers. An extremely short supply of skilled mechanics and machinists led to competition among employers for workers and consequently high rates of labor turnover. As a result, these early auto workers developed a spirit of individual power and independence. They moved from job to job, enticed by high wages. Also, on the shop floor, they refused to tolerate overbearing foremen pushing for production. Thus, in these early years, much discontent found expression in the individual escape of turnover rather than collective struggle.

Because of these obstacles to organized, collective struggle, early auto workers' resistance to managerial demands was more often covert, clandestine, and only partly conscious. Because they were aware at some level that it was the owners and not themselves who reaped the main benefits from production, workers were not particularly concerned with working very intensively or sometimes very accurately either, for that matter. Evidence of this clandestine struggle is found in a series of reports by a labor spy hired by the Ford Motor Company in 1906 to keep an eye on the workers in the shop. The spy reported that "many of the men neglected their work, malingered, put imperfect parts into cars, and cheated the timekeeper."[7] One trade journalist complained that, as a result of the free mobility of workers in the shops, "time is lost and it is impossible for the department heads to keep in accurate touch with the location of the men and at the same time to check the progress of the work."[8] A series of maxims labeled "Profit Chokers" that appeared in Ford's employee magazine indicated numerous ways in which skilled workers in control of their own labor could thwart capitalist attempts to intensify production. The series included the following: "Chronic strollers and time killers," "Killing time under day-work pay," "Sulkers, grunters, back-talkers, mumblers, knockers," "Employees not doing what they are told," "Antagonism to improved methods," "Employees working 'their' way instead of the 'Company's,' " and "Padded pay rolls through tardiness and shirking."[9]

Automobile companies seeking to tap the potentially large market for cheap cars realized that they could ill afford to leave the control of the labor process to the discretion and skills of a class of recalcitrant workers. Within the context of the antagonistic production relations of capitalism, to leave the control of the pace and accuracy of labor in the hands of workers inevitably meant to settle for less than maximum output and accuracy. So capital began to transform the craft labor process in order to seize control of work from the workers themselves. The foundation of this transformation of automobile work was the fragmentation of the unitary, skilled crafts into a plethora of unskilled detail jobs.

STAGES IN THE DIVISION OF LABOR

The employers first attacked the skilled craft process of assembling cars. Around the middle of the first decade of this century, they began to divide the actual labor of assembly from that of transporting materials by hiring a group of unskilled workers exclusively to carry parts from the stockroom to the assembly station. By 1907, many of the larger auto companies began to assign specialized tasks to the members of the small assembly team. "In place of the jack-of-all-trades who formerly 'did it all,' there were now several assemblers who worked over a particular car side by side, each one responsible for a somewhat limited set of operations."[10] This initial division of assembly work was made possible by the advent at this time of interchangeable parts, which rendered the various assembly operations independent and invariant. However, this method was limited by the number of specialized assemblers who could crowd around one assembly station. This problem was solved by the invention of a system of rotating, specialized "assembly gangs." At Ford around 1907, for example, about 50 highly specialized gangs of workers rotated around a circle of the same number of cars, doing their fragmentary tasks on each. There were gangs specialized in frame assembly, motor mounting, wheel mounting, fender assembly, body assembly, and so on. As soon as the last gang had finished its work, the completed car was removed, and an uncompleted frame was put in its place.

A similar division of labor in the machine shops of early industry was preceded by a change in the layout of work. As soon as the volume of production reached a level at which it was feasible to devote a machine to a single task, corporate managers began to arrange machines progressively within departments specialized in a single part or product. Instead of grouping machines by the function they performed—milling, turning, boring—all those devoted to one part were grouped together and arranged in order of their work on it. Such an arrangement was known as progressive layout. Although Ransom Olds seems to have been the early leader in progressive layout, Henry Ford was not far behind. In 1906, Ford arranged his engine-machining department progressively. Each machine tool and its operator performed one, and only one, operation on the engine block, after which it was passed to the adjacent machine and its operator, who did likewise.[11]

This progressive layout of machine work was accompanied by a heightened division of labor. No longer was the worker engaged in a variety of tasks on a number of different machines. He was confined to one specific operation on one specific machine in the progressive line, and because he performed the same operation time and time again, day in and day out, there was no need for skill or discretion on his part. In fact, as the labor of machine shops became more and more divided, the remaining operations that required skill and knowledge were split off from the ordinary machine operator and concentrated into specialized occupations. Machine setters adjusted and set up machines; tool grinders sharpened and replaced cutting tools; oilers cleaned, oiled, and performed routine maintenance on machines; and repair workers repaired them.

By the beginning of the second decade of the twentieth century, the skilled craft worker was becoming a rare commodity in the rapidly changing automobile factories. A survey of automobile manufacturing occupations in Cleveland revealed that only 11 percent of the work force required more than one year of training, and 44 percent required one month or less.[12] Henry Ford spoke for the entire industry when he stated that the basic principle of his shop organization was "the reduction of the necessity for thought on the part of the worker and the reduction of his movements to a minimum. He does as nearly as possible only one thing with only one movement. . . . Dividing and subdividing operations, keeping the work in motion—those are the keynotes of production."[13]

CAPITAL'S MOTIVES BEHIND THE DIVISION OF LABOR

Some of the motives for minutely dividing labor offered by automobile companies parallel those cited by classical political economists over a century earlier. In his classic treatment, Adam Smith argued that dividing labor increases its productivity.[14] Following Smith, Karl Marx also endorsed this notion.[15] By being forced to concentrate on one task day in and day out, the detail worker develops a certain dexterity that is lacking in the versatile worker, whose switching from task to task prevents him or her from doing one job long enough to get good at it. Auto managers also recognized this advantage of increased productivity, citing it as a motive behind their push toward a greater division of labor. Henry Ford thus wrote that "it is necessary to establish something in the way of a routine and to make most motions purely repetitive—otherwise the individual will not get enough done to be able to live off his own exertions."[16] Upon examining the division of labor in the Ford shops in 1914, two engineering journalists similarly concluded:

> Minute division of operations is effective in labor-cost reducing . . . by making the workman extremely skillful, so that he does his part with no needless motions. . . . Where a workman can perform absolutely similar successions of movement, he very soon gains great skill combined with great rapidity of muscular action.[17]

Recent Marxist critics of the division of labor have raised doubts about this argument endorsed by Marx himself. In *Labor and Monopoly Capital*, Harry Braverman is skeptical about whether dividing labor actually increases its productivity.[18] So is Stephen Marglin, who states that the division of labor increases labor productivity only to the extent that work skills are difficult to acquire and thus improve with experience.[19] He argues, however, that most of the tasks that early industrialists minutely divided were quickly learned and that consequently the potential increase in dexterity afforded by this division was quickly exhausted. The complex skills of automobile assembly and machine-tool operation, however, are the type that are acquired only through long experience and hence benefit from the concentration on one task allowed by the division of labor.[20] So these recent doubts would seem unfounded.

Braverman argues that the main motive behind the division of craft labor is another principle of classical political economy, which he labels the "Babbage Principle."[21] Following Charles Babbage, he holds that the minute division is introduced by capitalists mainly to lower wage rates. Dividing a craft cheapens its parts by allowing employers to hire low-wage labor to perform unskilled tasks and to use high-wage, skilled labor solely on skilled tasks. Although the Babbage Principle may have been a major factor in the division of labor of other industries, there is little evidence of the operation of this motive among automobile managers. General labor market conditions made the lowering of wage rates an impossibility. In the first decade of the century, there were great shortages of labor, skilled and unskilled, to fill the growing auto factories. These shortages empowered worker resistance and struggle, forcing auto employers seeking to attract and hold workers to pay high wages, often above those paid for similar work in other industries. As a result, despite an increasing division of labor during this period, real wages of auto workers rose steadily.

If auto manufacturers could not use the division of labor to slash wages, they could and did use it to achieve a third economic advantage—overcoming the shortage of skilled workers. The supply of skilled workers available to the burgeoning auto industry was not large enough to meet its growing demand. Although unskilled industrial labor was also relatively scarce, it was more abundant than skilled labor. Hence, auto employers were motivated to divide skilled jobs into a myriad of unskilled fragments, each of which could be filled by the unskilled immigrants or farm migrants. Henry Ford thus stated:

> As the necessity for production increased it became apparent not only that enough [skilled] machinists were not to be had, but also that skilled men were not necessary in production. . . . If every job in our place required skill the place would never have existed.[22]

The answer to this problem, Ford continued, was the division of labor, for this "subdivision of industry opens places that can be filled by practically any one."[23]

If the motives advanced by auto managers for the division of labor are examined closely, however, an entire set of motives qualitatively different from these simple economic arguments emerges. It is clear, especially from their more private communications in trade publications, that employers also fragmented skilled craft jobs in order to break the power of skilled workers and exert greater control over the labor process.

Control over Labor

Skilled craft workers exercised a great deal of power over their own work because of their knowledge and skills. Also, because of a recalcitrant shop culture of class conflict, they often thwarted attempts by their employers to produce in a manner and pace that maximized output and minimized costs. One way that managers sought to overcome this resistance of workers to greater production and profits was by eliminating their skills and power through dividing labor into unskilled fragments. Their ultimate motive was the same economic one of increasing the production and profitability of their firms. The way this end was achieved, however, was qualitatively different from simply increasing labor productivity and overcoming labor shortages, the other aims of the division of labor. The enhanced managerial control over the process of production that accompanied the division of labor increased the output and profits of mass-production automobile manufacturers solely by overcoming the resistance of workers. Hence, this motive behind the division of automotive labor was necessitated solely by the antagonistic class relations of capitalism. A different set of social relations—one that was more cooperative and less exploitative—would have rendered this control motive unnecessary and superfluous.

The use of the division of labor to overcome shortages of skilled labor was actually motivated as much by attempts to exert greater managerial control over the labor process as it was by the attempt to secure sufficient labor for expansion. The shortage of skilled auto workers not only made industrial growth difficult; it also enhanced the power of workers on the shop floor. Tight labor market conditions severely attenuated the major sanction used by managers to maintain control of the early labor process—firing. Realizing that their bosses were reluctant to fire them because of the difficulty of finding replacements, skilled workers were strengthened in their struggle with managers on the shop floor. This relationship between worker power and labor shortages was obvious to managers, as evidenced by a trade-journal editorial during World War I, when the industry again suffered tight labor market conditions:

> High wages coupled with extraordinary demand [for labor] create a situation where workers may be independent, not only of their jobs, but also of the employer, with a result that includes costly labor turnover, increased accidents, extravagant time demands, exorbitant accident compensation and other evils.[24]

Given such conditions, automobile employers were motivated to divide labor and draw on the more plentiful—but not altogether abundant—supply of unskilled labor in order to enforce stricter discipline on the shop floor. With skilled jobs shattered into unskilled fragments, managers could fill them with even the "greenest" workers with a minimum of training. As a result, workers in the shops were more reluctant to defy managerial authority because of the fear of losing their jobs to the numerous immigrants and rural migrants.

Not willing merely to create the potential for a greater labor supply by dividing labor, the employers actively sought to expand this supply of unskilled workers with control motives in mind. As one critic of the auto industry observed: "The charge is often made that individually, if not concertedly, the big plants stimulate the coming of workers to Detroit in order to have a sizable labor pool to pick from, to spread the fear of losing your job, and to keep control in their hands."[25]

In Detroit, the vehicle of labor market manipulation was the EAD. This association worked in a number of ways to control the competition for labor and to expand the labor supply. The EAD sought to persuade U.S. immigration authorities to divert a large part of the incoming stream of immigrants to Detroit. Also, the association financed a nationwide advertising campaign to draw on the internal labor resources of the United States. The EAD's *Labor Barometer*, a weekly bulletin on the Detroit labor market, was also used to manipulate labor supply. Instead of reporting factually, Detroit employers used inflated reports of employment opportunities in this publication to stimulate the flow of workers to the city. Individual auto companies used similarly erroneous newspaper reports about increased employment to attract the labor supply to their factories.[26]

Until World War I, the auto industry drew mainly on immigrants as its primary source of unskilled labor. The war, however, stopped the flow of immigrants to the rapidly expanding auto shops, forcing manufacturers to turn to alternative sources of labor supply, namely rural workers, blacks, and women. Recruitment from the rural hinterlands, a traditional source of automotive labor, was intensified by offering "farm boys" incentives, like special deals on tractors. Southern black workers were enlisted by labor agents, who often brought them back en masse on trains. By 1930, about 4 percent of all auto workers were black. Women were also actively courted to fill labor shortages, resulting in an auto labor force composed of up to 12 percent women during World War I. While blacks maintained a relatively permanent and growing presence in the auto shops, however, most women were turned out as soon as shortages of male workers were overcome.[27]

That the stimulation of the supply of unskilled labor was a conscious managerial strategy aimed at greater control of workers on the shop floor is evident from an editorial in *Automotive Industries*. After stating that an "over-supply of labor is far from furnishing the ultimate answer to the labor question," the author observed that:

> During the recent labor shortage, some manufacturers looked to the importation of unskilled labor from Europe as the solution to our labor problem. They believed that the solution consisted chiefly in getting so many men for every job that each individual would work harder because he feared losing his job. That situation has come about to some extent at present.[28]

The division of labor had another effect upon the struggle for control of the labor process, apart from its effect on the labor market. By replacing skilled with unskilled workers, the division of labor greatly reduced the power that the former exerted over the labor process. Because the craft labor process required workers to use their knowledge to determine the precise nature of work, they had a wide range of discretion with respect to its productivity, intensity, and accuracy. The employers realized that this exercise of discretion lowered the intensity of labor in their shops. Recalcitrant workers could use this power to slow down operations to a human pace and take breaks between tasks. The division of automotive labor centralized the skill and intelligence of work into the hands of capital. By fragmenting the crafts into minute, unskilled jobs, capital eliminated the workers' need to think and, along with it, the pores in the working day. As the two engineering journalists wrote of bench assembly work at Ford: "If the routine of the workman's movements is broken, he must inevitably call his brain into action to find the best means of bridging his troubles, and must lose some time in devising and executing his unusual line of procedure." The minute division of labor "allowed" the worker "to perform his unvaried operation with the least possible expenditure of will-power and hence with the least brain fatigue."[29] In reality, managers were less concerned about workers getting tired brains than their using the discretionary time to decrease the intensity of labor.

The division of automotive labor destroyed one large area of workers' discretionary time by eliminating the necessity of movement about the shop. With specialized "stock chasers" to bring parts to assembly locations, workers no longer had an excuse to take long and leisurely trips to the stockroom. Assembly could now proceed "without there being any need for the mechanics to walk more than a yard between the stand and the supply."[30] Also, in the machine shop, with workers similarly tied to one position and one machine: "No time is lost by the operator. The parts come to his machine and are removed to the next automatically. His attention is only on his job."[31] His foreman was sure to see to that. With workers confined to specific work positions, their foremen could maintain constant surveillance of their work and thus exercise stricter supervision.

The drastic reduction in skilled workers effected by the division of labor also strengthened capitalist control of the labor process by eliminating the inhibiting traditions of these workers. They had developed through long experience traditional norms governing how work should be done—the speed, feed, and setup of machines; a normal day's work; the quality of output. These traditions quickly proved to be a major obstacle in the path of complete capitalist control of labor. By dividing labor into unskilled fragments, the auto companies sought to eliminate these skilled workers and their traditions, and replace them with unskilled workers who, having no memory of craft traditions, put up little resistance to the absolute control of capital. As one academic spokesman for capital wrote: "The unskilled or semiskilled worker is more apt to be content with the simple and repetitive task. He will perform the work for which he is trained and is not so likely to question the method of doing the job or to fuss over unnecessarily good quality."[32] However, perhaps engineering journalists Horace L. Arnold and Fay L. Faurote best captured this employer disdain for the skilled and preference for the unskilled when they wrote:

> As to machinists, old-time, all-around men, perish the thought! The Ford Company has no use for experience, in the working ranks, anyway. It desires and prefers machine-tool operators who have nothing to unlearn, who have no theories of correct surface speeds for metal finishing, and will simply do what they are told to do, over and over again, from bell-time to bell-time.[33]

Progressive Layout and Intensity of Labor

Similar capitalist motives of greater control over work and consequently greater work intensity were in back of the progressive layout that often accompanied the division of labor. There were, of course, advantages to this spatial arrangement of work that had nothing to do with control. For example, placing successive work operations close to one another cut down on the amount of back-breaking labor necessary in hauling heavy parts from place to place. Further, progressive layout reduced substantially the amounts of resources tied up in stock and inventory. These advantages certainly played a part in motivating capitalists and managers to adopt this new method. However, an examination of the historical record reveals that attempts of employers to exert greater control over the *intensity of labor* formed the *main* motive.

Progressive layout increased capitalist control of the work pace in several ways. First, it made supervision of work closer and easier. With workers crowded together in a small area, foremen could maintain a large force under constant surveillance. Further, one engineering professor noted that: "The steady flow of work through the line automatically leads to the quick detection of delays. It also holds operators at their work; on certain lines each worker must be on the job continuously."[34]

Second, progressive layout gave capital greater control over work intensity by allowing "stretch out," the operation of more than one machine by a worker. Because machines were grouped close together, it was possible for the first time for a worker to cover the short distance between them. The stretch out that often accompanied progressive layout was illustrated at the Cadillac plant, where a change in the layout of connecting-rod production forced half the previous number of workers to operate all the machines.[35]

The main way, however, that progressive layout enhanced capitalist control of work intensity was by ensuring a rapid, continuous flow of work past operators. Even though work at this time was simply passed by hand between operations, this movement exerted a certain "pull" on workers and forced them to work rapidly so as not to fall behind. As the engineering journalists noted of progressive layout in the Ford shops of 1914, "it succeeds in maintaining speed without obtrusive foremanship."[36] Another engineer noted generally that progressive line production produced a "tautness in operating sequence":

One of the psychological advantages of the line production is the tendency to draw closely upon the work ahead. In most cases there will be but a few parts between operations. Employees will make a constant effort to keep this material from building up ahead of them and to pass the work along promptly to the other workers on succeeding operations. This results in a steady pull from operations down the line which tends to increase production.[37]

Auto companies and their managers were not content, however, to allow the natural "pull" of the line to speed up work. They used other methods to seize control actively of the pace of line work. One was time study.[38] By setting and enforcing job times that allowed no discretionary actions by workers, the companies could control work intensity. Once labor became divided and no longer unified by the individual craft worker, capital imposed itself as the unifier and coordinator of the fragmented labor process. It had to determine the proper timing and manner of all tasks in order to ensure a smooth, uninterrupted flow between them. Furthermore, automobile companies and their managers did not miss the opportunity afforded them by this new role to speed up workers by eliminating their discretionary time. Standard times for jobs were set so as to allow workers little or no time between operations. For example, a Bureau of Labor Statistics (BLS) researcher reported that in one auto body factory that had recently instituted progressive layout and applied time study, "much of the slack between operations was obliterated, and a steady flow of work was secured throughout the establishment, so that an operation on one body would be finished just in time to make way for the next body."[39]

The results of such time study in the auto industry were reported from the workers' point of view in a letter to the *Industrial Worker*, organ of the Industrial Workers of the World (IWW):

Calculations made by the pushers [time-study agents] are based upon what a man could turn out by working the lathe, drill press, milling machine, gear cutters, etc., at top speed; cut out the too frequent sharpening of tools, bumming a chew from a fellow worker on the other end of the floor, going after a drink too often, etc.... (When the men ran their (?) [editorially inserted question mark] machines at slow speed, they had a chance to sit down and watch while resting, but now the dirt is flying.) . . . No more loafing 'round the grindstone to sharpen drills and tools, no more excursions to the tool crib or stock room and many more scientific schemes of working while a fellow is resting. As a matter of fact, those seeming little time killing tricks are absolutely necessary, for no man can work steady at top speed and not get bughouse and worn out in short order.[40]

The other method of controlling the pace of progressive line production was the use of "pacesetters." These were particularly fast and loyal workers who were placed in strategic points along the line to maintain a rapid work pace. Of one such pacesetter on a progressive milling operation at Ford, a researcher wrote that "when he worked very rapidly he passed the materials on to the others at the same rate, and the others had to either keep up or pile up an excess of parts and thus call the attention of the boss to their delay."[41]

An MIT expert on progressive line production summed up its effects on control of work intensity in this way:

The operator in a production line has less control over his working speed than the job-shop employee. . . . The fact that the pace of work is more directly under management's control in line production is an important one. The power which management is thus given to set the speed of the line is not to be taken lightly. Used wisely, it may maintain production at a high level.[42]

Thus, both the minute division of automotive labor and the progressive layout that accompanied it were motivated in large part by the conscious efforts of capitalists and managers to centralize the control of the labor process out of the hands of skilled craft workers. These measures resulted in higher levels of production and higher profits not mainly because they made work more productive or efficient, but because they overcame the resistance of a recalcitrant work force to capitalist exploitation. Under different relations of production, in which workers were not alienated from the means of production and thus labored willingly for the social good, these methods would be superfluous.

Yet in the capitalist mode of production, the minute division of labor formed the foundation for the subsequent transformation of the automotive labor process. Once the various tasks were fragmented and laid out progressively in a line, it was only a short leap of the imagination to the idea of continuous, mechanical movement of work in progress—that is, the moving assembly line. The division and specialization of machine-tool work also laid the basis for mechanization and automation. Once a machine was devoted to one task alone, it could be rigidly specialized and automated so as to operate itself virtually without worker intervention. As with the division of labor, each of these innovations had as a major motive the further erosion of worker discretion and centralization of control into the hands of capital.

Workers in the early auto factories did not, however, passively accept these managerial assaults on their power over the labor process. These early stages in the transformation of work were met with an explosion of worker resistance. Most of this took place at the individual level and was unorganized, as when workers quit and stayed away from the transformed factories in droves, sending turnover and absentee rates soaring. Some of this struggle, however, was collective and class conscious, as when the IWW led a strike against Studebaker in 1913 and the United Automobile, Aircraft, and Vehicle Workers' Union organized a series of strikes and walkouts after World War I. Ironically, the changes originally introduced in the labor process to overcome the resistance of skilled craft workers actually ended up strengthening the collective power of the unskilled industrial workers who replaced them. Not only did the new Fordist methods concentrate a growing mass of discontented workers into large factories and remove the divisions of skill and wages between them, but they also enhanced the power of auto workers by rendering production more interdependent and hence vulnerable to disruption.[43]

Realizing that one ironic result of the division of labor was the creation of a homogenized and powerful collective work force, auto manufacturers sought to reassert their authority by creating artificial divisions within it. This divide-and-conquer strategy took the form of hierarchical job structures. Jobs fundamentally similar in skill were arrayed in steps differentiated by wages and benefits. New workers entered the job ladder at or near the bottom, and progressed up the steps as they demonstrated their reliability and subservience to managers. Such schemes encouraged workers to seek individual advancement in the artificially differentiated promotional ladder and diverted their energies from collective advancement through class struggle.

The divisive effects of these job hierarchies were enhanced by the superimposition upon them of racial and gender divisions. The sexist and racist hiring practices of auto manufacturers resulted in blacks and women being occupationally segregated in divisions at or near the bottom of the hierarchy, with little chance for promotion. Women were confined to a narrow range of jobs related to the unpaid labor they performed at home: sewing, fitting fabric, small-parts assembly. Also, blacks were ghettoized in the hottest, hardest, and most dangerous work: painting, sanding, foundry work, manual labor. Although such discrimination by manufacturers does not seem to have been consciously aimed at furthering divisions within the work force, this was the effect nonetheless. Privileged white male workers found it more difficult to identify and cooperate with workers separated from them not only by wages, but also by deeply rooted racial and gender hatreds and hostilities. Blacks and women at the bottom of job hierarchies often resented the privilege of white males who monopolized the better jobs as much as the discrimination of managers. Furthermore, auto manufacturers were not reluctant to use the hostilities and divisions fueled by job discrimination to weaken the collective resistance of workers. They played off race against race and gender against gender to speed up workers, cut wages, and break strikes.[44]

By the mid-1930s, however, the contradictions of the labor process, together with the deprivations of the Great Depression, overpowered the divisive efforts of auto manufacturers and produced an explosion of militant conflict in the auto industry. Under the leadership of class-conscious Communists, Socialists, and syndicalists, auto workers launched a wave of sit-down strikes. Some manufacturers tried to manipulate black workers as a strike-breaking force, but close cooperation between some far-sighted black leaders and union forces thwarted these efforts, and auto workers finally forced the employers to recognize their union—the United Auto Workers union. However, adamant managerial resistance to repeated worker demands for increased control over the labor process succeeded in containing this struggle within the bounds of a bureaucratic collective bargaining system focused on wages and benefits. By the early 1950s, workers had completely bargained away any claim to control their own labor within the increasingly automated and fragmented auto factories.[45]

RECENT INNOVATIONS: AN END TO THE DIVISION OF LABOR?

By the early 1970s, these hitherto inviolable assumptions about the production of automobiles were being fundamentally questioned. Experiments began in U.S. factories that enlarged work tasks and, in some cases, gave teams of workers responsibility for organizing their own work. What had come over auto capitalists and managers? Had they suddenly abandoned a hard-nosed concern for efficiency and profitability to adopt a humanitarian concern for the quality of employees' work experience?

This latter conclusion flows from a naive perspective that sees aspects of work organization as neutral instruments for the achievement of efficiency under all circumstances. Thus, if a neutral technique like the division of labor is rolled back, then it certainly must be at the expense of industrial efficiency. However, the perspective adopted here views techniques as conditioned by social relations of production. The division of labor increases productive output only under specific conditions of class antagonisms. Altering this staid method of production may signal not abandoning profitability as the key criterion of production, but rather an attempt to achieve it under changed conditions of class struggle.

In the mid-1960s, the U.S. system of collective bargaining began to be undermined by class struggles at home and abroad. In the Third World, national liberation struggles challenged U.S. economic hegemony abroad. On the domestic front, workers excluded from the bargaining system demanded a better dispensation, while workers in large industries began to shift their attention to the previously excluded issues of health, safety, and workers' control.[46] The U.S. auto industry was a center of this renewed class struggle. Black workers, who faced discrimination inside and outside of the auto plants, struggled against both with militant new organizations, like the League of Revolutionary Black Workers.[47] Young workers of all races who had never known the harsh discipline of economic scarcity began to question the trade-off of monotonous, degrading work for relatively high wages. Soaring rates of absenteeism, turnover, and work stoppages reflected a rebellion against the nature of Fordist work and authority. As the plant manager of a General Motors assembly plant stated:

> It was during this time that the young people in the plant were demanding some kind of change. They didn't want to work in this kind of environment. The union didn't have much control over them, and they certainly were not interested in taking orders from a dictatorial management.[48]

This rebellion came to national attention in 1972 with the three-week strike at the GM plant in Lordstown, Ohio, whose central issue was not wages, but working conditions.[49]

Managers responded to this renewed struggle with a shift toward control structures emphasizing responsible autonomy. Although retaining overall control of production, they allowed workers some discretion over the immediate labor process.[50] In the auto industry, managerial programs of job enlargement, worker participation, and quality of work life were initiated to overcome the renewed struggle of workers. As the director of employee research at GM stated: "We know that we have to take action to avoid situations like Lordstown. We've got to learn how to prevent those problems."[51] Regardless of their ostensible motives of enhancing the quality of work life, it is clear that the real managerial motives remain increased output per dollar cost. By making unskilled jobs a little less monotonous and giving workers largely formal decision-making responsibilities, managers hope to increase job satisfaction and "promote employee identification with [managerial] goals. Such positive identification increases not only workers' motivation to work but also their sense of belonging in the workplace and their pride in the plant's achievement."[52] In a detailed analysis of many such programs that enlarge the previously minute division of labor, one study found that they increased labor productivity in ways unrelated to worker identification and satisfaction—namely, by reducing the labor force, cutting balance delay time between line jobs, and eliminating idle time.[53]

There is another managerial objective behind this alteration in the division of labor, one that explains the persistence of such programs under the quiescent labor relations of the 1980s and 1990s. It is flexibility. As many students of industry have pointed out, the rigidly and minutely specialized work process is difficult to alter rapidly in response to the fluctuating quantity and quality of product demand.[54] Workers who are narrowly specialized are difficult to shift to different tasks when new products are introduced or new levels of production are required. In addition, union struggles have rendered the specialized system even more inflexible. Accepting the prevailing division of labor as inevitable, unions built programs of job security and rights around narrowly defined occupational positions, thus hindering arbitrary transfers of workers at managerial discretion. These problems of inflexibility have become serious only recently in the auto industry, when new international competition and realization problems have forced a shift to new and more diversified products, and placed a premium on rapid change in the labor process.

Programs that enlarge job skills and definitions promote this much-needed attribute of flexibility. As one social scientist has recently written with respect to these industrial experiments:

> Industrialists, you will have guessed, are not eager to cede wide-ranging authority over product design and manufacture to the workers. Their strategy as it emerges from dozens of experiments in core countries is to use a combination of innovative technologies and organizational devices to increase the flexibility of production while holding to a minimum and sharply circumscribing discretion exercised at the workplace.[55]

Thus, one of the major benefits of the famed group assembly method of the Saab-Scania plant in Sweden is, according to its production manager, greater flexibility in the use of labor power,[56] and the quality-of-work-life programs in GM plants are reported to have drastically reduced the number of grievances filed by workers during production changeovers and cutbacks, thus giving managers a freer hand in such changes.[57]

That the final aim of these efforts restructure the labor process remains the maximization of surplus value is clear from the way in which managers evaluate them. As one Italian researcher found: "Almost no one measures the effects of the content of work on the workers' well-being, while instead even the amount of grease consumed is measured with absolute precision."[58] Profitability remains the sole criterion of evaluation. General Motors measured the benefits of one experiment in work teams as a 20 percent increase in productivity and a 35 percent increase in profitability.[59] Also, although the production manager of the plant that initiated a pilot quality-of-work-life program could not so precisely measure the benefits, his criteria are clear:

> From a strictly production point of view—efficiency and costs—this entire experience has been absolutely positive, and we can't begin to measure the savings that have taken place because of the hundreds of small problems that were solved on the shop floor before they accumulated into big problems.[60]

Although, under crisis conditions, auto companies and their managers have begun to alter somewhat the traditionally minute division of labor in the industry, this in no way signals a change in the basic capitalist logic driving development of the labor process. The same capitalist attempt to increase the production of surplus value through exerting absolute control over production and overcoming the resistance of an exploited and recalcitrant working class lies behind both the initial fragmented division of labor and the recent experiments in its alteration. As long as this capitalist logic based upon antagonistic relations of production persists, the fundamental enlargement of the work tasks and responsibilities of workers will remain an unrealized dream rather than a palpable reality.

NOTES

1. Adam Smith, quoted in Karl Marx, *Capital*, Vol. I (1867) (New York: International Publishers, 1967), p. 362.
2. Ibid.
3. Harry Braverman, *Labor and Monopoly Capital: The Degradation of Work in the Twentieth Century* (New York: Monthly Review Press, 1974).
4. Herbert Gutman, *Work, Culture, and Society in Industrializing America* (New York: Knopf, 1976).

5. David Montgomery, *Workers' Control in America* (Cambridge: Cambridge University Press, 1979); and id., *The Fall of the House of Labor* (Cambridge: Cambridge University Press, 1987).

6. Allan Nevins and Frank Hill, *Ford: The Times, the Man, the Company* (New York: Scribner's, 1954), pp. 376–80; William E. Chalmers, "Labor in the Automobile Industry" (Unpublished Ph.D. dissertation, University of Wisconsin, 1932), pp. 188–93.

7. Nevins, *Ford*, p. 381.

8. "Mills on All Three Sides," *The Automobile* 29 (1913), p. 279.

9. Stephen Meyer III, *The Five Dollar Day: Labor Management and Social Control in the Ford Motor Company, 1908–1921* (Albany: State University of New York Press, 1981), p. 74. On informal and unorganized worker resistance in the early years of the U.S. auto industry, *see also* Joyce Shaw Peterson, *American Automobile Workers, 1900–1933* (Albany: State University of New York Press, 1987), Chapter 7.

10. Keith Sward, *The Legend of Henry Ford* (New York: Rinehart, 1948), p. 32.

11. Nevins, *Ford*, p. 325.

12. R. R. Lutz, *The Metal Trades* (Cleveland: Survey Committee of the Cleveland Foundation, 1916), p. 97.

13. Henry Ford, *My Life and Work* (London: Heinemann, 1923), pp. 80, 90.

14. Adam Smith, *The Wealth of Nations* (1776) (New York: Penguin, 1982), pp. 112–13.

15. Marx, *Capital*, Vol. I, pp. 519–20.

16. Ford, *My Life and Work*, pp. 103–104.

17. Horace L. Arnold and Fay L. Faurote, *Ford Methods and the Ford Shops* (1915) (New York: Arno, 1972), pp. 245, 275.

18. Braverman, *Labor and Monopoly Capital*, pp. 76–78.

19. Stephen Marglin, "What Do Bosses Do? The Origins and Functions of Hierarchy in Capitalist Production," *Review of Radical Political Economics* 6 (1974), pp. 37–38.

20. Chalmers, "Labor in the Automobile Industry," pp. 72, 84.

21. Braverman, *Labor and Monopoly Capital*, pp. 79–83.

22. Ford, *My Life and Work*, pp. 77–78.

23. Ibid., p. 209.

24. "Industrial Relationship," *Automotive Industries* 37 (1917), p. 887.

25. Paul U. Kellogg, "When Mass Production Stalls," *Survey* 59 (1928), p. 726.

26. Chalmers, "Labor in the Automobile Industry," pp. 192, 200–201.

27. August Meier and Elliot Rudwick, *Black Detroit and the Rise of the UAW* (New York: Oxford University Press, 1979); Ruth Milkman, *Gender at Work* (Urbana: University of Illinois Press, 1987); David Gartman, *Auto Slavery: The Labor Process in the American Automobile Industry, 1897–1950* (New Brunswick, NJ: Rutgers University Press, 1986), pp. 138–41.

28. "The Manufacturer's Opportunity," *Automotive Industries* 43 (1920), p. 284.

29. Arnold and Faurote, *Ford Methods and the Ford Shops*, pp. 275, 245.

30. W. K. White, "What Some New England Makers Are Doing," *The Automobile* 20 (1909), p. 434.

31. "Twenty Operations to Make Knight Sleeve," *The Automobile* 29 (1913), p. 649.

32. Richard Muther, *Production-Line Technique* (New York: McGraw-Hill, 1944), p. 239.

33. Arnold and Faurote, *Ford Methods and the Ford Shops*, pp. 41–42.

34. Muther, *Production-Line Technique*, p. 24.

35. Fred H. Colvin and Frank A. Stanley, *Running a Machine Shop* (New York: McGraw-Hill, 1948), p. 51.

36. Arnold and Faurote, *Ford Methods and the Ford Shops*, pp. 6–8.

37. Muther, *Production-Line Technique*, pp. 22–23.

38. Time study was part of the program of scientific management promoted by Frederick Taylor. However, the first managerial efforts in the auto industry to time and study minutely divided jobs do not seem to have been directly inspired by Taylor. Auto managers independently discovered and applied time study without knowledge of Taylor's work. *See* Nevins, *Ford*, pp. 468–69. For an insightful treatment of Taylorism in general, *see* Dan Clawson, *Bureaucracy and the Labor Process: The Transformation of U.S. Industry, 1860–1920* (New York: Monthly Review Press, 1980).

39. Mortier W. La Fever, "Workers, Machinery, and Production in the Automobile Industry," *Monthly Labor Review* 19 (1924), p. 17.

40. "Scientific Management," *Industrial Worker* 3 (1911), p. 3.

41. Chalmers, "Labor in the Automobile Industry," pp. 155–56.

42. Muther, *Production-Line Technique*, p. 233.

43. On the contradictory strengthening of collective struggle by the new Fordist methods, *see* Richard Edwards, *Contested Terrain: The Transformation of the Workplace in the Twentieth Century* (New York: Basic Books, 1979), pp. 126–29; David M. Gordon, Richard Edwards, and Michael Reich, *Segmented Work, Divided Workers* (Cambridge: Cambridge University Press, 1982), pp. 162–64; Jerry Lembcke, *Capitalist Development and Class Capacities: Marxist Theory and Union Organization* (Westport, CT: Greenwood Press, 1988), pp. 4–9.

44. Gartman, *Auto Slavery*, pp. 233–57.

45. On the rise and decline of militant industrial unionism in the auto industry, *see* Nelson Lichtenstein, "Auto Worker Militancy and the Structure of Factory Life, 1935–1955," *Journal of American History*, 67 (September 1980), pp. 335–53; Roger Keeran, *The Communist Party and the Auto Workers' Unions* (Bloomington, IN: Indiana University Press, 1980); Martin Halperin, *UAW Politics in the Cold War Era* (Albany: State University of New York Press, 1988).

46. *See* Samuel Bowles, David Gordon, and Thomas Weisskopf, *Beyond the Wasteland* (London: Verso, 1984).

47. Dan Georgakas and Marvin Surkin, *Detroit: I Do Mind Dying* (New York: St. Martin's Press, 1975); James Geschwender, *Class, Race, and Worker Insurgency* (Cambridge: Cambridge University Press, 1977).

48. Quoted in Robert H. Guest, "Quality of Work Life—Learning from Tarrytown," *Harvard Business Review* 57 (July–August 1979), p. 78.

49. *See* Stanley Aronowitz, *False Promises: The Shaping of American Working Class Consciousness* (New York: McGraw-Hill, 1973), pp. 21–50; Emma Rothschild, *Paradise Lost: The Decline of the Auto-Industrial Age* (New York: Random House, 1973), pp. 97–119; Barbara Garson, *All the Livelong Day: The Meaning and Demeaning of Routine Work* (New York: Penguin Books, 1975), pp. 86–98. Twenty years later, in 1992, a massive shutdown of the Lordstown plant, which brought most of GM's operations to a halt across the nation, attested to the continuing problems of worker alienation and morale which have not been (and cannot be) fully resolved under capitalist production.

50. Andrew Friedman, *Industry and Labor: Class Struggle at Work and Monopoly Capitalism* (London: Macmillan, 1977).

51. Quoted in David Jenkins, *Job Power: Blue and White Collar Democracy* (New York: Penguin, 1974), p. 199.

52. Richard E. Walton, "Work Innovation in the United States," *Harvard Business Review* 57 (July–August 1979), p. 89.

53. John Kelly, *Scientific Management, Job Redesign, and Work Performance* (London: Academic Press, 1982). "Balance delay time" is the idle time of workers whose job cycles along a production line cannot be made equal to the duration of other workers' job cycles. Hence, it is the productive time lost when balancing the various jobs on the line.

54. Friedman, *Industry and Labor*, pp. 106–8; Charles Sabel, *Work and Politics: The Division of Labor in Industry* (Cambridge: Cambridge University Press, 1982), pp. 209–14; Michael Piore and Charles Sabel, *The Second Industrial Divide* (New York: Basic Books, 1984); Stephen Wood and John Kelly, "Taylorism, Responsible Autonomy, and Management Strategy," in Stephen Wood (ed.), *The Degradation of Work? Skill, Deskilling, and the Labor Process* (London: Hutchinson, 1982), pp. 74–89.

55. Sabel, *Work and Politics*, p. 211.

56. Jenkins, *Job Power*, p. 270.

57. Guest, "Quality of Work Life."

58. Quoted in Sabel, *Work and Politics*, p. 213.

59. Walton, "Work Innovation in the United States," p. 92.

60. Quoted in Guest, "Quality of Work Life," p. 85.

3 Transformations in Hierarchy and Control of the Labor Process in the Post-Fordist Era: The Case of the U.S. Steel Industry

Harland Prechel

Applications of scientific management have provided mechanisms to exercise managerial control over the labor process throughout the twentieth century. Until recently, scientific management has taken the form of Taylorism and Fordism, which have established modes of control that focus on production functions and the separation of conception from execution.

Taylorism was the first method to identify discrete manufacturing activities and reunify them into an integrated production system. Taylorism reduced jobs to their elemental components, and then timed and recorded the necessary motions as they were completed. These "time-and-motion" studies were used to define the "one best way" to produce a product and provide management with a standard to evaluate workers. Top management relocated this information in centralized engineering and planning offices, which articulated work rules that were presented by managers to workers. This centralization of control separated conception from execution by removing many of the production decisions previously incorporated into the craft tradition and placing them into the hands of management, which reduced production work to tasks that required fewer skills and less knowledge.[1]

In response to the accumulation crisis that resulted in the Great Depression, Fordism gradually replaced Taylorism, but was only fully implemented in the post–World War II era. Fordism continued the trend of centralizing control by incorporating worker's "know-how" into the production machinery and the emerging managerial hierarchy. Fordism also continued to fragment tasks and specialize work activities. A primary characteristic of Fordism was the mechanization of the production process by reincorporating the various tasks into an assembly line. This reorganization of the labor process required several layers of management to supervise the various tasks and specialized work activities.

This chapter analyzes the emergence of post-Fordism, the third mode of control based on principles of scientific management. I will demonstrate how post-Fordism further centralized control, made it possible to eliminate several layers of management, and reduced the decision-making authority of lower and middle managers in an American steel corporation. There are several dimensions of this analysis. First, I discuss how top management ensured centralized control over the expanding number of lower and middle managers within the Fordist mode of control. Second, I analyze the source of contradiction and inefficiency within Fordism. Third, I demonstrate that the corporation's response to the crisis of accumulation that followed the recessions in the early 1980s was to overcome the inefficiencies of Fordism. Fourth, I identify three types of control and discuss how each specified control over a distinct sphere of the corporation.

FORDISM AND CAPITAL ACCUMULATION

There are several changes that have undermined the capacity of the Fordist mode of control to ensure accumulation. First, the oil crises of 1973 and 1979–1980 raised fuel costs in energy-intensive industries. Second, although quality standards increased in the marketplace, the capacity of Fordism to increase manufacturing quality reached its technical limits. The cost of "defective" products constituted a considerable proportion of production costs and eventually became an impediment to capital accumulation. Third, the tall managerial hierarchies necessary to enforce the wide range of rules and regulations within the Fordist mode of control represent a significant operating cost. Moreover, bureaucratization within Taylorism and Fordism removes decision making from the point of production, which impedes the decision-making process and reduces manufacturing flexibility. Fourth, in contrast to the immediate post–World War II era when wages steadily increased, earning power declined for blue-collar workers after the mid-1970s, which has undermined the consumption capacity of society and reduced demand. Fifth, the emergence of Newly Industrializing Countries (NICs) in the global economy and their success at penetrating markets in the United States increased economic competition. In conjunction with the decline in consumer buying power, the penetration of U.S. markets by NICs reduced utilization rates of domestic manufacturing corporations. Sixth, economic competition undermined the capacity of oligopolistic industries (e.g., steel, automobile) to set prices, which was a primary mechanism to ensure accumulation in the post–World War II era; when production costs increased, oligopolistic industries would automatically increase their prices.

Together, changes in the global economy and the technical limits of Fordism have become impediments to capital accumulation in the late twentieth century.[2] To ensure an acceptable rate of accumulation, Fordist task fragmentation, specialization, and mechanization (e.g., assembly line principles) are being replaced with a post-Fordist social organization of production.[3]

COMPETING EXPLANATIONS OF THE TRANSITION TO POST-FORDISM

Post-Fordism attempts to overcome the limits of Fordism where individual reaction time, faculties of perception, and the speed at which individuals can coordinate their actions limit productivity increases. Post-Fordism includes the application of science to organizational control systems to reduce the cost of maintaining managerial hierarchies, labor costs, and inventory and manufacturing cost, while increasing control over the manufacturing process to enhance product quality.

Several arguments associate the decentralization of decision-making authority with recent changes in the mode of control.[4] For example, managerial theory suggests that decision-making authority has been decentralized to lower levels within the managerial hierarchy throughout the twentieth century[5] and especially in the 1980s.[6] Even recent critical analyses suggest that post-Fordist applications of automatic production controls and integrated production complexes are based on work teams, cooperative decision making, and participation on the shop floor.[7] If these arguments are correct, decision-making authority should become more equally distributed.

In contrast, I argue that a very different dynamic is occurring in response to recent increases in economic competitiveness. Specifically, my analysis suggests that the mode of control is being redefined in such a way that it centralizes control, while decentralizing responsibility for decisions. Rather than encouraging participation and cooperative decision making, post-Fordist controls result in a significant decline in the autonomy of both traditional production workers and lower and middle management.

I have selected a corporation in the steel industry for study, because the low quality of steel produced in the United States and competition in the global economy resulted in a serious accumulation crisis in this industry in the early and mid-1980s. For example, the steel industry did not realize a profit between 1982 and 1986. Although the industry reported a 4 percent rate of return in 1987, it reported a net loss again in 1988.[8] Moreover, to avoid bankruptcy, several large steel corporations filed protection under Chapter 11 (e.g., Wheeling-Pittsburgh, LTV). Therefore, if a new mode of control is emerging in corporate capitalism, it should be readily observable in the steel industry where an extended accumulation crisis existed.

TECHNICAL LIMITS OF CENTRALIZED CONTROL

This study suggests that in addition to the increased competition, the crisis of accumulation in the 1980s is a consequence of contradictions within the Fordist mode of control. It demonstrates that the particular social organization of Fordism shaped the interest of managers.[9] However, dimensions of the Fordist mode of control were opposed to one another because Fordism shaped the interest of middle managers in such a way that their decisions were in opposition to the interest of top management; these oppositions will be considered contradictions.

Contradictions express themselves as crises when they undermine the efficient use of resources and make it impossible to realize a profit. There are two contradictions that are of concern here: (1) those that occur between dimensions of the Fordist mode of control and the corporation's accumulation goals, and (2) those that occur between the corporation's accumulation goals and the economy. A contradiction emerges within the firm when the mode of control generates a course of action that undermines the corporation's accumulation goal. Contradictions emerge from the economy when oscillating business cycles create overproduction and underconsumption, which result in a falling rate of profit.[10]

Historically, top management attempted to resolve these contradictions by extracting more labor from the workers. Scientific management (e.g., Taylorism, Fordism) was applied to more spheres of the corporation, which created a central role for middle management and steadily removed control from the point of production.[11]

However, there were technical limits to the centralization of decision making within Taylor's "one best way" that stemmed from the complexities of the manufacturing process. In steelmaking, for example, it is often easier to provide general guidelines over production decisions than definitive solutions to specific problems. The manufacturing process itself restricts the effectiveness of identifying, establishing, and incorporating rules into the production process. Steel manufacturing includes numerous variables and countless permutations of these variables for each product.

Moreover, large integrated steel corporations make hundreds of products that have unique production specifications. Establishing and implementing a separate set of rules for each product create an enormously complex managerial system, and restrict the necessary flexibility at the point of production to adjust the manufacturing process to meet product specification.

Hence, despite top management's efforts to increase control by establishing managerial hierarchies within the steel industry, the technical limits to scientific management resulted in comparatively high skill levels among workers and lower level managers (e.g., foremen), and required some decentralized control over production. Similar to other manufacturing industries, to ensure flexibility, many decisions remained at the point of production.[12]

THE PROFIT-MAKING STRATEGY AND ORGANIZATIONAL CONTROL

Beginning with the foundation of the corporation in the late nineteenth century through the mid-twentieth century, top management monitored a wide range of operating and coordinating decisions (e.g., scheduling manufacturing line-ups). This centralized managerial system allowed top management to oversee cost inputs directly within the various organizational units. However, as the corporation's size and complexity increased in the post–World War II era, its centralized managerial system became inadequate. As organizational complexity exceeded top management's cognitive capabilities, it was no longer able to make decisions and exercise control over the wide range of day-to-day manufacturing activities.[13] To overcome this problem, top management implemented a decentralized managerial system, which delegated decision-making authority to the managers of the various organizational units.

Once top management relinquished direct control, it implemented bureaucratic controls (e.g., rules, regulations) to specify the limits of middle managerial authority over operating units. However, the complexity of steelmaking, in conjunction with the corporation's wide product line, placed limitations on the degree to which bureaucratic controls could be implemented. On the one hand, bureaucratic controls could not govern coordinating decisions because it is difficult to establish rules governing changes in the linkage of the manufacturing facilities when those linkages frequently change. Similar to other expanding corporations, coordination of the flow of materials (i.e., scheduling, alignment of production units) through the manufacturing process was achieved by personal cooperation among the middle managers. On the other hand, the large number of individual products and the numerous variables in the steelmaking process made it difficult to routinize production. Hence, many steel manufacturing decisions remained at the point of production. Knowledge of craft traditions continued to govern many manufacturing activities.

The complexity of steel manufacturing restricted the degree to which Taylorism and Fordism and the concomitant bureaucratic controls could be implemented to: (1) coordinate the various production units and (2) exercise control over the manufacturing process. To retain control over costs, top management established more intensive budget controls by specifying operating budgets for each organizational unit.

ORGANIZATIONAL EXPANSION AND THE CONTRADICTIONS OF BUDGETARY CONTROLS

During the rapid economic growth of the 1960s and 1970s, the corporation increased its manufacturing capacity by 24 percent. By the late 1960s, the lower and middle segments of the managerial hierarchy expanded to seven levels. Budgetary controls remained top management's primary means to exercise control over the middle managers who had decision-making authority within the organizational units. The primary purpose of these controls was to determine if middle managers remained within their budgets, which was the primary criterion to determine if these managers merited a salary increase. However, middle managerial decisions to keep operating costs low within the organizational units often contradicted the corporation's profitability goal, because these decisions frequently undermined product quality. For example, if mill superintendents stopped the manufacturing process to reroll defective steel, their operating cost increased, which reflected poorly on their managerial abilities. Hence, this system of control encouraged production managers to pass flawed products to the next stage in the manufacturing process.

This contradiction within the mode of control undermined accumulation by reducing the quality of the final product. In addition, the longer the defective product remained in the manufacturing process, the higher the capital investment (e.g., labor, energy, raw materials) in that product. Moreover, the defective product must be sold at a lower price, scrapped, or rerolled. Each of these alternatives undermined the corporation's profitability goal. Whereas low-quality steel must be sold at a lower price, reprocessing the product increased manufacturing cost. Although these decisions were the most rational means to realize the subunit goal to remain within assigned budgets, they undermined the corporation's profitability goal.

Two interrelated issues contributed to this contradiction between the mode of control and the corporation's accumulation goals. On the one hand, because middle managers were evaluated by their ability to remain within assigned budgets, they often made decisions based solely on how they would affect their budgets. These decisions often undermined product quality. On the other, as steelmaking became more complex and the organizational units expanded (e.g., some units had over 500 employees), middle managers focused increasingly on the day-to-day supervisory responsibilities within their operating units. In both cases, the Fordist mode of control generated interest among managers that resulted in decisions that undermined the profitability goals of the corporation.

The Fordist mode of control did not change because it was cost-effective enough to realize an acceptable rate of accumulation in this oligopolistic industry, where the steel corporations set prices. Moreover, the high cost of production was not detected, because as long as middle managers remained within their assigned budgets, they met the technical criteria of success as defined by the budgetary controls.

THE RESPONSE TO GLOBAL COMPETITION

Several changes in the economic environment in the early 1980s undermined the corporation's capacity to accumulate capital. Competition intensified because global steel manufacturing capacity exceeded demand, several foreign corporations were dumping steel into U.S. markets,[14] and foreign steelmakers were producing lighter, higher quality steel.

Although these trends had been emerging throughout the late 1970s, they did not result in an accumulation crisis until the recessions in the early 1980s, when domestic steel demand dropped from 100 million tons in 1979 to 61.5 million tons in 1982. In 1980, the corporation's utilization rate declined to 67 percent and its rate of return dropped to 2.3 percent. These higher costs restricted accumulation even more during the 1981–1982 recession, when the corporation did not realize a profit for the first time since the Great Depression. To regain its competitive position in the marketplace, top management had to reduce cost while improving product quality.

These contradictions within the corporation's Fordist mode of control that undermined efficiency together with the increased competitiveness in its economic environment restricted the corporation's capacity to accumulate capital. The core dimension of the corporation's strategy to improve its profitability position was to increase efficiency by intensifying control. The first step in this process was to identify cost inputs in more detail. The calculation of detailed input cost was necessary before the corporation could identify where cost could be cut.

THE EXTENSION OF BUDGETARY CONTROL

By 1984, the accounting department had identified and calculated over 50,000 cost points, which were used to establish more precise controls in two ways. Initially, managerial accounting was extended to more decisions: the dimension of accounting that transforms data into decision-making information. Managerial accounting provides production managers with predetermined standard cost data, which can be compared to actual cost inputs. If variances are located between standard and actual costs, production managers are responsible for determining why variances exist and attempting to reduce those costs. The specification of cost also made it possible to intensify responsibility accounting: cost accounting by area of responsibility. Responsibility accounting specified the location in the manufacturing process where cost inputs occurred.

These changes in the accounting system made it possible to identify where specific cost inputs occurred, and evaluate the cost efficiency of specific manufacturing activities.

THE EXTENSION OF BUREAUCRATIC CONTROLS

There were two dimensions of top management's efforts to increase efficiency with more precise bureaucratic controls. Top management created a decision-making center that specified rules governing how to manufacture each product, which extended premise controls over production decisions. Premise controls establish guidelines within which a decision can be made. Technical experts in the decision-making center established these premise controls by calculating the most cost-efficient means to manufacture each product and, through a complex computer system, transmitted the rules governing production decisions to the manager on the shop floor. Premise controls were established to extend decision-making criteria to those dimensions of the decision-making process that previously escaped control. In addition, top management and its administrative staff specified the span of control and lines of authority in more detail. More precise rules identified the manager accountable for each input cost and ensured that every manager was directly accountable to a more senior manager.

Budget and bureaucratic controls together made it possible to hold the lowest level decision makers accountable for input costs by incorporating more spheres of the decision-making process within the formal mechanism of control. Whereas budget controls provided the information to determine where the cost inputs occurred, bureaucratic controls identified the production manager responsible for each cost input, which allowed top management to identify even the lowest level decision maker and hold that person accountable for costs. In the past, only middle managers were held accountable for costs.

Premise controls established more precise guidelines within which decisions could be made, which made it possible to push decision making down to the level where inputs occurred to increase organizational responsiveness. The rules that specified the span of control and lines of authority in more detail made each manager accountable to a more senior manager. Together, these bureaucratic controls made it possible to push decision-making responsibility down the organizational hierarchy, while centralizing control over the decision maker.

THE EXTENSION OF TECHNICAL CONTROLS

Once the bureaucratic and budget controls were specified in more detail, top management established a decision-making center to implement two interrelated technical controls. These controls facilitated continuous processing: the reconceptualization and reorganization of steelmaking by moving the product steadily through the manufacturing process (i.e., raw materials to finished steel).[15] Continuous processing increases efficiency by lowering capital investment in unfinished inventories[16] and the energy cost associated with reheating steel at each discrete stage of production.

The first technical control is the cybernetically controlled plant planning and scheduling system, which coordinates and integrates the manufacturing process from beginning to end. Once this centralized decision center receives an incoming order, it is entered into the plant scheduling model, which determines production line-ups.

The second technical control incorporates statistical analysis with computer controls. Statistical process control analyzes statistical variances to determine the tolerance capabilities of particular technologies. These tolerance levels are programmed into the production control computer, which measures the product as it is being manufactured, assesses product quality, and automatically adjusts the manufacturing process when levels of error move beyond predetermined standards. That is, if the production process goes out of statistical control, these cybernetic controls readjust the production technology while the product is being manufactured. Technical controls increase standardization by incorporating many operating decisions into the manufacturing process. Like budget and bureaucratic controls, technical control centralizes control over the production process.

The plant planning and scheduling system and statistical process control are components of a three-layer integrated computer system designed to increase automated management: the application of cybernetic information processing systems to aid in decision making and controlling the production process. At the first level, statistical process control standards are programmed into the production control computer, which operates individual pieces of equipment responsible for a single phase of the production process. A second level of the system coordinates the lower level control computers and integrates the various steps of the process into a smooth, continuous processing flow. A third level of the system schedules production line-ups that generate the fewest semifinished inventories; this level requires the least number of adjustments in the manufacturing process. The ultimate goal of this multilevel computer system is to provide a fully integrated set of computer controls to reduce inputs into the decision-making process that were previously not specified by the formal control system.

By 1987, the corporation located computer monitors at each work site, which made it possible to transmit the manufacturing specifications established by technical experts in the centralized decision-making center to the shop floor. Top managerial control was increased, because the standardization of information was conveyed to all levels of management from operations to sales to general management. The system was an attempt to overcome the contradiction created by budgetary controls and ensure that decisions at all levels were consistent with the profitability goals of the corporation.

Since supervision over manufacturing is built directly into the system itself, technical control reduces the need for human decision makers. As a result, once the multilevel computer system was implemented, the corporation reduced the lower and middle levels of the managerial hierarchy from seven to three layers, and reduced its managerial work force by 20 percent. In short, the applications of post-Fordism reduced both the need for decision-making skills at the point of production and the number of managers necessary to manufacture steel.

THE EXTENSION OF TOP MANAGERIAL CONTROL

The intensification of formally rational control ensured that decisions conformed to top managerial agenda. The formally rational controls ensured standardization of manufacturing decisions by programming a wide range of product specifications directly into the production control computer, which automatically adjusted the manufacturing facility to predetermined specifications. In addition, technical experts established decision premises that were transmitted through the computer system to the point of production to establish narrowly defined parameters within which production decisions had to be made.

In the past, top managerial decisions were dependent on experience in service and information obtained from the large staff of middle managers.[17] However, with the intensification of formal control, top management and its small administrative staff have the information to govern a wide range of organizational activities. These controls make it possible to reorganize the entire managerial system into one hierarchical system. The corporation has the organizational capacity to centralize decision-making information, and either implement that information directly into the production process or establish the premise of decisions. This system of control centralized authority and reduced the autonomy of both semi-skilled and skilled blue-collar workers, and lower and middle management.

CONCLUSION

The application of science to the social organization of production has increased the capacity of top management and its administrative staff to establish controls that ensure consensus and standardize decisions. Taylorist and Fordist controls were replaced, because their technical limits generated contradictions that restricted capital accumulation in the increasingly competitive economic environment.

There are three dimensions of this control system. First, technical controls made it possible to incorporate production guidelines directly into the manufacturing computers at the point of production. Second, whereas more precise rules were established to identify the manager or production worker responsible for a specific cost, premise controls stipulated guidelines governing the decisions made by these organizational members. Third, budgetary controls compare the actual cost of specific manufacturing cost to predetermined costs. If managers fail to follow the rules governing manufacturing, the new budgetary/cost controls simultaneously identify the location of the subsequent cost variation and the manager responsible for that cost.

Most importantly, the establishment of decision-making centers placed lower and middle managers at a greater distance from decision making, while providing the organizational capacity to increase surveillance over these managers. These decision centers increased top managerial control over more spheres of organizational activity. This post-Fordist mode of control has redefined the traditional responsibilities of lower and middle level managers, which has reduced their decision-making autonomy.

The emergence of post-Fordism has far-reaching implications for the distribution of authority. In addition to extending more precise control over production workers, post-Fordism demands that lower and middle level managers base their decisions on criteria established in decision centers.

In contrast to previous conceptions of corporate change that suggest decision-making authority is being decentralized, this study demonstrates that authority is being centralized. In addition to increasing control over traditional blue-collar work, post-Fordism extends top managerial control over the technical and social organization of production. Whereas Taylorist and Fordist modes of control required extensive managerial hierarchies, which restricted top management's control over the labor process, post-Fordism reduces these managerial hierarchies and simultaneously establishes formal controls that ensure managers adhere to formally rational decision-making criteria. These efforts to eliminate costs and thereby increase the rate of accumulation project the corporation toward a higher level of mechanization, standardization, and centralization of authority. The decision centers, in conjunction with the multilevel computer system, have reduced the capacity for lower and middle managers and workers to have inputs into the decision-making process.

In this chapter, I have attempted to identify more precisely the lines along which decision making is simultaneously becoming diffused throughout the organization and located in decision-making centers. On the one hand, my analysis supports the arguments that suggest the new mode of control increases participation on the shop floor. However, because these researchers fail to analyze control, they do not recognize that authority is being centralized. Although cooperative decision making has been encouraged, the definition of an "appropriate decision" is predetermined within the centralized decision-making centers. Cooperation, therefore, must be understood as the process of establishing a means of coordination and control under the centralized authority of top management, who, when faced with competition, progressively tightens the authority structures and control mechanisms within the work place. Although the layers of management within post-Fordism declined, the authority structures became more formalized and centralized to ensure cooperation. The presentation of post-Fordist strategies as based on work teams, cooperative decision making, and participation on the shop floor mask the basic relation of domination and subordination that necessarily prevails when centralized controls are implemented.

Premised on production technologies and decision-making criteria, post-Fordism is more subtle and integrated than the more direct exercise of authority within previous modes of control. Similar to Taylorism and Fordism, post-Fordist controls may generate new unanticipated forms of work place conflict. The post-Fordist mode of control that employs complex information technology to increase surveillance not only sharpens the traditional opposition between workers and management by intensifying control over traditional blue-collar occupations, but it may create a new dynamic that generates opposition between operating management and top management and its staff of technicians and engineers. Subjecting previous "unrationalized" areas of the corporation to centralized control, reduces and/or eliminates the discretion previously exercised by workers and managers. This may direct attention to the issue of autonomy, give rise to new forms of strain and conflict, and is a potential source of organizational transformation.

NOTES

1. Frederick Taylor, *The Principles of Scientific Management* (New York: W.W. Norton & Company, 1967).

2. Accumulation is the mobilization, transformation, and exploitation of inputs—labor, materials, and so forth—in such a way that the total capital of the corporation increases. *See* Paul M. Sweezy, *The Theory of Capitalist Development* (New York: Monthly Review Press, 1942); Samuel Bowles and Richard Edwards, *Understanding Capitalism* (New York: Harper & Row, 1985). Capital accumulation is used here, rather than profits, because it reflects the overall financial position of the corporation. In addition to profits, accumulation includes maintaining a strong liquidity position for capital investment and reducing debt. These variables determine the financial strength of the corporation, the value of its stock, and its financial worth. Most importantly, accumulation includes reinvestment of capital, which is necessary in the long term to realize profits.

3. Several theorists characterize the response to global competition as neo-Fordism, which suggests that these changes represent an intensification of Fordist-type regulation. I use the term post-Fordism because recent changes in the mode of control represent a significant transformation in social organization. *See* Michel Aglietta, *A Theory of Capitalist Regulation* (New York: New Left Books, 1979); Annemieke Roobeek, "The Crisis of Fordism and the Rise of a New Technological Paradigm," *Futures* 19 (April, 1987). This chapter moves beyond Aglietta's description, which only gives attention to the introduction of information technology and automation in the labor process.

4. There are numerous other dimensions of post-Fordism, including changing consumption patterns, the dwindling power of trade unions, and the deregulation of industry, that cannot be adequately addressed in this essay.

5. *See*, for example, Alfred Chandler, *Strategy and Structure: Chapters in the History of the American Industrial Enterprise* (Cambridge: The M.I.T. Press, 1962); and id., *The Visible Hand: The Managerial Revolution in American Business* (Cambridge: Belknap-Harvard University Press, 1977); Oliver Williamson, *Markets and Hierarchies* (New York: The Free Press, 1975).

6. George Huber and Reuben McDaniel, "The Decision-Making Paradigm of Organizational Design," *Management Science* 32 (1986), pp. 572–89.

7. Aglietta, *A Theory of Capitalist Regulation*; Martin Kenney and Richard Florida, "Beyond Mass Production: Production and the Labor Process in Japan," *Politics and Society* 16 (1988), pp. 121–58; Charles Sabel, *Work and Politics: The Division of Labor in Industry* (Cambridge: Cambridge University Press, 1982).

8. American Iron and Steel Institute, *Annual Statistical Report* (Washington, DC: AISI, 1989).

9. For further discussion on this point, *see* Harland Prechel, "Irrationality and Contradiction in Organizational Change: Transformations in the Corporate Form of a U.S. Steel Corporation, 1930–1987," *The Sociological Quarterly*, Vol. 32, No. 3 (Fall 1991).

10. Karl Marx, *Capital*, Vol. I (New York: International Publishers, 1967); Sweezy, *The Theory of Capitalist Development*; Ernest Mandel, *Late Capitalism* (London: Verso, 1975).

11. *See* Harry Braverman, *Labor and Monopoly Capital: The Degradation of Work in the Twentieth Century* (New York: Monthly Review Press, 1974); Dan Clawson, *Bureaucracy and the Labor Process: The Transformation of U.S. Industry, 1860–1920* (New York: Monthly Review Press, 1980); Richard Edwards, *Contested Terrain: The Transformation of the Workplace in the Twentieth Century* (New York: Basic Books, 1979); Stephen Marglin, "What Do Bosses Do? The Origins and Functions of Hierarchy in Capitalist Production," *Review of Radical Political Economy*, No. 6 (Summer, 1974).

12. *See* Michael Burawoy, *Manufacturing Consent: Changes in the Labor Process under Monopoly Capitalism* (Chicago: University of Chicago Press, 1979); and id., "Between the Labor Process and the State: The Changing Face of Factory Regimes under Advanced Capitalism," *American Sociological Review*, 48 (1983); William Staples, "Technology, Control, and the Social Organization of Work at a British Hardware Firm, 1791–1891," *American Journal of Sociology*, Vol. 93, No. 1 (July, 1987).

13. The organizational literature refers to the expansion of organizational complexity beyond the cognitive capacity of managers as bounded rationality. *See* Herbert Simon, *Administrative Behavior*, 2nd ed. (New York: Macmillan, 1957), p. 79; James March and Herbert Simon, *Organizations* (New York: John Wiley & Sons, 1958), pp. 168–71.

14. The definition of dumping has varied historically, but generally refers to selling steel below prices the U.S. government negotiated with foreign steelmakers. For more details, *see* Harland Prechel, "Steel and the State: Industry Politics and Business Policy Formation, 1940–1989," *American Sociological Review*, Vol. 55, No. 5 (October, 1990).

15. Traditionally, steel production was organized in segments.

16. For manufacturing corporations, semifinished inventory cost is a major source of capital investment. For example, in the early 1980s, this corporation had between $750 and $900 million invested into semifinished inventories.

17. *See* Chandler, *The Visible Hand: The Managerial Revolution in American Business*.

4 The Labor Process and Control of Labor in the U.S. Computer Industry

Navid Mohseni

Under capitalism, nothing is protected from becoming a commodity, available to be bought and sold. In fact, what distinguishes the capitalist system from its predecessors is that labor power has become a commodity. This continual process of striving for "commodification" of everything does not constitute the ultimate goal of the system, however. Rather, it is the maximization of profit through the exploitation of labor that is the motive force of capitalism. The continuous process of commodification has incorporated many things, but, above all, the "commodification of creativity" has produced, and will continue to produce, a profound ramification on the development of capitalism and on the whole notion of control of the labor process.

This chapter has a dual purpose: to present theoretically how and why creativity is commodified under capitalism and to evaluate the effects of the commodification of creativity on the computer industry. In doing so, I will illustrate the dialectical relationship between the labor process and the creative process, and show how each is controlled and organized in computer and hi-tech industries. This should help situate the controversy of Fordism and post-Fordism (as systems of control of the labor process) into a larger context that takes into account the development of capitalism and capitalist control of the labor process and of creative labor in the computer industry.

THE DEVELOPMENT OF THE COMPUTER INDUSTRY IN THE UNITED STATES

One of the requirements of a system that rests on the maximization of profit is rational calculation. With the concentration and centralization of capital, this need becomes more urgent for the owners of capital.

The Early Years

Although the first large computer-like calculating machine, the "Difference Machine," was built by Charles Babbage in 1822, it was not until the late nineteenth century that the first mechanical computer was built. The U.S. Census Office needed some kind of mechanical machine to speed up the process of tabulating census results, which required the work of hundreds of workers for several years.[1] At that time, Herman Hollerith, who was working for the U.S. Census Office, invented the first punched card machine, the "Counting Machine."

The main customers for Hollerith's machine were government departments within the large bureaucratic agencies of the state and large business firms that were expanding in the United States and abroad.[2]

During and following World War II, the need for computing became stronger. However, in spite of the initial development and financing of computers by the government, the first commercial computer was not completed until after the war. By late 1945, John Mauchly and John Eckert at the University of Pennsylvania finished building the first complete electronic computer, Electronic Numerical Integrator and Computer (ENIAC). ENIAC was operated on the technology of vacuum tubes; it contained 18,000 vacuum tubes, occupied 15,000 square feet, and could perform seven instructions per second.[3] Vacuum tubes were very large, expensive, and, because they consumed so much power, were unreliable when they overheated.[4] When Harvard Mark I (a 51-foot long and 8-foot high computer) was built with the assistance of IBM in 1947, Thomas J. Watson, Jr., then president of IBM, did not believe that such computers would have much commercial success. Mauchly and Eckert left the University of Pennsylvania in 1946 and set up their own company. They later received a contract to build a computer for the Census Bureau. Facing a lack of funds, they sold their company to Remington Rand. In 1951, UNIVersal Automatic Computer (UNIVAC) was completed and delivered to the Census Bureau.[5] IBM, which until then had controlled the sales of calculating punched card machines to the Census Bureau, was threatened by the sale of UNIVAC and began to design the production of its own computers. It delivered its 700 series in 1953 to compete with UNIVAC computers.[6]

By the late 1950s, there were five major companies producing computers based on vacuum tube components. Despite Remington Rand's first start in the market, by 1956, IBM was the number-one computer producer carrying 75 percent of the market share; Remington Rand followed with 19 percent.[7]

Since the 1950s, several waves of new-generation computers have poured into the market.[8] What determines the separation of one generation of computers from another is basically the utilization of more advanced electronic components. Thus, the second generation of computers was produced when vacuum tubes were replaced by transistors. The transistor was invented in 1948 at Bell Laboratories. In comparison with the vacuum tube, a transistor is much smaller, more reliable, requires less power, and is less expensive.[9] Transistor or solid-state technology had a tremendous effect on the development of faster, smaller, and cheaper computers. By 1958, transistors were being built so small that 1,000,000 of them could have been placed into a cubic foot.[10] From 1958 to 1965, many companies entered the computer industry, and the market was expanded drastically. In 1959, $1 billion, and in 1965, $6 billion worth of equipment was installed.

Compared to 1955 when there were only 250 computers in use, in 1965 alone, 7,400 computers were produced, which increased the total number of computers in use to 31,000.[11] As new companies entered the computer business, IBM's share dropped. However, IBM still remained the number-one producer with a 65 percent share of the market.

The third generation of computers emerged in 1965 with the utilization of another innovation from the semiconductor (or electronic component) industry (i.e., the integrated circuit). Integrated circuits were more a breakthrough in the realm of production technique than a new product innovation. Integrated circuits connected a number of transistors on the surface of semiconductor material (germanium or silicon) instead of wiring them together.

As in the past, IBM was not the first company to utilize new components. RCA, in 1964, announced the development of its new computer, "Spectra," which utilized an Integrated Circuit (IC). General Electric also produced its 600 series with time-sharing features. The era of third-generation computers represents the beginning of a greater diversification among computer manufacturers, and the entrance of many small firms into the computer market. During this period, IBM had a large market share for standardized input-output and peripheral equipment. According to IBM "internal" figures, IBM's share of the market between 1964–1970 was in the range of 70 percent to 75 percent.[12]

During the 1970s, the development of faster, cheaper, and smaller microchips, known as Large Scale Integrated Circuit (LSIC) or Very Large Scale Integrated Circuit (VLSIC), furthered the growth of smaller and more powerful computers. The innovation of the microprocessor (a computer on a chip) by Intel in 1971 also tremendously affected the structure of the industry, the computer market, and the composition of the computer producers in the industry. Thanks to the rapid development of semiconductors, the market for minicomputers expanded in the 1970s. Minicomputers were cheaper and smaller than mainframes. Hence, by being affordable and more specialized,[13] they became attractive to small businesses.

During this period IBM still continued to produce mainframes and did not foresee a substantial profit in the minicomputer market. That was a serious miscalculation on the part of IBM, since its market share decreased by 20 percent in the 1970s and its profit margin fell from 28 percent in the 1960s to 21 percent in the 1970s.[14] In contrast, other companies, like Digital Equipment Corporation (DEC), dominated the market for minicomputers.[15] Between 1970 and 1977, 50,000 minicomputers were sold by DEC at $250,000 each.[16] From 1970 to 1979, the number of computers purchased or installed increased ninefold.

Recent Developments

The great diversity of computer products differentiates the character of the computer industry of today from that of the past. The computer industry began by producing UNIVAC, a large, general-purpose computer. Today, the computer industry manufactures large mainframe computers, minicomputers, personal microcomputers, supercomputers, and interbreeds of computers that are highly specialized and task-oriented, such as work station computers.

In the 1980s, a huge wave of expansion of the computer market occurred via microcomputers or personal computers (PC). Small companies, like Apple and Commodore, began selling personal computers and had 100 percent of the market share to themselves. After several years of lagging behind, IBM entered the microcomputer market in the early 1980s, and by 1986, had captured 73 percent of the market. The market share for Apple microcomputers, which was the number-one producer in 1981 with 28.6 percent market share, dropped to 4 percent in 1986.[17] In 1982, a year after IBM entered the microcomputer market, total sales of microcomputers exceeded that of minicomputers by 8 percent.[18] The unit and dollar sales of microcomputers have been increasing ever since. In 1984, 34.8 percent of the total dollar sales of computers belonged to microcomputers.

Besides producing computers, the computer industry also provides software and services, and manufactures peripheral equipment for computers, such as printers and terminals. The market share of parts, peripherals, equipment, and software products in 1985 was 83.1 percent. Only 16.9 percent of the total revenue of $141.7 billion in 1985 was generated by the sale of mainframe, mini-, and microcomputers. Software alone captured 28.7 percent of total sales.[19]

In the production of early computers, software costs had comprised only 20 percent to 30 percent of total cost. By the mid-1960s, the cost of software had became equal to the cost of hardware. By 1976, close to 80 percent of the total system cost of computers was devoted to software production.[20] This percentage today has passed a landmark 90 percent level. According to *Electronic Market Data Book*, "software . . . is not only emerging as the decisive factor in the computer market, but it is also one of the fastest growing markets in the world."[21]

Like hardware, diversity among software products is a dominant feature of the software market today. Each general category of "system software" and "application software" is further subdivided, representing slower or faster growing segments of the market. Not only is there different system software to run different brands of mainframe computers, but there is also software for each kind of hardware, like minicomputers and personal microcomputers, which require their own system software. This diversification is also true for application software. For example, office automation software, such as database management, CAD/CAM/CAE, and desk-top publishing, has had the highest rate of growth in recent years.[22]

Software production/development is carried out by hundreds of small and large specialty and conglomerate companies. The *Computer Industry Almanac 1991*, in its list of the top 10 U.S. software producers in 1989, ranks IBM, with more than $8.4 billion in software sales, number one.[23] As described earlier, IBM is the number one producer of hardware as well as software in the United States. In fact, IBM is the top computer producer in the world. In 1981, close to one-fourth of the world market belonged to IBM. In 1989, $36.9 billion of IBM's revenue came from outside the United States, ranking IBM number two in the European market. However, in the Japanese computer market, IBM's total sales in 1989 was $6.9 billion, compared with the total Japanese electronics output of about $165 billion.[24]

Although IBM has always been the number-one computer producer, with a gigantic market share, it has never been free of competitors. There have always been companies that have threatened IBM's dominance of the market, through new innovation, better management, aggressive marketing, and market differentiation.

New Contradictions

Following Ernest Mandel's argument in *Late Capitalism*, one can contend that the computer industry is not qualitatively different from any other industry in that although the introduction of innovations is expected to bring a surplus-profit for the first introducer, the surplus-profits are soon lost when new companies begin to adopt these innovations and hence enter the market.[25] Mandel argues that the introduction of such innovations is speeded up under monopoly capitalism, but not indefinitely; his argument is based on the logic that accelerated technological innovations increase labor productivity, but the productivity of labor cannot be increased forever—it is finite.

Mandel's analysis of innovations is primarily based on labor-saving technologies that are designed to reduce labor costs. However, the history of the computer industry also suggests some subtle aspects of capitalist development. Computers are not only designed as labor-saving technologies, but are also designed (especially recently) as new "consumer goods." It is this aspect of computers as "new" commodities (i.e., in their usage) that points out the role that designers, engineers, software producers, and a whole group of "creative workers" play in the production process.

THE COMMODIFICATION OF CREATIVITY

Capitalism by the late ninteenth century had become monopolistic. By the middle of the twentieth century, it began facing the problem of overaccumulation[26]—that is, more capital had become available under monopoly capitalism than there were outlets for its investment. As a result, during the same period, there was an immense internationalization of capital. In addition to the widespread phenomenon of corporations moving overseas, the excess capital was also invested domestically in the production of new commodities, commodities that also created new markets. Producing these new commodities, however, involved creation of new use-values. New use-values, in turn, required new ideas and imagination, or what I call "creativity." For capital, creativity became, and still is, the potential source of both new commodities and new markets.

In the early twentieth century, monopoly capitalism was also faced with the problem of control of the labor process. Taylorism, and later Fordism, were introduced to increase the efficiency of control by management over the labor process.[27] This entailed the separation of the worker's knowledge and creativity and their transfer to the managers. This separation not only increased control by the managers over the workers, but it also generated the condition for knowledge and creativity to become autonomous. The autonomization of knowledge/creativity produced the possibility for its commodification. The two trends, the overaccumulation of capital and the application of Taylorism to the labor process, made possible the commodification of creativity. In the first trend, it took the form of the application of science to the creation of new commodities. In the second trend, it became the knowledge of scientific management.

Creativity was incorporated in the form of science in the emerging hi-tech industries of the late 1950s—mostly in the electronics, pharmaceutical, and plastics industries. The commodification of creativity brought about a work force of "knowledge workers."[28] The question that arises is: How does this new work force both control and be controlled by capital? In other words, how does the commodification of creativity affect the notion of industrial growth and control of the labor process? This question can be examined by focusing on the contradictions in the commodification of the creative process.

Contradictions in the Creative Process

When scientists and engineers in large corporations are faced with the contradictory character of their R&D departments and the opportunity to make profits well above their salaries, they are likely to start their own firms. This is possible only because of two additional conditions that hold under monopoly capitalism. First, the existence of surplus capital (overaccumulation) in the form of venture capital, which seeks outlets for higher rates of profit. Second, the existence of commodified "ideas." The commodification of ideas in the form of knowledge, information, or creativity defies control, and makes the start-up of small firms possible. Large corporations desperately undertake legal and other measures to prevent their employees from using their knowledge to start up their own firms or to go to work for competitors for higher salaries.

The newest, most recent generations of computers have originated in small companies that have introduced several generations of computers and that were, by and large, all new to the computer industry. Large corporations, however, were able to organize the production side of the computers so that mass production was made possible.

The growth of small companies was in part the result of the attempt of monopoly capitalism to overcome its contradictions; that is, the generated overabundance of capital, which needed outlets, created the condition for creative ability to become a commodity in order to absorb the existing excess capital and produce profits. The constant introduction of new generations of computers into the market has produced so much instability that it has required companies to be short-term oriented. This situation is characteristic of a new era that has surfaced as a result of the commodification of creativity. In this era of instability, one can argue that capital, as a system, and by necessity of its dynamics, must operate looking toward a long-term process of accumulation. Ironically, to survive the accumulation process, capital now has turned into its own denial by becoming either short-term oriented or by facing instability.

This process of continual short-term decision making and chronic instability is experienced by industries where ideas are more systematically commodified and the flux of new commodities is continual. As a result, companies have attempted to control the production process, and hence regulate the production of new commodities. To do so, managers of corporations operating in the high-tech industries have tried to implement new policies for control of the creative process.

CONTROL OF THE CREATIVE PROCESS

For large corporations, the question facing them now and in the next decade is how to control the creative process, or how best to organize the creative process so that it produces the highest and most secure profit? Organizing creative ability, like organizing labor power, denotes the effort of securing control of capital over the process of transformation of creative ability into something useful and, hence, marketable. From the management point of view, they must ascertain that what they have purchased (creative workers' abilities) is worth it—that is, the work of creative workers produces more value than it costs. Therein lies the crucial uncertainty. It is in this uncertainty, coupled with the desire to increase profits, where the rationale for the control of scientists and other knowledge workers' labor takes root.

The Creative Process and Productivity

To create something new requires investment in Research and Development (R&D)—the cost of creativity, excluding the cost of lab equipment and other constant capital investments. The cost of R&D has increased tremendously since the end of World War II, as has the concern for the profitability of a firm's R&D expenses. The question that is raised from the point of view of the capitalist is: How can research or creative process become more productive? Productivity implies profit. What we see is the effort of the capitalist system to organize "the brains" in order to increase the productivity of creativity for an ever higher rate of profit. For capitalism as a whole to increase productivity implies, most of all, the *measurement* of productivity.[29] There has been, however, controversy over the validity of these measurements, since there is no single way to measure the productivity and efficiency of the creative process.

There cannot be any form of measurement of productivity without implementing procedures to save costs and increase the innovative power of the R&D organization. This effort to save costs has led to the procedures of simplification of some lab operations and implementation of automated machines and computers in these departments. Simplification and automation of lab procedures have enticed some critics of R&D organizations to follow Harry Braverman's critique of Taylorism in their analysis of the organization of the creative process under capitalism.[30] The common argument of these studies is that computers are used in order to *simplify*—and hence deskill—the work of scientists, engineers, and software programmers.[31]

The critics rightfully contend that computers have provided the technical possibilities for management to implement the philosophy of Taylorism for knowledge workers as it was previously enforced on workers on the shop floor. Following Braverman, for example, Clement argues that "computerization is the technology of control. . . . Those who work with information in large organizations are in the process of being subjected to greater managerial control through their use of information systems."[32] In a similar vein, Philip Kraft applies Braverman's model to the work of computer programmers:

> Programmers, system analysts, and other software workers are experiencing efforts to break down, simplify, routinize, and standardize their own work so that it, too, can be done by machines instead of people. Computers are the most sophisticated instruments available to managers in their efforts to de-skill production workers and now they are being used against the very people who made it possible for managers to use them.[33]

Although Clement and Kraft's arguments have much validity in applying Braverman's framework to a phenomenon that is different from the traditional labor process, they have overlooked the subtleties in ideologies of the new forms of control. What distinguishes the creative process from the labor process, in spite of their organic connection, is that the outcome of the creative process is a new commodity not yet produced, whereas the end result of the labor process is a commodity not yet sold. These two processes are connected; their separation is inconceivable. Yet, in so far as a new not-yet-made commodity is the beginning of the labor process that ends with its real production, the creative process ceases and becomes part of the labor process when what is created at the end of the creative process is no longer a new not-yet-made commodity but a finished product. In other words, what makes a process creative is the production of "new ideas." However, when what is created is no longer a "new idea," the process is transformed into a labor process, even if it takes the form of "mental labor"—creative labor that has lost the element of creativity because of its standardization.[34]

Standardization and Control

It is the transformative mechanism of the creative process into the labor process that makes it appropriate for control and able to assume the form of Taylorism. It is when the creative process stops generating new ideas that the process can be routinized, standardized, and even computerized! Accordingly, then, at the very instance when the creative process becomes a labor process, Braverman's critical framework becomes most applicable, and the analyses of Kraft, Clement, and others become the most appropriate. Similarly, one can also argue that when the labor process becomes a creative process, Braverman's model becomes inapplicable. This happens whenever capital injects the notion of creativity back into the labor process in order to increase the productivity of labor (by generating consent) or to create new forms of the production process. This is, in fact, the heart of post-Fordism, which is well demonstrated by Harland Prechel in the previous chapter.

When the creative process is still a "creative" process, we can no longer apply Braverman's framework. Alternatively, management can standardize the creative process when it is only a labor process in disguise (i.e., mental labor), but it can also do so when standardization itself transforms the creative process into a labor process. As a result, of course, the creative process ceases to generate any new ideas. It is here that the contradiction in control over the creative process rests. That is, from the point of view of the capitalists, management should implement such forms of control over the creative process so that the generation of new ideas is not stopped.

The more highly routinized and systematized R&D organizations become, the less likely they are to produce new commodities. Large corporations, therefore, are caught in the contradiction of the transformation of the creative process into the labor process. In so far as large corporations and monopoly powers must remain creative (yet are not producing new commodities), the expense of R&D is a burden and a direct cost of production. To make R&D expenses cost-effective and productive, therefore, large corporations are tempted to implement scientific management in the control of their creative processes. Large corporations, being undercut by their own actions, become vulnerable by losing their competitive edge and market share to smaller companies that utilize greater creativity of their knowledge workers. For these companies, small size is a major advantage to their creativity, for it is only in this way that they can compete with the larger corporations and obtain a market share untapped by the monopolies because of the latter's routinization of the creative process to increase short-term profits, which inhibits them from generating new ideas and new products. Creativity means open communication, and communication is better established in small environments than in large ones.[35] Without large R&D expenses, small corporations do not need to routinize and standardize their creative activities for the sake of control.

New Forms of Control

It is this contradiction in the transformation of the creative process to the labor process that makes monopoly powers attempt to formulate and establish new forms of control over the creative process. The aim, without revoking its creative element, is to make it productive. "Team work," "open space," "freedom in the work place," "elimination of the distinction between management and scientists," and "decentralization" are all examples of a movement that departs from Taylorism in control of the creative process.[36] This does not mean, however, that all work is exempt from routinization and simplification in the computer industry. In fact, what operates in the computer industry, or other electronics industries, is the constant struggle between implementing control through Taylorism and Fordism over some work and applying some form of post-Fordism on others. Which one of these forms of control to be imposed depends, on the one hand, on the degree of monopolization of the industry, and on the other hand, on whether the product is mass-produced. Of course, these two are not totally separate phenomena, since the degree of monopolization can be affected by the uniformity of the demand and whether the product is mass-produced. Thus, the computer industry, for example, was dominated by the production of the mainframe, and it was highly monopolistic. When new generations of computers were introduced, the degree of concentration (i.e., total market share of the top few firms) was decreased, and the industry became more competitive, as more firms began producing mini- and later personal microcomputers. The standardization of computers, however, led to the possibility of their mass production, which, in turn, affected the price structure and, ultimately, the competitive-monopoly structure of the industry.

What makes the whole notion of control more complicated is that the monopoly structure is not fixed either, nor is the demand always standardized. So, what we have in reality is not just *one* form of control of labor or the creative process as some have argued,[37] but a mixture of the two, which also is in the process of transformation. Thus, when a product is yet to be "conceptualized," as with the creation of a new special-purpose microchip, the control of the scientists' work is more open-ended and the pressure to create is more indirect. When the product is mass-produced software, however, the work of programmers is routinized and systematized to increase their productivity. Likewise, when the product is a universal electronic chip that is mass-produced by a large company, we see that control of the labor process is nothing short of the assembly line championed by Ford.

Although the exploitation of creativity in the computer industry is an important source of its growth, as manifested in the introduction of generation after generation of new computers, the industry could not have expanded as it did without the mass production of computers. Hence, the control and exploitation of both the creative process *and* the labor process at the point of production are the sources of growth and expansion of the computer industry.

Looking at the latter, equally important aspect of the production process in the computer and electronics industries, I will in the next section examine the organization and control of the production process at the shop-floor level.

CONTROL AT THE POINT OF PRODUCTION

For a capitalist, a product is not a product until it is produced or materialized, and profit is not realized until the product is sold. What we see, then, is that the work of the creative workers is immanently connected to that of workers on the shop floor who mass produce the product in its material form. The value that capitalists appropriate from the creative worker makes up the surplus profit or monopoly-rent, because the product is new. This part can be forgone. The history of the computer industry shows that the larger monopoly firms, as long as they are the dominant power in the market, do not care for innovating something new, so the exploitation of the creative worker is not a major component of their profit. On the other hand, the value that they appropriate from the exploitation of their production workers is the *real source* of their existence; this they would not relinquish under any circumstance. By comparison, then, we see that the larger and more monopolistic firms are more concerned with their labor costs and the control of their labor process in order to guarantee their high rates of profit.

The major cost of electronics and computer products is in the labor costs. A new breakthrough, like a new chip or a new-generation computer, creates for the innovator firm monopoly-rent (extra profit over and above the normal rate of profit when the new product is totally defused into the market). This situation, however, will not last for a long time. In fact, if a company relies only on monopoly-rent as the major part of its profit, it will face a major blow when other companies copy the new products or come up with their own variations. In the 1980s, the major shakeup of the computer industry was due in part to the fact that many firms had relied on the extraordinary profits that they had made because of the newness of their products. When other firms entered the market to produce similar products, that extraordinary profit dried up. Then, those who could save on labor costs became the survivors.

Struggle over saving labor costs is the major battleground in the current computer industry. The production of electronics components is very labor-intensive. This has resulted in computer and electronics firms moving to other parts of the world, not for expansion of their markets or to have outlets for their excess capital, but primarily to save on labor costs.

The Nature of the Work Force

The work force in the electronics and computer industry consists mainly of women, especially women of the peripheral regions of the capitalist world. What the companies argue is that women are better suited than men to assemble intricate electronics components. To understand how the labor process is controlled in this context, we need also to consider the ideological component of labor control, which in this case includes sexism and racism.[38]

In Silicon Valley, where most production workers are women and women of color, and the foremen are male, the control of the labor process is not only enforced through the detailed routinization and standardization of work, but also through sexism. For example, women are positioned to view their work implicitly and explicitly as "women's work." This is done through color coding of employee uniforms. As Karen Hossfeld points out, a company's policy is that work smocks of all employees are to be color-coded, but "while the men's smocks are color-coded according to occupation, the women's are color-coded by sex, regardless of occupation."[39] Women's work is also viewed as secondary. Since traditionally women's primary job has been working at home, working in the factory is viewed as temporary and just "helping out." Although this claim defies the reality of women's lives, it is in part accepted and internalized by women workers, especially by women of color who come from societies where men are viewed as the main breadwinners. Challenging this custom, either by earning higher wages or by occupying the traditional role of men, is very difficult for women. When women workers view their job as temporary—"only till their financial situation gets better"—it makes it easier for management to impose harsher work regimens on them and get away with it. Referring to the Philippino female workers, the chairman of the board of INTERLEK (USA) and DYNETEICS (Philippines) justifies the terrible conditions of working with high-powered microscopes by saying that "these girls are all high school and college girls; they can take a lot of abuse; they like abuses."[40] Another example of management's view is that "Third World women genuinely enjoy doing the very things that would drive men to assault and sabotage."[41]

The companies can justify the low wages they pay to women workers by viewing them as not being primary breadwinners, and regarding them as only either supplementing the family's income or as earning extra pocket money for personal enjoyment. It is in the companies' interest to perpetuate this ideology both by their hiring and firing policies and the way they treat women in the work place. By having mostly males as their supervisors and foremen, the companies make sure women's feelings of powerlessness and docility are reinforced. Sexual harassment of women workers also makes it possible to increase the work pressure without confronting any opposition. Perpetuating the sexist ideology is advantageous to the corporations. Hiring young women and women of color with low education,[42] whether in the U.S. or overseas, depresses overall wages below the average. Low wages, coupled with the fragmentation of work and the standardization of the electronics products, make it possible for companies to hire semiskilled workers who are overworked and easily fired.

Working Conditions

The work conditions, from working with high-powered microscopes for assembling components, to using hazardous chemicals for washing the wafers, to working in "clean rooms," where the most sensitive computer components are fashioned, are dangerous and unbearable. In his book *Behind the Silicon Curtain*, Dennis Hayes points out that "electronics production work must be counted among the most dangerous occupations"[43] Yet the companies can afford to overlook and ignore the dangers while there exists an overpopulation of unemployed workers who accept these jobs. They can afford to ignore these, because the constant capital (machinery, tools, plant equipment) in the computer and electronics industry is lightweight and mobile. In fact, one of the features of the computer industry is its low capital/labor ratio. In Silicon Valley, most companies lease their equipment and plant facilities. Having leased their constant capital, companies can curtail their operations or move to overseas locations, whenever they are faced with market contractions.

The instability of the industry, which is due to a constant influx of new commodities (i.e., faster and more powerful computers) with a low capital/labor ratio, both requires and facilitates the organization of labor to be based on temporary hiring and maximum flexibility in conditions of work. It is sobering to realize that, contrary to the favorable publicity of the computer and other high-tech industries, what makes these industries the most advanced and progressive is also what makes them the most ruthless and cruel exploiters of their work force. The conditions that make an industry constantly innovative are also those that make it unstable. It is this instability that is transferred into policies that most directly affect the workers. Although one of the most innovative industries can be argued to be one of the most cruel and exploitative, this is not uniformly so. The creative process is controlled differently and with more freedom than the labor process (whether mental or physical), and it is this difference in control strategy that at the same time creates class division and, potentially, class solidarity among workers.

CONCLUSION

What I have argued in this chapter is that two conditions under monopoly capitalism—the existence of excess capital and the Taylorization of the labor process—have created the prerequisites for the commodification of creativity. This commodification (which is best shown by the incorporation of scientific work into the production of new commodities), in turn, has created instability. Any new innovation, although it absorbs excess capital and fetches high profit for venture capitalists, also affects the monopoly-competitive structure of an industry. This results in instability. No firm can count on a long, steady profit from new innovations. Any company that follows this policy is bound to be eliminated by competitors who imitate the new products. What makes a company successful is its adoption of a combination of two factors—a strategy of low-cost production with constant innovation. Low-cost production means moving to the peripheral regions of the capitalist world and hiring cheap labor. Constant innovation implies establishing lean R&D in the industrialized regions that have a highly educated work force.

The variation of the monopoly-competitive structure affects the patterns of control over the labor and creative process. As they relate to the work of scientists, engineers, and other knowledge workers, they can be subsumed under the category of neo- or post-Fordism, since creativity is the element that ultimately produces something "new." Control over the work of production workers is considered easier; because their work is highly routinized and Taylorized, no creativity is allowed. Their employment policy is designed to be flexible and their work is considered to be temporary. Unionization is discouraged, and if the wages increase or the opposition to work conditions escalates, the companies wrap up and move to a new region.

Although the differences in the forms of control of the labor process and the creative process by management stem from the kind of labor performed, these forms of control also affect and alter the nature of labor itself. Hence, the creative process (i.e., the work of scientists, engineers, and programmers) is not only organically linked to the labor process, but, depending on the nature of control, it *can* also become a labor process. This double linkage, one could argue, provides the potential common ground for class solidarity between manual workers and knowledge workers.

NOTES

1. *See* Richard T. DeLamarter, *Big Blue: IBM's Use and Abuse of Power* (New York: Dodd, Mead Publisher, 1986).

2. In 1914, when he was unable to cope with financial problems, Hollerith sold his company to the Computing Tabulating Recording Company (CTRC), which later became International Business Machines (IBM).

3. John T. Soma, *The Computer Industry* (Lexington, MA: D. C. Heath, 1975), p. 16. Today the speed of computers is measured by million instructions per second (MIPS). *See* Katherine Davis Fishman, *The Computer Establishment* (New York: Harper & Row, 1981), p. 28.

4. Brian C. Twiss (ed.), *The Managerial Implication of Microelectronics* (London: Macmillan, 1981), p. 25; Robert E. Freund, "Competition and Innovation in the Transistor Industry," Ph.D. dissertation (Duke University, 1971), p. 10.

5. Gerald W. Brock, *The U.S. Computer Industry* (Cambridge, MA: Bollinger Publishing Company, 1975), p. 11; Soma, *The Computer Industry*, p. 16.

6. Ibid.

7. Brock, *The U.S. Computer Industry*, p. 13; Stephen T. McClellan, *The Coming Computer Industry Shakeout* (New York: John Wiley and Sons, 1984), p. 54.

8. *See*, for example, Soma, *The Computer Industry*.

9. Freund, "Competition and Innovation in the Transistor Industry," p. 12.

10. Ernest Braun and Stuart Macdonald, *Revolution in Miniature* (Cambridge: Cambridge University Press, 1982), p. 90.

11. Ibid.

12. Brock, *The U.S. Computer Industry*, p. 21.

13. *See* Soma, *The Computer Industry*, p. 28.

14. McClellan, *The Coming Computer Industry Shakeout*, p. 59.

15. Other companies that entered the computer market via minicomputers were Data General, Hewlett-Packard, and Wang Laboratories. *See* Kenneth Flamm, *Creating the Computer* (Washington, DC: Brookings Institution, 1988), p. 103.

16. Ibid., p. 128.

17. Robert Eckelmann, "A Study of Competitive Position of the U.S. Computer Industry," in *The Future of the Semiconductor, Computer, Robotics, and Telecommunications Industries* (Princeton, NJ: Petrocelli Books, 1984), p. 45; E. Julivessen and P. Isaacson (eds.), *Computer Industry Almanac* (Dallas, TX: Computer Industry Almanac, 1987), p. 73.

18. Marcus Einstein and James C. Franklin, "Computer Manufacturing Enters a New Era of Growth," *Monthly Labor Review* Vol. 109, No. 99 (September 1986), p. 10.

19. *See* Mark L. Goldestein, "Slump or Shakeout? U.S. Computer Industry Assesses Its Future," *Industry Week* (January 6, 1986).

20. Soma, *The Computer Industry*, p. 29; Eckelmann, "A Study of Competitive Position," p. 47.

21. Electronic Industry Association, *Electronic Market Data Book* (Washington, DC: E.I.A., 1986), p. 68.

22. *See* "1988 U.S. Market Report," *Electronics* (January 7, 1988), p. 70.

23. Egil Julivessen and Karen P. Julivessen, *Computer Industry Almanac 1991* (New York: Simon & Schuster, 1990), p. 2.48.

24. Ibid., pp. 12.9 and 12.11.

25. *See* Ernest Mandel, *Late Capitalism* (London: Verso, 1975), p. 538.

26. For a discussion of the overaccumulation of capital and stagnation, *see* Paul A. Baran and Paul M. Sweezy, *Monopoly Capital* (New York: Monthly Review Press, 1966); John Bellamy Foster and Henryk Szlajfer (eds.), *The Faltering Economy: The Problem of Accumulation under Monopoly Capitalism* (New York: Monthly Review Press, 1984).

27. *See* Frederick W. Taylor, *Scientific Management* (New York: Harper, 1947).

28. Philip Kraft, *Programmers and Managers: The Routinization of Computer Programming in the United States* (New York: Springer-Verlag, 1977).

29. Michael J. Stahl and Joseph Steger, "Measuring Innovation and Productivity," *Research Management*, Vol. 20, No. 1 (1977), pp. 35–38; Alfred H. Schainblatt, "How Companies Measure the Productivity of Engineers and Scientists," *Research Management*, Vol. 25, No. 3 (1982), pp. 10–18.

30. Harry Braverman, *Labor and Monopoly Capital: The Degredation of Work in the Twentieth Century* (New York: Monthly Review Press, 1974).

31. *See* Mike Cooley, *Architect or Bee? The Human/Technology Relationship* (Boston: Hand and Brain Publications, 1980); Kraft, *Programmers and Managers*; Joan Greenbaum, *In the Name of Efficiency: Management Theory and Shop Floor Practice in Data-Processing Work* (Philadelphia: Temple University Press, 1979); Andrew Clement, "Office Automation and the Technical Control of Information Workers," in Vincent Mosco and Janet Wasko (eds.), *The Political Economy of Information* (Madison: University of Wisconsin Press, 1988).

32. Clement, "Office Automation," pp. 217–18.

33. Kraft, *Programmers and Managers*, p. 22.

34. On the same line of logic, I would argue that the kind of work a craftsperson does is also creative work. When the knowledge is taken away, the end result of the work process loses the possibility for creating something "new" and thus becomes part of a mere physical labor process.

35. *See* Robert N. Noyce, "Creativity by the Numbers," *Harvard Business Review*, Vol. 58 (1980), pp. 122–32.

36. I have found these terms in books written by R&D directors and managers, and in articles published in trade journals over the past 30 years on how to measure and increase the creativity and, hence, productivity of scientists and engineers. *See*, for example, James K. Brown and Lillian W. Kay, *Tough Challenges for R&D Management* (A Report of The Conference Board, 1987) and various issues of the journal *Research Management*.

37. *See*, for example, Charles Sabel, *Work and Politics: The Division of Labor in Industry* (Cambridge: Cambridge University Press, 1982). There are others who see post-Fordism as egalitarian and a new phase in the development of industrial society—a view effectively debunked by Harland Prechel in the previous chapter.

38. This segment of the chapter is based on Karen Hossfeld, "Their Logic Against Them: Contradictions in Sex, Race, and Class in Silicon Valley," in Kathryn Ward (ed.), *Women Workers and Global Restructuring* (Ithaca, NY: ILR Press, 1990); and Dennis Hayes, *Behind the Silicon Curtain* (Boston: South End Press, 1989).

39. Hossfeld, "Their Logic Against Them," p. 160.

40. Film titled *The Global Assembly Line*, directed and produced by Lorraine Gray.

41. Barbara Ehrenreich and Annette Fuentes, "Life on the Global Assembly Line," *Ms.* (January 1981), p. 54. *Also see* Annette Fuentes and Barbara Ehrenreich, *Women in the Global Factory* (Boston: South End Press, 1983).

42. An advertisement in a Mexican newspaper reads: "We need female workers; older than 17, younger than 30; single and without children; minimum education primary school, maximum education first year of preparatory school [high school]; available for all shifts." Quoted in Ehrenreich and Fuentes, "Life on the Global Assembly Line," p. 54.

43. Hayes, *Behind the Silicon Curtain*, p. 65.

5 Gender and Control over the Labor Process: Women's Power as Wage Earners

Marina A. Adler

Women have entered the labor market in increasing numbers, and they currently make up about 45 percent of the American labor force. Women continue to be employed predominantly in white-collar occupations labeled as "traditionally female," such as sales, clerical, and nursing. These occupations are also associated with low income, limited career advancement opportunities, and low levels of authority.[1] An extensive amount of literature examines variations in the work experience and occupational segregation of men and women in the labor force.[2] These researchers suggest that gender affects the differential allocation of individuals into occupations, and that labor market realities and on-the-job experiences vary by gender. Research also documents that women are less likely to be policy makers or supervisors, and have less job autonomy than men.[3] Since women are overrepresented in the working class, they also are more likely to be separated from the labor process than men. Part of the reason for this pattern is grounded in the traditional gender division of labor, which transcends the home and impinges upon the organization of work in modern capitalism.

This chapter will explore women's position in the relations of production and in the workplace. After reviewing various approaches to the issues relevant to the analysis of women's power as wage earners, empirical data are presented to support the claim that women continue to occupy a disadvantaged position *vis-à-vis* men at work.

GENDER AND CLASS

In all societies, an individual's position in the social structure is derived from his/her relationship to economic and kinship systems in general, and control over scarce resources in the market and family in particular. In advanced capitalist societies, there has traditionally been a separation of human activity into a "male-centered" public sphere (labor market) and a "female-centered" private sphere (family).[4] Consequently, researchers have assumed that men gain their class position through their employment in the labor market, whereas women's position is defined by their family ties to men, and hence only indirectly by economic relations. However, by the 1990s, most American women have become active participants in the labor force, and the question of how to incorporate the gender dimension of stratification into a class-based analysis arises.

Joan Acker has pointed out that "sex stratification always involves economic and power inequalities: these inequalities are produced and maintained within the system of relationships that also constitute the class structure."[5] Consequently, one of the major premises underlying this essay is that power structures and social stratification are not gender-neutral. This argument is grounded in the assumption that there is a division of labor by gender at home and at work, and that access to societal power positions is not equal for men and women.

Although the general social organization of work is defined by class relations, these class structures are internally stratified.[6] Since most women are gainfully employed, the analysis of women's position in the work place has become a major aspect of gender stratification research. As part of the work force, women are overrepresented in low-paying, gender-typed occupations with low career advancement opportunities. Therefore, in addition to the inequalities arising from the labor process (social class), sources external to the market (gender, race) serve to divide groups of workers into different jobs and activities, irrespective of individual qualifications.

Patriarchy as a form of power that is based on gender is related to economic domination at work and in the family. Thus, one may argue that ascribed characteristics, such as gender, may facilitate the access to and use of economic control, which then increases the inequality between the genders. These patterns are particularly evident in the history of the dynamics between kinship and economic systems. The patriarchal family form in Western society with its emphasis on the male breadwinner role has influenced the social relations of production related to women's employment patterns; consequently, women do traditionally different work than men, are paid on average lower wages, and are less likely to be protected by unions.[7]

Several researchers have recognized the need for increased attention to intraclass variation in worker power and rewards, particularly with respect to gender.[8] It is clear that stratification research grounded in class analytical frameworks needs to confront the linkage between gender and access to the work power. In this context, Arne Kalleberg and Larry Griffin search for "additional sources of within-class positional inequality," and Robert Thomas argues that "it is necessary to connect status inequalities external to the labor process more directly with the way in which activities and positions are structured internal to economic organization."[9] In other words, the link between ascribed characteristics, such as gender, and work stratification must be made more explicit.

The neo-Marxist position on ascription is essentially one of "class first." In other words, since in modern capitalist societies class is considered to be the most fundamental social category, the origin of inequality is considered to be located within the labor process, not external to it.[10] This poses the challenge of how to regard gender as a fundamental basis of inequality and stratification, without simultaneously having to reject Marx's analysis of the labor process in its entirety. Thus, Thomas's question is restated: "Can non-class categories impact on the organizational labor process?"[11] In order to answer this question, one has to accept the view that gender as a nonmarket status distinguishes among workers, regardless of their skill levels. Therefore, the consequences of gender for work stratification include occupational gender typing as well as the division of workers into different jobs and work activities. In addition to separating workers by gender, this selection process ranks "gendered" tasks by importance, resources, and remuneration. "Women's work" is an example of this phenomenon. According to Rosabeth Kanter, occupations containing high proportions of women often come to reflect the gender of the incumbents rather than the actual skill requirements for the job.[12] However, gender not only affects the occupational structure and work content, but it also causes differences in workers' power at work.

ALIENATION AND POWER AT WORK

Work is a fundamental human activity, and most American men and women spend a large amount of time in paid employment. According to Marx, alienation is the separation of the worker from the work process, the products of work, from fellow workers, and from his/her "species being" (lack of creativity). The literature on alienation contains approaches focusing both on the social psychological aspects and the objective aspects of the concept. Robert Blauner conceptualizes alienation in terms of four dimensions: powerlessness, meaninglessness, isolation, and self-estrangement.[13] Powerlessness refers to the worker's lack of control over the work process, working conditions, and policy decision making. Meaninglessness of the labor performed is based on routinization and the subdivision of work into minute tasks. The worker's isolation is also referred to as social alienation, and self-estrangement relates to lack of creativity and fulfillment in work. In a similar vein, others have developed the concept of "occupational self-direction," which is defined as the "use of initiative, thought, and independent judgment" at work.[14] This concept has three empirical dimensions: substantive complexity, routinization, and lack of supervision.

Most of these empirical analyses stress the subjective expression or social psychological interpretation of alienation. However, one of the Marxist premises related to alienation deals with the underlying objective conditions of the capitalist mode of production: Lack of ownership or control of the means of production (hence, control over work and exploitation) results in worker alienation.[15] Thus, both the process and product of labor become "alien" to workers, and they do not have control over their work activities.[16] The problem arises from the contradiction between the profit requirements of capitalist production and work as being autonomous, nonalienating, and creative.[17] Alienation clearly goes beyond subjective feelings of job satisfaction or control over the immediate work environment. However, for the analysis of gender and power at work, the exercise of control over work activities is crucial. Relations of production become exploitative when one group has more power in the work place in relation to another group. This uneven distribution of power facilitates the extraction of surplus value from those with less power and, hence, less control over the production process. If it can be shown that women are more likely than men to be in a disadvantaged position with respect to work power, they also may be more likely to be alienated.

The Marxist framework views alienation and workers' lack of control over the work process under capitalism as an outcome of the socioeconomic structure of capitalist society (i.e., social relations of production or property-based class relations).[18] The bulk of this literature is concerned with the empowerment of the working class *vis-à-vis* the capitalist system and its exploitative nature; another focus is on proletarianization and unionization processes as they relate to the collective power (or lack thereof) of workers as a group.[19]

As an extension of traditional class analysis, another approach acknowledges the existence of hierarchies not only between classes, but *within* them; it focuses on the various forms and degrees of worker control over work resources, positions, and personnel. It is argued that

> economic inequality is generated by differences in the *power* of economic actors and that inequalities in job rewards are determined both by work structures that reflect the relative power of employers in product markets and by those that represent the relative power of workers in labor markets.[20]

In relation to women's disadvantaged position in the labor market, this means that in addition to individual characteristics, such as educational and skill levels, structural factors determine unequal rewards by gender. Members of the working class are differentiated by gender and by the characteristics of the firms and markets they work in. It is also acknowledged that individuals may have different amounts of power within these broader categories.

Alienation has also been associated with deskilling processes, proletarianization, and increasing routinization of the modern work place.[21] Harry Braverman argues that in modern capitalist societies, the separation of mental and manual labor under capitalist relations of production has led to the destruction of "crafts."[22] Conceptual control becomes separated from the execution of production, and work tasks become increasingly minute; not only blue-collar work but also white-collar work is shown to become increasingly routinized, menial, and controlled. This has been attributed to a shift from earlier, small-scale manufacturing to more recent large-scale corporate and bureaucratic organizations as the main employers. Bureaucracy has become a part of the capitalist production process, and thus, white-collar skills have been downgraded and their craft dimension destroyed. However, low-level, white-collar work continues to be associated with higher training and educational levels than blue-collar work. Professional white collar workers, scientific workers, or semiautonomous workers are less alienated than lower level white-collar and blue-collar workers because of education and autonomy.[23]

Since World War II, the service sector of the economy and white-collar work in general have expanded. According to Val Burris, there has also been a dramatic shift from self-employment to the salaried middle class since 1900.[24] This can be attributed to the large growth in white-collar occupations, which resulted from the transformations in the nature of modern capitalism related to declines in profit rates and consumption. These processes have led to mechanisms to increase rationalization and control of the labor process. Consequently, clerical work has changed as well. The proportion of women in secretarial and clerical occupations has risen drastically from about 5 percent in 1870 to about 95 percent by 1930.[25] The combination of high demand in the labor market and the opportunity to pay less to women than men has created the gender segregation of the modern office in terms of male managers and female secretaries.[26]

THE DEFINITION OF WORK POWER

In defining work power, some authors conceptualize authority as "legitimated control over the work process of others," whereas others specify job power as "control over organizational resources."[27] When specifically addressing women's power in the work place, emphasis is placed on women's "capacity to shape their work environment."[28] In a similar vein, "empowerment" is seen as crucial for women, because it generates "more autonomy, more participation in decisions, and more access to resources."[29]

The concept of job autonomy or discretion is usually treated as separate from power. However, it can be argued that in the work context, autonomy becomes a form of power because it entails independence and control for the worker. Erik Olin Wright defines job autonomy as the "extent to which an individual controls the conceptual aspects of work."[30] Job autonomy or self-direction may be regarded as both a dichotomous or a gradational concept: Whereas the employer/supervisor may categorically have the ability to determine the amounts of responsibility delegated to individual employees, these employees then vary in terms of their degree of job autonomy. Therefore:

> Autonomy . . . designates a social relationship between supervisor and subordinates which structures the range of activities over which the subordinate has discretion. It is possible to measure this range as a continuous variable while still regarding it as an indicator of the underlying social relation.[31]

Thus, whereas an employee as a member of the working class may not have much power as part of his or her relationship *vis-à-vis* the employer, he or she may have some degree of autonomy in terms of the actual work activities performed. Women are overrepresented in the working class in general, but they may also be disadvantaged in regard to the amount of control they have over their own work, when compared with working-class men.

Autonomy as a structural aspect of work power can be derived from arguments about proletarianization and deskilling. By breaking down comprehensive production into minute tasks requiring minimal skill levels, the contemporary production process has stifled most of the workers' conceptual input. The separation of mental and manual labor under capitalism is seen as a key element in power relations at work.[32] According to Stewart Clegg and David Dunkerly, "de-skilling represents a loss of control by the worker over a given task because of a re-design of the job by which the task is accomplished."[33] In other words, the nature of work in industrial society has changed in as much as it partitions skills originally embodied in one craft and thereby reduces the worker's power, autonomy, and creativity. Nevertheless, industrialization has also created new positions and occupations (professional occupations in particular) that have relatively high levels of autonomy.

Technological innovation is based on efforts to increase the organization's efficiency and, thus, as in the case of authority, is likely to curtail some of the worker's control over his/her work environment. In other words, the workers' abilities to make decisions regarding their own work processes, pacings, timings, and conceptual structures will be reduced. Increased routinization and regulation, as well as supervision, reduce the independence and responsibilities of the worker. Since the literature suggests that women have historically been closely supervised at work and that women are in jobs characterized by high levels of routinization,[34] one may expect that they have less autonomy at work than men.

Overall, although an individual may be subject to rules, supervision, and control by superiors, he or she may be able to exert some input on how and when his or her work is done. Being the "recipient" of authority (supervision) is not necessarily the same as lacking job autonomy. In other words, although authority is "other-directed," autonomy entails the worker's immediate decisions about his/her own work situation or the degree of independence in the performance of the job, and therefore it is self-directed.

RESEARCH ON GENDER, OCCUPATIONAL SEGREGATION, AND POWER

The literature on gender differences in work power is limited. Nevertheless, studies show that men generally have more power and autonomy at work than women.[35] Although Wright's theory focuses on class relations, his exploitation-centered analysis is relevant to the study of gender inequality. Throughout recent history, women as a group have been systematically subordinated by exclusion and the exploitative relations of production. Originally excluded from paid labor, women were relegated to the class status of their male family members (fathers or husbands). Upon entering the labor force, women were initially excluded from various occupations, particularly those involving crafts and the professions, and later they were concentrated in certain industries and economic sectors, such as textiles and services, all the while being subjected to lower pay scales than men. Furthermore, as a result of patriarchal capitalist relations, women were not only excluded from the protection provided by unions, but were denied access to power positions, such as supervisors, within factories and organizations. After the barriers of exclusion to paid labor were lifted, women's participation in the labor market was, like child labor, characterized by exploitation. Women's labor was relegated to cheap, unprotected, and "secondary" labor. Even when doing the same work as men, women were paid lower wages, thereby increasing the employers' profits as well as consolidating the patriarchal family form.[36]

The entire idea of "women's work" bears on this history of exclusion, exploitation, and powerlessness. Occupations that have traditionally led to high-level power positions or high rewards, such as professional or managerial jobs, have until recently been out of reach for women. The types of work women have traditionally engaged in are invariably jobs that are not in direct contradiction to the normative "female role." Occupations involving care for children and homes, such as teacher, governess, or maid, exemplify this kind of work. Another occupational category that was opened relatively early for women is factory work. The nature of this work is characterized by a lack of unionization, low wages, and occupations with limited advancement opportunities to power positions. This combination of disadvantaged conditions is likely to affect the collective position of women, as well as the individual power distributions among men and women at work.

Research demonstrates that "the lower the level of authority considered, the more egalitarian is the process of acquiring that level of authority, at least with respect to education."[37] Wendy Wolf and Neil Fligstein have found that when controlling human capital and family characteristics, women's access to higher levels of authority, as measured by the ability to hire/fire, is restricted. Nevertheless, they argue that generally most of the gender differences in authority returns are due to differences in job characteristics, such as gender typing. Overall, even though different indicators of authority are used, this and other such studies conclude that despite occupational status similarity, men have more authority than women.[38]

In general, women are overrepresented in lower paying, lower authority occupations that lack job ladders. White-collar occupations, such as secretary, for example, have very limited routes for career development. This is consequential for gender differences in power at work, because collectively and individually, women encounter lower ceilings with respect to advancement opportunities than men within occupations and careers. It has been suggested that women forgo career opportunities, authority, and higher wages in order to "buy" flexibility of work schedules to accommodate their family responsibilities. In other words, women trade higher paying jobs and increased power for the ability to control, leave, and resume their work.

Recent findings indicate that segregation tends to be higher in those industries that are characterized by higher profitability.[39] These are located in the core sector of the economy, which is the sector with high incomes, unionization, and job stability. Thus, it is argued that these increased assets may offset the costs of inefficient labor practices, such as gender segregation. Another study demonstrates that in general firms are highly gender segregated and that the nature of work performed by employees varies by gender: Even when women are in the same occupations as men, they tend to perform different tasks and receive less pay.[40] Those tasks labeled as "women's work" are consistently assigned a lower value than activities considered to be "men's work."

Research on the relationship between occupational gender segregation and wages indicates that when controlling the type of tasks performed, women are paid less than men.[41] Consequently, in an attempt to counteract the negative effect of gender typing on income, the concept of "comparable worth" (i.e., equal pay for equal work) was developed.[42] Work tasks that entail similar skill and educational levels, disregarding the proportion of women in the job, are assigned the same income. This strategy aims at elevating the "systematically undervalued" women's work to equalize male and female incomes.

Consistent findings indicate that part of the income gap between the genders and races is due to differences in access to high positions in authority hierarchies and restrictions of job ladders. Specifically, Charles W. Mueller and Toby Parcel argue that "differential access to authority resources explains racial earnings differences, whereas differential resource efficacy is more important in explaining sex inequality."[43] Thus, power in the work place contributes to the explanation of the gender income gap by showing that women with similar power as men are not rewarded the same. In other words, blacks may generally be barred from power positions, but if they reach them, they are paid the same as whites in those positions. Women, however, even if they do attain high levels of power, cannot convert that power into income to the same extent as men.

Overall, in terms of "span of responsibility" (task and sanctioning authority) and "span of control" (number of subordinates), white males benefit more from authority than women, because they are selectively promoted and rewarded.[44] Thus, gender discrimination exists in both access to and benefits from power. This finding also gives credence to Kanter's analysis of informal power networks and their exclusionary effect on women in organizations.[45] In addition, research on the relationship between work power and income indicates that although both "control over monetary resources" and "control over personnel" are the key work variables determining women's income, men benefit mainly from monetary control alone.[46] This finding is somewhat in contradiction to Mueller and Parcel's, who found control over personnel to be less important for the income of female managers than male managers. One possible explanation may be that female managers are more likely to supervise female employees and thus are rewarded less.

EMPIRICAL PATTERNS IN OCCUPATIONAL SEGREGATION AND POWER AT WORK

In order to assess whether women are less likely than men to have control over the work process, some descriptive analyses are performed. It is evident from the Census data presented in Table 5.1 that male and female workers are not equal in terms of rewards for their work and in their occupational distribution. The table shows that although about 57 percent of all American women (and 76 percent of the men) are employed in the labor force, on average they only earn about 70 percent of men's median weekly earnings. Even when taking marital status into account, the majority of women are employed outside the home. When comparing the median earnings of men and women in each occupational category, it becomes clear that women consistently earn less than men, disregarding particular occupations. However, women's incomes come closest to men's for mechanics (3.3 percent female) and agricultural jobs (16.3 percent female), and are least similar to men's in sales (48.9 percent female). Overall, the female/male income ratio is lowest for traditional white-collar jobs categorized as technical, sales, and administrative support occupations, and it is highest for traditional blue-collar jobs in the precision, craft, repair and operators, fabricators, and labor categories. Thus, female workers may do better *vis-à-vis* male workers in traditional working-class labor, partly because these jobs are not as "feminized" as the white-collar support jobs.

Analysis of the occupational distribution of women and men reveals evidence of occupational gender segregation. Not only are women concentrated in certain large occupational groupings, such as technical, sales,

Table 5.1
Average Earnings in Various Occupations by Gender, 1988

Employment	*Women*	*Men*	
Percent employed,	56.6	76.2	
married	56.5	78.6	
single	65.2	72.1	
widowed, divorced, separated	46.1	66.9	
Earnings ($)	*Women*	*Men*	*$ Ratio*
Median weekly earnings, full-time	315	449	.70
Occupation (% females)			
Managerial & professional (44.7)	465	666	.70
execut., administ., manag. (39.3)	430	682	.63
prof. specialty (49.8)	485	651	.75
Technical, sales, adm. support (64.8)	305	472	.65
techn. & related support (47.9)	384	510	.75
sales (48.9)	264	488	.54
adm. support, clerical (80.1)	305	418	.73
Service (60.5)	208	299	.70
private household (96.3)	139	na	--
protective (14.1)	347	424	.82
other (65.1)	210	247	.82
Precision, craft, repair (8.7)	302	446	.68
mechanics (3.3)	392	441	.89
construction (2.1)	335	423	.79
other (23.5)	284	477	.60
Operators, fabricators, labor (25.7)	238	352	.68
machine, assembly, inspector (40.8)	236	366	.64
transport, material movers (9.0)	286	394	.73
handlers, equipment cleaners, helpers, labor (17.2)	237	287	.83
Farming, forestry, fishing (16.3)	201	234	.86

Source: U.S. Bureau of the Census, *Statistical Abstract of the United States, 1990.*

Table 5.2
Percentage of Women and Men in Various Categories of Control at Work

	Women (502)	*Men (591)*	*Difference*
Making decisions about organizational			
policy in general	25.1	36.1	-11.0**
employee pool	7.3	15.0	- 7.7**
production	14.6	22.2	- 7.6**
pace	18.6	29.5	-10.9**
procedures	14.5	22.5	- 8.0**
budget	14.6	22.4	- 7.8**
	Women (507)	*Men (595)*	*Difference*
Making decisions about subordinates			
in general	35.4	49.2	-13.8**
tasks at work	26.7	37.6	-10.9**
procedures	24.0	35.5	-11.5**
pace of work	18.6	29.5	-10.9**
getting raises	12.6	24.1	-11.5**
not getting raises	21.2	30.5	- 9.3**
being fired	15.6	25.1	- 9.5**
being warned	19.9	31.6	-11.7**
	Women (507)	*Men (600)*	*Difference*
Making decisions about			
own work	76.8	83.4	- 6.6**
own ideas	38.6	52.6	-14.0**
new tasks	60.0	63.5	- 3.5
when to work	35.8	40.0	- 4.2
when to take off	31.3	38.8	- 7.5*
when to slow down	55.0	65.5	-10.5**

Notes:
* Significance level of difference $p<.05$, Chi-Square Test
**Significance level of difference $p<.01$, Chi-Square Test

Source: Erik Olin Wright, *1980 U.S. Class Structure and Class Consciousness Survey,* 1985.

administrative support, and service, but they are overrepresented within particular job categories. Thus, based on the percentage of women in occupations, women are predominantly employed in administrative support, clerical, and service occupations. Men are more likely to be managers, blue-collar, and agricultural workers than women.

After providing evidence for gender differences in the occupational and income distribution, the extent to which control at work varies by gender is assessed. The data in Tables 5.2 and 5.3 come from the 1980 Class Structure and Class Consciousness U.S. Survey.[47] This nationally representative sample consists of 1,760 adults living in the United States.[48]

Table 5.2 reflects the fact that relatively few workers in general, disregarding gender, have policy-making or supervising responsibilities. The probability of having autonomy seems somewhat greater. The table also shows that for this sample, men have consistently more control over organizational policies, subordinates, and their own work environment than women. Women are generally less likely to be policy makers and supervisors than men with a difference of 13.8 and 11 points, respectively. Male and female workers are somewhat more similar with respect to having any autonomy. The percentile differences for particular work tasks by gender are largest (above 10 points) with respect to most supervisory activities, making decisions about the organizational work pace, slowing down at work, and the implementation of ideas (conceptual autonomy). The gender differences are smallest in terms of introducing new ideas at work and deciding when to work or when to take off from work.

In order to assess the effect of occupational segregation (traditional female occupations, such as teacher, white-collar service, nurse, secretary) on control at work, Table 5.3 presents the percentage of men and women having any policy decision-making and supervisory capacity or autonomy by gender type of occupation. Within traditional female occupations, the distribution of work power by gender seems relatively similar. In other words, in female-typed jobs, women are as likely as men to be policy makers, supervisors, or autonomous workers. Turning to the other occupations, it becomes clear that women are disadvantaged *vis-à-vis* men in all dimensions of control at work. Therefore, in order to improve the status of women in the labor market, it is insufficient to combat occupational segregation *per se*. Although it may be advantageous for women to enter less traditional occupations in terms of increased economic rewards, they continue to lack equal control over their work. Consequently, since women have less control at work, they are more likely to be separated from the labor process, that is, more likely to be alienated than men. Moving into less gender-typed occupations will not change that fact. One may argue

Table 5.3
Policy Decision-Making and Supervisory Capacity and Autonomy by Gender and Traditional Female Occupation

	Traditionally Female Occupation		
	Women (249)	*Men (51)*	*Difference*
Policy Decisions	23.8	36.4	ns
Supervision	35.8	30.4	ns
Autonomy	81.1	82.4	ns
Flexibility	68.4	78.2	ns
	Nontraditionally Female Occupation		
	Women (257)	*Men (544)*	*Difference*
Policy Decisions	26.3	36.0	<.01
Supervision	34.9	51.0**	<.001
Autonomy	72.6*	83.5	<.001
Flexibility	63.0	77.4	<.001

Notes:
* Significance level of difference from traditionally female occupation $p<.05$, Chi-Square Test
**Significance level of difference from traditionally female occupation $p<.01$, Chi-Square Test

Source: Erik Olin Wright, *1980 U.S. Class Structure and Class Consciousness Survey,* 1985.

that although the majority of American workers lack significant control over their work environment, gender is an additional dimension that serves to stratify the modern work place. The dynamic relationship between capitalism and patriarchy has created a gendered division of labor that is evident in occupational gender segregation.

CONCLUSION

The theoretical and empirical literature has produced various approaches to the question of gender as it affects work-related phenomena. The Marxist analysis locates the source of economic inequality in the nature of capitalist relations of production rather than in gender relations. Structural labor-market theorists argue that the capitalist economy has segmented the labor market, industries, and occupations, which in turn confounds women's disadvantages. The Marxist-feminist tradition emphasizes the dynamic cooperation of capitalism and patriarchy in establishing the structures that now place women in a disadvantaged position *vis-à-vis* men in the labor process. This chapter has attempted to provide some empirical evidence for the effect of one such structure, that is, occupational gender segregation, on discrepancies in power over the labor process.

A fundamental issue revolves around the "place" of women in the class and occupational structure. This chapter has documented that women remain segmented within contradictory class positions as well as segregated in particular occupations. This does not suggest that women voluntarily choose female-typed occupations. Furthermore, women earn less than men even in male-dominated occupations. Overall, it has been shown that women are consistently outranked by men in the labor market.

Another question is: If women workers are in a different structural position *vis-à-vis* male workers, how does that affect their control over the labor process? The empirical patterns presented here demonstrate that women are generally less likely than men to have power at work. In other words, not only do women earn less than men and are working in different kinds of occupations than men, within similar work situations, women have less power over the process and product of their labor than men. One consequence of this separation from the labor process is increased alienation.

It has been argued in the literature that women are willing to trade high income, power, and career opportunities for flexible work schedules and convenience so that they can more easily combine work and family responsibilities. Another line of thought urges women to pursue nontraditional occupations in order to combat low incomes, occupational segregation, and lack of power at work. Neither of these arguments seem supported by the empirical evidence presented here. Both the gender wage gap and occupational segregation persist in the face of rising numbers of female professionals. Increased demand for lower level white-collar workers, such as clerical and service workers, continues to reinforce existing occupational structures.

Expansion of the modern work place continually erodes the control of the workers in general. The empowerment of women at work does not seem to be, however, a byproduct of the empowerment of male workers. In addition to creating a work environment devoid of alienating conditions, the gender-based structures related to the traditional division of labor and gender typing of occupations need to be eradicated. Beyond the requirements of capitalist production, the traditional division of household labor consolidates the existing patterns of female disadvantage. As long as women are assigned a disproportionate share of household maintenance and child-rearing responsibilities, their choices in finding creative and nonalienating work outside the home are severely restricted.

NOTES

1. Shelley Coverman, "Occupational Segmentation and Sex Differentials in Earnings," in R.V. Robinson (ed.) *Research in Social Stratification and Mobility* (Greenwich, CT: JAI Press, 1986); Rosabeth Moss Kanter, *Men and Women of the Corporation* (New York: Basic Books, 1977); Wendy C. Wolf and Neil D. Fligstein, "Sex and Authority in the Work Place: The Causes of Sexual Inequality," *American Sociological Review* 44 (1979).

2. *See* Francine D. Blau, "Women in the Labor Force: An Overview," in Joe Freeman (ed.), *Women: A Feminist Perspective* (Palo Alto, CA: Mayfield, 1984); Shelley Coverman, "Occupational Segmentation and Sex Differentials in Earnings," in Robinson (ed.), *Research in Social Stratification and Mobility*; (Greenwich, CT: JAI Press, 1986); Rachel A. Rosenfeld, "Sex Segregation and Sectors: An Analysis of Gender Differences in Returns from Employer Changes," *American Sociological Review* 48 (1983).

3. Charles W. Mueller and Toby Parcel, "Ascription, Dimensions of Authority, and Earnings," *Research in Social Stratification and Mobility* 5 (1986); Erik Olin Wright, C. Costello, D. Hachen, and J. Spraegue, "The American Class Structure," *American Sociological Review* 47 (1982).

4. Elise Boulding, "Familial Constraints on Women's Work Roles," *Signs* 1 (1976); Heidi Hartman, "Capitalism, Patriarchy and Job Segregation by Sex," *Signs* 1 (1976).

5. Joan Acker, "Women and Stratification: A Review of Recent Literature," *Contemporary Sociology* 9 (1980), p. 26.

6. Joe L. Spaeth, "Structural Contexts and the Stratification of Work," *Research in Social Stratification and Mobility* 3 (1984).

7. Shelley Coverman, "Occupational Segmentation and Sex Differentials in Earnings," in R.V. Robinson (ed.), *Research in Social Stratification and Mobility*; (Greenwich, CT: JAI Press, 1986) Tamara K. Hareven, *Family Time &*

Industrial Time. The Relationship Between the Family and Work in a New England Industrial Community (New York: Cambridge University Press, 1982); Hartman, "Capitalism, Patriarchy and Job Segregation by Sex."

8. Toby Parcel and C. W. Mueller, *Ascription and Labor Markets: Race and Sex Differences in Earnings* (New York: Academic Press, 1983); Robert J. Thomas, "Citizenship and Gender in Work Organization: Some Considerations for Theories of the Labor Process," *American Journal of Sociology* (Suppl.) 88 (1982). *See also* Arne L. Kalleberg and Larry J. Griffin, "Class, Occupation and Inequality in Job Rewards," *American Journal of Sociology* 85 (1980); Robert V. Robinson and Jonathan Kelley, "Class as Conceived by Marx and Dahrendorf: Effects on Income Inequality and Politics in the United States and Britain," *American Sociological Review* 44 (1979).

9. Kalleberg and Griffin, "Class, Occupation and Inequality in Job Rewards," p. 765; Thomas, "Citizenship and Gender in Work Organization," p. S109.

10. Thomas, "Citizenship and Gender in Work Organization." *See also* Erik Olin Wright, "Race, Class, and Income Inequality," *American Journal of Sociology* 83 (1978).

11. Thomas, "Citizenship and Gender in Work Organization," p. S86.

12. Kanter, *Men and Women of the Corporation.*

13. Robert Blauner, *Alienation and Freedom* (Chicago: University of Chicago Press, 1964).

14. Melvin L. Kohn and Carmi Schooler, *Work and Personality: An Inquiry into the Impact of Social Stratification* (Norwood, NJ: Ablex Publ. Co, 1982), p. 22.

15. Stephen Hill, *Competition and Control at Work: The New Industrial Sociology* (Cambridge, MA: MIT Press, 1981).

16. Douglas M. Eichar and John L. P. Thompson, "Alienation, Occupational Self-direction, and Worker Consciousness: An Exploration," *Work and Occupations* 13 (1986).

17. Beverly H. Burris, *No Room at the Top: Underemployment and Alienation in the Corporation* (New York: Praeger, 1983).

18. Albert Szymanski, *Class Structure* (New York: Praeger, 1983).

19. *See* Jerry Lembcke, *Capitalist Development and Class Capacities: Marxist Theory and Union Organization* (Westport, CT: Greenwood Press, 1988); Rick Fantasia, *Cultures of Solidarity: Consciousness, Action and Contemporary American Workers* (Berkeley: Univeristy of California Press, 1988).

20. Arne L. Kalleberg and Ivar Berg, *Work and Industry: Structures, Markets and Processes* (New York: Plenum Press, 1987), p. 29.

21. Harry Braverman, *Labor and Monopoly Capital: The Degradation of Work in the Twentieth Century* (New York: Monthly Review Press, 1974); Margery Davies, "Women's Place Is at the Typewriter: The Feminization of the Clerical Labor Force," *Radical America* 8 (1974); Evelyn Nakano Glenn and Roslyn L. Feldberg, "Degraded and Deskilled: The Proletarianization of Clerical Work," *Social Problems* 25 (1977).

22. Braverman, *Labor and Monopoly Capital.*

23. *See* Val Burris, "Capital Accumulation and the Rise of the New Middle Class," *Review of Radical Political Economics* 12 (1980); Erik Olin Wright, *Classes* (London: Verso, 1985).

24. Burris, "Capital Accumulation."

25. Davies, "Women's Place Is at the Typewriter."

26. Ibid. Kanter, *Men and Women of the Corporation.*

27. *See* Wolf and Fligstein, "Sex and Authority in the Work Place," p. 236; Joe L. Spaeth, "Job Power and Earnings," *American Sociological Review* 50 (1985), p. 603.

28. Dorothy Remy and Larry Sawers, "Women's Power in the Workplace," in Liesa Stamm and Carol D. Ryff (eds.), *Social Power and Influence of Women* (Boulder, CO: Westview Press, 1984), p. 167.

29. Kanter, *Men and Women of the Corporation*, p. 166.

30. Erik Olin Wright, *Class Structure and Class Consciousness Study U.S. Survey, 1980: A User's Guide to the Machine-Readable Data File* (Ann Arbor, MI: University of Wisconsin at Madison, Institute for Political and Social Research, 1985), p. 324.

31. Wright et al., "The American Class Structure," p. 712, footnote 6.

32. Braverman, *Labor and Monopoly Capital.*

33. Stewart Clegg and David Dunkerly, *Organization, Class and Control* (London: Routledge and Kegan Paul, 1980), p. 465.

34. Hareven, *Family Time & Industrial Time*; Hartman, "Capitalism, Patriarchy and Job Segregation by Sex"; R. Stolzenberg, "Occupations, Labor Markets, and the Process of Wage Attainment," *American Sociological Review* 40 (1975).

35. Parcel and Mueller, *Ascription and Labor Markets: Race and Sex Differences in Earnings;* Wolf and Fligstein, "Sex and Authority in the Work Place"; Spaeth, "Job Power and Earnings."

36. Hareven, *Family Time & Industrial Time* ; Hartman, "Capitalism, Patriarchy and Job Segregation by Sex."

37. Wolf and Fligstein, "Sex and Authority in the Work Place," p. 244.

38. Ibid. *Also see* Patricia Roos, "Sexual Stratification in the Workplace: Male-Female Differences in Economic Returns to Occupation," *Social Science Research* 10 (1981).

39. William P. Bridges, "The Sexual Segregation of Occupations: Theories of Labor Stratification in Industry," *American Journal of Sociology* 88 (1982).

40. James N. Baron and William T. Bielby, "The Organization of Work in a Segmented Economy," *American Sociological Review* 49 (1984).

41. Paula England and Steven D. McLaughlin, "Sex Segregation of Jobs and Income Differentials," in Rudolfo Alvarez et al. (eds.), *Discrimination in Organizations* (San Francisco: Jossey-Bass, 1979).

42. Ronnie Steinberg, "From Laissez-Faire to a Fair Wage for Women's Work: A Technical Fix to the Labor Contract," *Contemporary Sociology* 13 (1984).

43. Mueller and Parcel, "Ascription, Dimensions of Authority, and Earnings," p. 212.

44. Ibid.

45. Kanter, *Men and Women of the Corporation.*

46. Spaeth, "Job Power and Earnings."

47. Erik Olin Wright, *Class Structure and Class Consciousness Study U.S. Survey, 1980: A User'sGuide to the Machine-Readable Data File*, (Ann Arbor, MI: University of Wisconsin at Madison, Institute for Political and Social Research, 1985).

48. Since this study focuses on wage labor employment, those aged over 65, the unemployed, full-time housewives, and self-employed individuals are excluded. The final sample size prior to deletion of missing values is 1,150 (531 women and 619 men).

6 Race, Nationality, and the Division of Labor in U.S. Agriculture: Focus on Farm Workers in California

John C. Leggett

Farm workers by the hundreds of thousands migrate annually from both north-central Mexico and the U.S. Southwest to the California southlands—the Imperial and Coachella valleys. Then up the West Coast they motor through either Pacific central coastal California or the San Joaquin Valley to the American Northwest. There they labor in the vegetable rows and on the orchard ladders of Oregon and Washington. Subsequently, they return, either to northwestern Mexico or southern California.

Toward south-central America, and residing largely in Texas during the winter months, can be found hundreds of thousands of Mexicans—some have been "legals," and others "illegals." They move north each year to work the fields, until they finish up in northern Michigan, Wisconsin, Minnesota, and the Dakotas. Once through working the crops, most return to Texas. Still, many of these working-class Mexican-Americans have left this Texas-based farm labor behind to settle in northern Midwestern communities, such as Chicago, Minneapolis, and Omaha, to work in their steel mills or meat-packing houses. In some cases, they have settled to labor as permanent small-town residents inside service employment, plus the occasional but seasonal bout within fruit or vegetable harvesting, as in northwestern Ohio and southern Michigan.

On the East Coast, the major migratory farm worker groups are American blacks, Jamaicans, Puerto Ricans, Mexicans, Laotians, Cambodians, and Vietnamese, although there can be found a residual group of whites, winter-based in Florida, Georgia, and the Carolinas. Also, like their Texan-Okie-Arky cousins in California, these whites have descended from essentially Scot-Irish background. They have worked the ripened green vegetable produce and fruits, from southern Florida up through the Carolinas, the Chesapeake Bay, on into Delaware and New Jersey, and from there to Upstate New York, into Connecticut, and even onward for the few to join local high school children involved in the potato harvest of northern Maine.[1]

Here it should be noted that type of work done generally depends upon nationality grouping. For example, on the East Coast, American blacks, and Haitians work the vegetables; Belle Glade Florida Jamaicans serve as contract laborers for six months every year to harvest the sugar cane; Mexicans work fruit and vegetables; and Philadelphia-based Indo-Chinese labor primarily in vegetable fields in southern New Jersey.

Out West, the same patterning occurs in the San Joaquin and Imperial valleys, where corporate farms, such as those owned by DiGiorgio Corporation, have channeled each nationality grouping into a limited range of crop-harvesting occupational choices. Thus, there has been cross-nationality competition for the better, high-paying manual jobs, and a largely contained but nonetheless real animosity has developed among the various nationality groupings, thereby limiting possibilities for labor solidarity within agriculture—a situation that works to the benefit of the white growers.[2]

RACE, NATIONALITY, AND THE ORIGINS OF COMMERCIAL FARMING IN CALIFORNIA

During the eighteenth century, the Spanish colonialists came to California as conquerors, took the land, entrusted the reworking of the agricultural division of labor to the Franciscan missions, and enslaved Indians within this division of labor. The Franciscan missionaries gave way during the Mexican governmental period (1821–1846) to Spanish nonclerical ownership of estates whose secularized division of labor continued focus on production of many agricultural products rendered by Indians. The Anglo-Americans began to arrive during the 1840s, adopted the Mexican large estate structure, and eventually imposed a violent and rapacious servitude-based division of labor upon California Indians. The subordination of the Indians by Anglo-Americans within a division of labor where Indians had no choice but to accept their ranch field supervision without pay became a causal precedent for white ranch owners' violent treatment of nonwhite laborers in general.

In the early 1860s, the Anglo-American land owners moved toward the substitution of Chinese tenantry in place of a more than decimated Indian quasi-slave labor force, until by 1870 much of white dependence on Indian labor had all but disappeared—a situation that coincided with a 95 percent decline of the Native American population in northern California between 1840 and 1900.

The Chinese succeeded the American Indians on both Anglo-American and residual Spanish *haciendas*. These essentially Han Chinese from China's Kwangtung and Fukien provinces cut a path quite different from this country's indigenous native population.[3] In the main, the arriving Chinese worked initially for pecuniary rewards as California land tenants.

The Anglo-Americans leased subsections of land to Chinese tenants who, in turn, employed free, noncoolie Chinese field gang labor procured for the tenants by labor contractors also of Chinese descent. The labor contractor system rested upon wages and occupied a crucial link within the all-Chinese vertical chain of command, except at the very top where the owners were generally white.

Barred from almost all California labor unions, the Chinese laborers employed by the Chinese tenant farmers were able to protect themselves by way of their cross-class Chinese protective associations, the "tongs."[4] From the 1860s until World War I, Chinese laborers and their fellow Chinese allies did fashion for themselves a modest amount of protection through these self-help associations made up exclusively of Chinese. These tongs were used as the bases for bargaining with white owners to obtain better wages for Chinese workers.

Violence against the Chinese and anti-Chinese immigration legislation (most notably the 1882 law passed by the U.S. Congress to forbid further Chinese immigration) paved the way for extensive Japanese emigration into California agriculture.[5] Initial, turn-of-the-century Japanese migration into California agriculture essentially overlapped with widespread Chinese participation in agricultural production, although between 1910 and 1920, the Japanese surpassed the Chinese in terms of numbers and importance within California's agricultural division of labor, often settling side by side within spatially proximate communities, such as those established in the Sacramento and San Joaquin Delta region.[6]

Carey McWilliams has noted how in the Sacramento, Santa Clara, San Joaquin, and Imperial valleys, it was the Japanese who for the most part proved responsible for the reclamation of waste lands. The hardships they experienced in the course of this pioneer activity took a stunning toll; in many cases, the Japanese laborers worked under exceedingly unhealthy conditions—in swamps, river deltas, and marshes. In Fresno County alone, during one period when water and sanitary conditions were bad, the Japanese lost an estimated 3,000 lives.[7]

The Japanese farm laborers were able to build up small, informal, work-group solidarity teams that through strikes made insistent wage demands upon the growers. Frequently, they made their wage demands known at the time of the harvest; they would declare a strike and walk out at that crucial moment of crop gathering.

Like the Chinese, many of the Japanese were to move from tenantry and wage labor to land ownership and truck gardening within the Delta and the surrounding valleys, whereas others farmed throughout the rest of the state down to southern coastal California.

The gang labor, tenantry, and land ownership success of the Japanese moved California populists during World War I to use California government to sponsor the settlement of whites only on lands to be purchased by veterans with intent to use these new properties to erect cooperatively based agriculture as an answer to large white holdings and their practice of leasing/selling properties to Orientals, especially the Japanese. By the late 1920s, the racialist experiment in white agrarian co-ops had failed, because white large-scale agribusiness came to rely successfully upon Filipinos, Sikhs, Hindus, blacks, and, most importantly, Mexicans.

During the 1930s, agribusiness turned increasingly toward the recruitment of hundreds of thousands of "dust-bowl refugees" from the U.S. Southern Great Plains (e.g., "Okies," "Arkies," and "Texans"); however, they did not become the labor base for California agriculture.[8] By the early 1940s, white agribusiness moved simultaneously toward the realization of two objectives: the absorption of Japanese-owned and leased landholdings, as the Japanese were escorted by the federal government to the detention camps, and the importation of unlimited numbers of *bracero* labor from Mexico.[9]

Hurriedly sent to incarceration centers by the federal authorities, the land-owning Japanese relocated and had no choice but to sell their properties at a fraction of their value, while other lands rented by Japanese from whites were left behind. In effect, Japanese landholdings were garnered by whites as all 110,000 Japanese, noncitizens and citizens of the United States, were forcibly removed to ten so-called internment camps, thereby permanently pressing tens of thousands of Japanese from the overall agricultural division of labor.

In 1942, the federal government initiated the widespread importation of *bracero* labor from Mexico to take the place of Japanese farm labor. This, coupled with the growth of large agricultural firms acquiring sizable plots of land during this period, gradually transformed the twentieth-century ranch into a modern-day *hacienda* based largely on Mexican labor.[10]

With the proliferation of late-twentieth-century corporate farming, involving thousands of acres of absentee-owned ranches, most of the arable land in the United States has now become the property of the great banks and oil companies. These production facilities have evolved into veritable factories in the field dependent overwhelmingly upon nonwhite labor drawn from a variety of nationalities, but fundamentally most dependent upon Mexican Indian/Mestizo farm workers.[11]

Racism against Native Americans, Chinese, and Japanese was to leave its indelible mark upon the California agricultural division of labor. That past historical condition, socially patterned and legitimated over the decades by dominant white institutions, functions as an ongoing causal force for the cruel treatment and minimal pay for today's Mexican farm workers. As a consequence, these nonwhite farm workers obtain but a fraction of what they have produced for large farms owned by white growers, and when these farm workers protest against such conditions through union struggles, their actions are met with violence.[12]

Hence, history appears to have come full circle. For today this patterning of battered exploitation has been reinforced by the fact that an ever-growing number of California field laborers derive their identity from a native heritage rooted in the northwestern Mexican countryside.[13] Over the centuries—from the exploitation of the first native American farm laborers to their present-day Mexican counterparts—race, racism, nationality, exploitation, and profits have all become inseparable.

CORPORATE FARMING AND THE DIVISION OF LABOR IN CALIFORNIA AGRICULTURE

In California during this century, certainly since World War II, the coordination of the agrarian subgroups has moved forward under circumstances of increased concentration and centralization of capital and control.[14] As the number of farm owners has shrunk from many millions to but a fraction of that number over the past century, the concentration of land ownership has become more pronounced and, consequently, decisions about the use of land and investment in water sources, seeds, fertilizers, pesticides, herbicides, general land improvements, soil conservation, and overall crop production are now made by an ever-smaller minority of corporate owners whose bottom line is to secure the highest rate of profit possible, whatever the human cost. These changes in the structure of ownership parallel the enlargement of farm size, reduction in overall farm count, and decrease in farm laborer employment. Thus, although by 1989 there were 2.95 million people who owned 833 million acres of private farmland, only 124,000 owners (or 4 percent of the total) held 47 percent of the land. Meanwhile, owners whose holdings were less than 50 acres, accounted for 30 percent of the total number of owners but held only 2 percent of the total acreage.[15]

Modern corporate agriculture involves a complex web of social relations that are based on the division of farm labor and the multilayered structure of work relations at the point of crop production in the fields. We find here the workers, crew leaders, farm labor contractors, growers, and boards of directors, as well as the judges, legislators, and the police. The essential elements of this collection of multiple interests come together in a contradictory way to generate foods to be marketed for private profit. The division of labor in corporate agriculture, as in other sectors of the capitalist economy, thus has as its end product the continued accumulation of capital—a process that facilitates further control and exploitation of labor in the fields, as on the shop floor.

Robert J. Thomas, in his study of lettuce cultivation in the Salinas Valley, California, in the late 1970s, provides some observations on the situation of farm workers, the role of the farm labor contractors, and the nature of the industry itself.[16] He observes how the large lettuce-producing firms have organized production around a large number of low-paid workers who labor much the same way as those in construction and mining operations, in an industry dominated by highly capitalized, bureaucratically administered multinational corporations. Thomas notes how lettuce harvesters work under physically destructive conditions, suffer the social and economic costs of seasonal migration, and lack legal protections within the larger community.[17]

A most informative book by William Friedland, Amy Barton, and Robert Thomas, titled *Manufacturing Green Gold: Capital, Labor, and Technology in the Lettuce Industry*, published in 1981, offers additional insight into the division of labor in California agriculture and documents the labor process at the point of production by providing a detailed description of lettuce cultivation in California's Salinas Valley.[18] In their depiction of supervised thinning and weeding operations in the lettuce harvest, the authors note that these tasks are performed by workers external to the lettuce firms, "sometimes by the grower-shippers who hire workers on a daily basis or often by specialists in the recruitment and management of temporary workers, for example, labor contractors."[19] This externalized labor force, they point out, is drawn from three major sources: (1) unskilled workers seeking to develop regular employment; (2) people who are not regularly or continuously in the labor force; and (3) casual workers who work only as forced to economically.

Unlike the thinning and weeding laborers, the higher status harvesters occupy a position as "the semi-internalized labor force."[20] This group consists of harvest workers. Harvesting activities have included two major kinds of arrangements, and therefore involve different kinds of workers and work organizations. The most significant category of harvest workers, although now in decline because of mechanization, has been those involved in the ground pack of lettuce—the cutting and packing of lettuce into cartons. Here the workers have been organized into crews usually consisting of 36 workers.

Cutters lead off the crew and move stooped through the rows cutting and trimming heads of lettuce, while the packers follow behind and squeeze the heads into empty cardboard cartons. The packer leaves the filled carton in the rows. He is followed by a sprayer who sprays the lettuce with water. The cartons are then glued, stapled, and loaded on trucks for transport out of the field. In moving through the fields, the truck (and any other equipment used) remains in the furrows so that heads left behind will remain undamaged and thereby permit future picking. With the exception of simple mechanical aids, all work is done by hand.

Crews are paid on a per-carton basis. Among crew members, the emphasis is on speed and coordination of their actions. Although the length of the workday may vary according to weather, field, or market conditions, the physical exertion required in the work is tremendous. The arduousness of the work can be compared to walking stooped for eight to ten hours a day or doing over 2,500 complete toe-touches over the same period. The speed and endurance required in harvesting take its toll on workers. Careers in the industry are short, since the length of a worker's career can range between ten and 18 years.[21] Most common among the physical complaints and reasons for quitting the harvest are back injuries, arthritis, hernias, and slipped disks.

During the early 1980s the average adult farm worker made $186 a week for 23 weeks, or $4,300 per year. The same average worker obtained another two weeks of nonfarm work for an additional $320 per year, which when added to his/her farm work income totaled $4,620. A typical family of four worked on the average for a total of 49 weeks per year and earned less than $9,000, whereas the poverty level in 1983, as defined by the federal government for a family of four, was $10,178.[22]

According to a survey by Mines and Martin, over 70 percent of the 168 four-member households in the sample were in poverty. They commented that although the average hourly rate ($5.10) and weekly wage ($186.00) for farm work may seem "high," yearly cash income levels have been low because of long periods of farm worker unemployment. Although workers do take advantage of governmental "transfer payments," including unemployment compensation and welfare, the tendency to do both has been much less the case among Mexican men who have migrated up from Mexico. These "undocumented" Mexican males almost never use welfare, perhaps because of a fear of county and state administrators and the police. Thus, despite Cesar Chavez's drive to organize farm labor through the United Farm Workers (UFW) union to improve their condition, the situation of the farm workers has steadily deteriorated, especially during the 1980s. By the early 1990s, the condition of farm workers has become worse than some 20 years earlier at the height of their initial unionization struggles.

The Growers and the Farm Labor Contractor

Whatever the changes in farm ownership and control, one role has proven to be central to the division of labor in California agriculture. Here we must stipulate as centrally powerful the coordinating role of the farm labor contractor. Over the centuries, the division of labor in California agriculture has moved through several very broad stages until one has emerged triumphant, and each stage has made a contribution to the overall, current definition of the contractor's role in the larger agrarian division of labor.

To impose proper controls on farm labor, both away from work and in the fields, the owners of the great estates, railroad construction sites, and placer mining ventures saw fit to accept the Mexican farm labor contractor. Being a member of the exploited nonwhite group in question, the labor contractor had the cultural understanding and leadership skills to impose order and to guide his labor gangs—and to do so within limits he could judge to be properly flexible, thereby avoiding rebellion among his charges.

He knew his subordinates well, for he had initially selected them into his work team not only annually, but often recurrently over decades of time. His intimate knowledge of field work allowed him over the years to examine and select the ones he preferred: for crew leaders, a selection often from his relatives; for work crews, choices from a wide array of fellow nationality subjects. In the process, he could drop those evaluated by him to be goldbrickers, reprobates, or troublemakers. He thus became an informal personnel manager for white ranchers simply not in positions to make the complicated evaluations and choices.

Spirited by a personal survival animus into the fields to guide the task performances of others, the frequently very intelligent labor contractor soon learned of his indispensability in the eyes of the Anglo growers. That being the case, he has over the decades found himself in a position where he can be ethically derelict, if only modestly, by ranch norms, as long as these gain-seeking proclivities did not go so far as to antagonize seriously his crew members, for crude transgressions could provoke labor stoppages and, consequently, harm the profit margins of the growers. So the contractor's gains from his flock proved to be measured, small in each instance, spaced to minimize the build-up of underlying anger, yet self-enhancing in amount in the long haul. As we shall see, the labor contractor's inspirations came to include the gleaning of small but additively over time significant amounts of spending money held by his 25 to 35 subordinates. These were the very ones he had brought together to labor on behalf of a whole string of growers. Composed by the contractor in late winter for the forthcoming year's field-to-field long march, these labor gangs moved from south to north, and returned in the fall, in effect both up and down as well as back and forth, zigzagging as it were, within a collective traverse, all sweated within the continent's particular crop-picking circuit.

At first glance, given the rationality of his coordination, the labor contractor's nationality may seem to be incidental. There is good reason, however, for there to exist an interrelationship among the nationality of the labor contractor, crew leader, and work team members, and this tie has been advantageous to growers. When the labor contractor belongs to a nationality identical with that of the bulk of his crew, he can connect to it through intimate knowledge of its cultural norms, values, and beliefs used to manipulate to exact sought outcomes, such as high labor productivity.

Richard Mines and Philip Martin have noted how, given the preponderance of short-term jobs, the rapid turnover of Mexican immigrants through the farm labor market, and the language barrier between white employers and Mexican crews, the contractors and crew leaders do the labor recruiting and managing for the growers.[23] Both the contractors and the crew leaders keep track of the demand for workers in an area, and with that information, they both scout and secure an adequate supply of laborers at a wage to meet the growers' demands.

The contractor (or crew leader, where a contractor is absent) has become an irreplaceable link in the rural employment chain. Also, employers, instead of hiring individuals, no doubt culturally incomprehensible to them, hire labor contractors who are bilingual, personally ambitious, and culturally sensitive managers who oversee the productive process in the fields and are directly responsible to the owners.

The labor contractor decides who will work and who will not, as he recruits and transports crews to the work site. At the point of production, he is the one who lines up his subordinates to be paced through specialized tasks. These he maps in his head before he walks into and about the fields. Later, he directs that expending of labor power among the vines, trees, and furrows, on occasion deciding that some of his charges should be fired and new ones hired. Although the contractor role takes multiple and complex forms, he ordinarily obtains a simple lump sum from the grower to hire workers and then deploys his blue-collar subordinates into field labor. With the all but total disappearance today of the UFW from California agriculture, the labor contractor has returned to positions of commanding heights at the point of production within almost every agricultural setting, but especially in the Imperial and San Joaquin valleys.[24]

In the overall labor process, the labor contractor arranges housing for crew members, sells work tools, sets up sources of food, and mediates conflicts among crew members. Also, he encourages agricultural workers to use the company (or nearby) store to purchase food and clothing essentials. He loans money to the farm workers, charges them interest, and sells them food as they work in the fields. He pays to his crew member subordinates approximately three-fourths of the money given to him by the growers for crew member pay. He keeps the remaining one-fourth of the cash for the services he provides to the growers and the crew members. In addition, he collects lump-sum money from the growers for the skilled labor provided—in effect charging the owners an added labor price for obtaining and directing crew members and crew leaders.[25] Altogether, he sets aside a goodly portion of the overall compensation to himself at the end of a work period—be it a day, week, or season—and often the amount set aside for his subordinates' net wages is not much once he has subtracted deductions.

Then there is debt peonage. When the migratory farm workers go into debt, the contractor proves eager to provide loans. In California, crew leaders also engage in money lending to crew members. Especially common on the East Coast is the propensity for workers to obtain loans just as they initiate their trip up from Florida, Georgia, or the Carolinas. The cash advance comes in handy. For at that moment, the field laborers' meager savings from the previous year have been spent to survive during the winter layovers. Given the usurious profits involved, the labor contractor will grant loans at the kick-off point of the north migration, plus many stops during the course of the trip, including the ride home. As a consequence, not a few farm workers end their winter-approaching harvests by returning to their base residence without earnings.[26]

These nonwhite field workers sometimes become bound to the labor contractor through debt on a permanent basis. Like bonded peasants of the eighteenth and nineteenth centuries, many of today's indebted laborers have remained firmly linked to the contractor until they have paid off the balance of their debts. That payback becomes difficult, given the excessive interest rates charged. Unable to eliminate the principal owed and dutifully subordinated to the contractor until that sum is paid, the indebted become locked indefinitely to their bosses.

The labor contractors also make difficult the enforcement of federal and state laws designed to protect workers from poisons at work. Often they can and will force workers to harvest fruits and vegetables long before they should enter the fields subsequent to their being sprayed by herbicides/pesticides that also happen to be carcinogenic. Further, the contractors make clear to their crew that should they question any work site practices that do in fact violate the law, such as entering aerially sprayed fields too soon or acts sometimes bordering on violation of the law (e.g., substitute recruitment of foreign labor to work as strike breakers to take farm laborers' jobs in an upcoming labor dispute), they can be dismissed, or be deported by the U.S. immigration service should they be foreign-born.[27] In fact, Mexican farm workers of U.S. citizenship status have been "deported" to Mexico during the course of agricultural strikes. That kind of episode has happened repeatedly, as James Cockcroft has documented.[28] Also, time and again, it has been the labor contractor who has singled out those eligible for deportation.

Most importantly, the labor contractor will go out of his way to destroy any bonafide union organizing activity among his crew members and to purge those judged by him to be ringleaders,[29] because unionization by legitimate unions means the elimination of the contractor role and the substitution in its place of the union hiring hall. That role elimination occurred wherever the UFW won union contracts during the 1960s and 1970s.

The growers have been absolutely opposed to nonsweetheart unionization of farm workers, especially those laboring in the fields where work stoppages risk the destruction of the harvest and indicate the questioning of white grower power. Thus, the growers have traditionally counted upon the contractor to function as a detective and to be able to scent the faint beginnings of unionization. Added to this has been the grower's fear that the coming of the union can only lead eventually to the purge of the person upon whom the grower has staked his point-of-production division of labor—that is, the labor contractor. Thus, the grower uses the contractor, as both field leader and labor spy, to stand alert against bonafide unions.

The net result of all these for the farm workers is clear. They are both humiliated and made to earn less by the presence of the labor contractor.

The Work Crew: Farm Labor and the Organization of Work in the Fields

The general portrait of farm labor should be broken down into specialties within the agricultural division of labor. In doing so, we should keep in mind both crop and task to give the reader a better idea of how work is allocated by recency of immigration, gender, and age, as well as nationality.

In California agriculture crew members are, with few exceptions, of Mexican extraction. Most are probably still Mexican citizens, many being legal immigrants to the United States, whereas others are undocumented workers. Although many crew members make their permanent home base in Mexico, directly across the border from the Imperial Valley, especially in cities such as Mexicali, an increasing number of farm workers are beginning to settle down in the United States (e.g., in the Salinas Valley).

Among farm workers, there are definite patterns of blue-collar job assignments. For example, the most recent immigrant workers do the most toilsome labor, whereas the other immigrants and the long-term U.S. residents obtain less laborious tasks. The longer farm workers remain in California, the more likely it is that they will locate themselves in contact situations attached to mature immigrant social networks. These mature, locally and job-site integrated members by definition have more experience and hence are better able to locate both themselves and the newly arrived friend workers in higher paying jobs. The aid is meted out generally to like workers of middle age.

Meanwhile, the young men tend to avoid such traditional social networks, and do seek to dominate most of the heavy harvesting tasks in ground citrus, tree fruits, melons, and piece-rate vegetable harvesting. This strength-demanding labor of necessity involves youthfulness of body, and hence, surplus of energy needed to stoop, climb, wrench, carry, and heave. It is not difficult to imagine how, after 10 to 15 years of back-breaking tasks, this cartilage pulling labor has taken its toll on workers' backs. Hence, they must move along, as they age, to jobs more in keeping with depleted tendons and vertebrae. Also, as they grow older, they seek and find supportive social networks to confirm their laboring in work slots where they can survive.[30]

Older workers specialize in the harvesting of strawberries, carrots, and certain vegetables, such as cauliflower; these crops are cut, placed on a conveyor belt, and packed in the field. In addition, the older men dominate in the semiskilled tasks of operating machines, supervising, irrigating, and tree pruning.

Farm worker children and women, by contrast, do a large share of the hoeing, thinning, and sorting. Older men may also be involved in these relatively lighter tasks. However, many of the older males drop out of farm work altogether by age 45. Very few of them remain after they reach age 54.[31]

Crew members were recruited, in the past, through existing members of crews, their crew leaders, and their farm labor contractors. When a new person was required, an individual crew member could bring a candidate into the crew. The crew member became, in effect, the new person's sponsor and was considered responsible for the work of the candidate. If there were any deficiencies in the work of the new person (e.g., an inability to maintain the pace), the sponsor was held responsible for making up the deficiencies. This system of recruitment placed serious obligations upon crew members who would not take such responsibilities lightly. Crews work at high speed, and sponsors might find themselves paying for their sponsorship through subsidizing a share of the income of the candidates. Sponsorship appears to have been based on kinship and friendship patterns.

Work crews develop norms for themselves with respect to earnings. In any given crew, there is what can be called a "target earnings level" of so many dollars per hour for each crew member. Some crews work much harder than others and therefore earn more. Thus, there is a hierarchy of work crews in terms of earnings that establishes the basis for individual movement among crews. Mobility, through this system, consists of individuals initially joining slower crews and then moving into crews with higher target earnings levels. Thus, young individuals could work their way through a hierarchy of crews by developing experience and maintaining their strength. However, as they grow older and are less capable of maintaining the pace, they begin to descend the hierarchy. The need for the reversal of such conditions became an important factor in farm worker organizing efforts to unionize the fields.

Unionism and its concomitants, especially seniority rights, have been instrumental in breaking down the self-recruitment and self-regulation of the crews, and have initiated the process of integration of workers into various agricultural firms. Several processes give rise to these changes. First, unionization tends to encourage restriction on "runaway" piece rates. Unions encourage situations in which earning levels become homogeneous and regular. Second, the establishment of seniority under union contracts creates the basis for an entirely different crew organization in which workers are assigned to work on the basis of length of individual service rather than membership in a crew or the length of the crew's service. This process also affects the situation in which crews used to determine their target earnings levels and therefore intercrew mobility. Once intercrew movement declines, the tendency toward homogenization of crew earnings also accelerates. Prior to the destruction of the UFW during the 1980s, the unionization of the fields had in this sense played an important role in bringing about the uniformity of farm labor in California agriculture.

FARM WORKER UNION STRUGGLES

The history of major farm worker organizing efforts and unionization struggles during this century goes back to the 1930s. As agricultural laboring conditions deteriorated appreciably between 1929 and 1931, and as the United States plunged into the Great Depression of the 1930s, the developing labor struggles of this period spread to the farms and fields of California and other states around the country.

By 1933, the California Communists had begun to use greater (however scant) resources to recruit significant numbers of agricultural workers to militant union locals. Relying partly on Carey McWilliams's full account of farm labor struggles in California during the 1930s, Walter J. Stein observed in his book *California and the Dust Bowl Migration* that California's Filipino and Mexican field workers had dropped their accustomed docility to generate a temporary alliance with multinational union organizers of left-wing commitment and considerable organizational skill. Stein noted that the massive 1933–1934 agricultural strikes mounted and directed by the Communist party within the Imperial and San Joaquin valleys provided the "immediate background" around which the California growers subsequently and gratefully received the essentially nonunion Great Plains migrants as replacements for the Mexicans and Filipinos. The growers were glad to see these Okies and Arkies, at least until the desperation strikes of 1938, when the dust bowlers proved to be the key participants within a "united front" labor drive.[32]

The Trade Union Unity League (TUUL), the affiliated Cannery and Agricultural Workers Industrial Union (CAWIU) of 1933–1935, and the United Cannery, Agricultural, Packing and Allied Workers of America (UCAPAWA) of 1938–1939 went all out but failed to win against their opponents, despite the at times massive participation of workers, especially in the 1933–1935 fights waged throughout California's Central Valley. In these extraordinary disputes, even though many farm workers no doubt believed they had little chance of winning, fight-or-starve laborers nonetheless organized and struck. As Stein noted when commenting on the conflagration of 1933, when the Mexican farm workers' demands for higher cotton-picking wages were refused by the San Joaquin Valley's growers and ginning companies, the field workers shut down the valley's cotton industry. Stein has commented: "Unheralded, indeed ignored, by historians of industrial labor, the San Joaquin cotton strike was a major labor conflict." According to Stein, between 15,000 and 18,000 workers went out on a 120-mile front for 24 days. The strike was ended through outside mediation, and the strikers returned to the fields.[33]

Stein has observed how the Communists, buoyed by their victory, moved south into the Imperial Valley. There the following year they supplied leadership in a strike of 3,600 Mexican vegetable workers and organized a host of lesser strikes throughout the State during the 1933–1934 period. In fact, by 1934, at the height of the great strike wave, the Communist-led drive had drawn approximately 70,000 farm workers into a union as yet unmatched in American farm labor history for its commitment to labor militancy.[34]

Three decades later, in the 1960s, another resurgence of farm worker militancy and unionization struggles took hold in the California fields. In the mid and late 1960s, California Central Valley farm workers rebelled and tried to organize. In September 1965, thousands of Delano farm workers joined either the Agricultural Workers Organizing Committee (mainly Filipino) or the National Farm Workers Association (overwhelmingly Chicano), and participated in the great marches and demonstrations that mobilized tens of thousands of supporters in favor of the farm workers' cause.

By 1970, the UFW launched and won a series of offensive and successful strikes against the growers of the San Joaquin and Salinas valleys. These victories brought tens of thousands of farm workers under UFW contracts. However, when UFW contracts came up for renewal in 1973, the growers adamantly opposed their renewal. To aid the growers and to destroy the UFW, the Teamsters hired professional strike breakers, many of them Chicanos, to beat up UFW workers. The Teamsters were joined by police in coming down hard on pro-UFW workers, whatever their nationality.[35]

In the 1980s, Latino farm workers scored a number of successes. Among them has been the spring 1986 triumph of the Mexican-American Farm Labor Organizing Committee (FLOC) against Campbell Soup and Vlasic Pickles, not to mention their supplier growers situated in both northwestern Ohio and southern Michigan.[36] More recently, unionized farm workers in New Jersey have won a historic pact. A southern New Jersey, Cumberland County farm has been the first to grant a contract to farm workers.[37]

Still, very real problems face farm worker unions today. For example, the California-centered UFW has, over the course of 17 years, lost approximately 70 percent of its membership, in large measure because of Teamster raiding offensives against the UFW, because of the courts, and in part because of the hostility expressed by successive state administrations at the local and national levels.[38]

Corporate agribusiness conflict with farm workers and their unions became most intense between the mid-1960s and 1973, at which time an alliance of growers, California government agencies, and the Teamsters union soundly defeated but did not eliminate entirely the fledgling Mexican/Filipino-based UFW union. Between 1974 and 1981, in particular, the UFW both conducted union drives and fought strikes intermittently, but the phantom alliance of the governor's office, the state legislature, the courts, the federal government, the growers, the banks, the mass media, the county and local governments, and the Teamsters Union simply overwhelmed the UFW. The decline in union activity and strikes by the UFW accompanied the union's propensity to give up on the impossible, namely, a fight for lasting union contracts for farm workers. Rather, the UFW turned toward education of the general public around the dangers of chemicals, especially those sprayed on grapes. Although in the 1980s the UFW relied on contributions from its supporters to keep the union afloat, today the union is one-fourth of what it was 20 years ago, and its overall strategy seems to be one of keeping it alive until times more conducive to labor organizing make their appearance in the California fields.

Historically, in the United States, farm labor struggles, like struggles of U.S. labor in general, have coincided with hard times, when the economy has plunged into cyclical crises of recessions and depressions. This cycle of economic downturn and social resurgence seems to reemerge approximately once every 30 years: the early 1900s, the 1930s, the 1960s, and perhaps again in the 1990s. If this is the case, we may soon pass into a period of significant labor battles and gains for farm workers as the decade of the 1990s unfolds into the early years of the coming twenty-first century.

APPENDIX: CHEMICALS IN THE FIELDS

The agricultural division of labor proceeds out of doors. With the enormous quantity of dangerous chemicals sprayed on crops, workers' bodies absorb liquid and vaporous toxins via lungs and skin as they labor in the fields.

The additive and the synergistic toxic effects of herbicides/pesticides fail to redound to the betterment of either underpaid workers or the consuming public. In fact, these chemical compounds are often deadly.

Among the chemicals most carcinogenic are the following:

1. *Methyl bromide* is an extremely poisonous substance to all forms of life. This fumigant is reportedly responsible for more occupationally related deaths than any other pesticide; even nonfatal exposure can cause severe, irreversible effects on the nervous system, with permanent brain damage or blindness.
2. *Parathion* and *phosdrin* are work site chemicals that can be fatal, producing illnesses in workers in as little as 20 minutes. These poisons are usually sprayed aerially and cause populations surrounding agricultural areas the same problems as those visited upon farm workers, since as much as 90 percent of aerially sprayed pesticides miss their target areas.
3. *Dinoseb* induces a poisoning at first resembling heatstroke; subsequently, cumulative doses cause extensive illnesses, including loss of vision. It is much too toxic to be used safely.
4. *Capatan* is a chemical sprayed on table grapes at the rate of 344,000 pounds each year. The residue of this compound is the most frequently discovered material on grapes in stores. Not only can capatan cause cancer, but it also originates birth defects and changes in body cells; it is structurally similar to thalidomide, which several decades ago caused thousands of babies in the United States and Europe to be born without arms and legs.

The net result of the use of such deadly chemicals in the fields has been disastrous to the farm workers. An estimated 78 percent of Texas farm workers studied in one survey had chronic skin rashes, whereas 56 percent had kidney and liver abnormalities, and 54 percent suffered from chest cavity problems. Nationwide, more than 300,000 farm workers are made ill every year through pesticide exposure, with pesticide poisoning incidents doubling over the last ten years. The miscarriage rate for female farm workers is seven times the national average. Disability days associated with pesticide illnesses have increased by 53 percent and hospital days by 61 percent since 1979.[39]

NOTES

1. *See* Gladys K. Bowles, "The Current Situation of the Hired Farm Labor Force," in E. E. Bishop (ed.), *Farm Labor in the United States* (New York: Columbia University Press, 1967); Carey McWilliams, *Factories in the Field* (Santa Barbara and Salt Lake City: Peregrine Publishers, 1971); Dorothy Nel-

kin, *On the Season: Aspects of the Migrant Labor System* (Ithaca, NY: New York School of Industrial and Labor Relations, 1970).

2. John G. Dunne, *Delano, The Story of the California Grape Strike* (New York: Farrar, Straus & Giroux, 1967); Alec Wilkinson, *Big Sugar: Seasons in the Cane Fields of Florida* (New York: Vintage Books, 1989).

3. *See* Sucheng Chan, *This Bittersweet Soil: The Chinese in California Agriculture, 1860–1910* (Berkeley: University of California Press, 1989); Stanford Lyman, *Chinese Americans* (New York: Random House, 1974).

4. Ibid. *Also see* Richard E. Lingenfelter, *The Hardrock Miners: A History of the Mining Labor Movement in the American West, 1863–1893* (Berkeley: University of California Press, 1974).

5. Harry Kitano and Roger Daniels, *Asian Americans: Emerging Minorities* (Engelwood Cliffs, NJ: Prentice Hall, 1988).

6. Chan, *This Bittersweet Soil.*

7. McWilliams, *Factories in the Field.*

8. *See* James Gregory, *American Exodus: The Dust Bowl Migrations and Okie Culture in California* (New York: Oxford University Press, 1989).

9. Ernesto Garlarza, *Merchants of Labor: The Mexican Bracero Story, an Account of the Managed Migration of Mexican Farm Workers in California* (Santa Barbara, CA: McNally and Lofton, 1964).

10. Kevin F. McCarthy and Burgiaga Valdez, *Current and Future Effects of Immigration in California* (Santa Barbara, CA: Rand Corporation, 1985).

11. Garlarza, *Merchants of Labor: The Mexican Bracero Story*; James D. Cockcroft, *Outlaws in the Promised Land: Mexican Immigrant Workers and America's Future* (New York: Grove Press, 1986).

12. McWilliams, *Factories in the Field*; John C. Leggett, *Mining the Fields: Farm Workers Fight Back* (Highland Park, NJ: The Raritan Institute, 1991).

13. Richard Mines and Philip L. Martin, *A Profile of California Farm Workers* (Berkeley, CA: The Giannini Foundation of Agricultural Economics, University of California, Berkeley, 1986); Cockcroft, *Outlaws in the Promised Land.*

14. Harland Padfield and William E. Martin, *Farmers, Workers and Machines* (Tucson, AZ: University of Arizona Press, 1965); Gigi M. Bernardi and Charles M. Geisler, *The Social Consequences and Challenges of New Agricultural Technologies* (Boulder, CO: Westview Press, 1984).

15. Cited in Chan, *This Bittersweet Soil.*

16. Robert J. Thomas, "The Social Organization of Industrial Agriculture," *The Insurgent Sociologist* (Winter 1981), pp. 5–20.

17. Ibid.

18. William Friedland, Amy Barton, and Robert Thomas, *Manufacturing Green Gold: Capital, Labor, and Technology in the Lettuce Industry* (Cambridge: Cambridge University Press, 1981), p. 58.

19. Ibid., p. 58.

20. Ibid.

21. *See* Mines and Martin, *A Profile of California Farm Workers.*

22. Ibid., pp. 38–41.

23. Ibid.

24. Truman Moore, *The Slaves We Rent* (New York: Random House, 1965); William Friedland and Dorothy Nelkin, *Migrant Workers in America's Northeast* (New York: Holt, Rinehart and Winston, 1971); Nelkin, *On the Season: Aspects of the Migrant Labor System*; Leggett, *Mining the Fields: Farm Workers Fight Back.*

25. Dunne, *Delano, The Story of the California Grape Strike*; Mines and Martin, *A Profile of California Farm Workers.* On the East Coast, the migratory crew chief takes on the contractor role and charges accordingly. *See* Dale Wright, *They Harvest Despair: The Migrant Farm Workers* (Boston: Beacon Press, 1965); Friedland and Nelkin, *Migrant Workers in America's Northeast.*

26. Moore, *The Slaves We Rent*; Nelkin, *On the Season: Aspects of the Migrant Labor System*; Herman L. Emmet, *Fruit Tramps* (Albuquerque, NM: University of New Mexico Press, 1989).

27. *See* Murray Campbell, "Withering on the Vine: As Conquests Fade, a New Nightmare Haunts Grape Pickers," *The Globe and Mail* (Toronto) (November 27, 1991), pp. A1, A10.

28. *See* Cockcroft, *Outlaws in the Promised Land.*

29. Ibid.; Campbell, "Withering on the Vine," pp. A1, A10.

30. Campbell, "Withering on the Vine," pp. A1, A10.

31. Only 5 percent of the females and 10 percent of the males studied by Mines and Martin were 55 or older. *See* Mines and Martin, *A Profile of California Farm Workers.*

32. Walter J. Stein, *California and the Dust Bowl Migration* (Westport, CT: Greenwood Press, 1973).

33. Ibid., p. 224.

34. Ibid., pp. 224–26; McWilliams, *Factories in the Field*, pp. 211–29.

35. Cockcroft, *Outlaws in the Promised Land*, p. 183; Linda C. Majka and Theo J. Majka, *Farm Workers, Agribusiness, and the State* (Philadelphia: Temple University Press, 1982).

36. Donald Warshaw, "Campbell and Workers Reach Pact," Newark *Star Ledger* (February 21, 1986), p. 56; Kenneth Barger, *Hasta LaVictoria, A Farm Labor Movement in the Midwestern U.S.* (Austin: The University of Texas Press, 1992).

37. Donald Warshaw, "Unionized Migrant Workers Win Historic Pact," Newark *Star Ledger* (May 7, 1986), p. 33.

38. Cockcroft, *Outlaws in the Promised Land*, p. 184. The estimated figures used by Cockcroft cite a drop from 100,000 to 30,000.

39. *See* Daniel M. Berman, *Death on the Job: Occupational Health and Safety Struggles in the United States* (New York: Monthly Review Press, 1978); Harry Weinstein, "The Health Threat in the Fields," *The Nation*, 240 (May 11, 1985), pp. 558–60; V. Wilk and D. M. Hancock, "Farmworker Occupational Health and Safety in the 1990's," *New Solutions*, 1 (Spring 1991), pp. 6–10.

7 The Labor Force in Transition: The Growth of the Contingent Work Force in the United States

Robert E. Parker

This chapter examines the emergence and growth of the contingent work force in the U.S. economy. Contingent workers are those who have a loose affiliation with their employers.[1] As the 1990s began, between one-quarter and one-third of all U.S. workers were a part of the contingent work force. Examples of contingent workers include temporary workers (the fastest growing category), part-time workers, and contract/subcontract workers (usually employed by business service firms). All of these categories are growing much faster than the U.S. labor force as a whole. Although some workers choose a contingent working status (often for family or other personal reasons), a large and growing percentage of these workers are finding contingent positions their only option as U.S. corporations continue to restructure their operations on a world scale.

Employers are increasingly turning to contingent workers to cut labor costs, to gain greater control over the labor process, and to increase their profits. Moreover, this strategy on the part of the employers can also thwart unions since contingent workers are inherently more difficult to organize. All these factors have led to the creation of a more transient and contingent work force.[2]

In this chapter, we will examine a number of theoretical and empirical issues surrounding the emergence and expansion of contingent employment in the United States. First, we will address the latent foundations of contingent work. We will argue that deskilling, increased profits, and greater control over labor and the labor process are three key factors that have contributed to the widespread adoption of contingent employment. We will then show that the corporate search for a cheap, docile, and flexible work force is closely related to the process of deskilling, exploitation, and control of labor, and that the movement toward a contingent work force is part and parcel of the changes in the capitalist labor process now taking place on a global scale—changes that have an enormous impact on full-time, year-round workers in particular, and the working class in general.

THE NATURE AND GROWTH OF CONTINGENT WORK

The contingent work force, whether in the core or peripheral sector of the U.S. economy, is demographically distinctive. Disproportionately, it is composed of the young, the elderly, minorities, and, most prominently, women. The transition to an increasingly contingent work force provides U.S. businesses with greater flexibility and other benefits, but implies several negative effects for workers, including lower wages, reduced health care protection, and the loss of pension and retirement benefits.[3] This essay provides an overview of these developments in the labor process, and examines the nature and implications of the move toward a contingent work force to secure greater control and exploitation of labor in the United States and around the world.

In the past decade, the marginal or contingent sector of the U.S. labor force has significantly expanded, easily surpassing the overall growth of the U.S. labor force. One study in the late 1980s reported a contingent labor force of between 29.9 million and 36.6 million workers, or approximately one-quarter of the work force.[4] According to U.S. Bureau of Labor Statistics (BLS) data, the U.S. civilian labor force grew by 14 percent between 1980 and 1988. During the same period, however, the number of temporary workers (those specifically recorded as employed by the temporary help services industry) increased by 175 percent; part-time workers (roughly 30 percent of whom work part-time "involuntarily") grew by 21 percent; and the business services industry (which expanded more rapidly during the entire decade of the 1980s than any other industry in the U.S. economy and is the primary provider of subcontracted human resource services to employers) advanced by 70 percent (*see* Table 7.1).

The above list is not exhaustive, but is indicative of the transformation of the labor process in the United States and other advanced capitalist countries. International competition, restructuring of the world economy, and the drive to reduce labor costs are frequently cited by employers as the reasons for using and expanding their payroll of contingent workers.

An important aspect of employment growth in the past two decades has been the creation of many part-time, impermanent positions. In the 1980s and early 1990s, employers have been actively avoiding any long-term

Table 7.1
Growth of the Contingent Work Force, 1980–1988

Contingent Work Force	*Millions of Workers* 1980	1988	*Percent Change*
Temporary Workers	0.4	1.1	175
Service Workers	3.3	5.6	70
Part-time Workers	16.3	19.8	21
Total Labor Force	106.9	121.7	14

Source: Adapted from Richard Belous, *The Contingent Economy: The Growth of the Temporary, Part-time, and Subcontracted Workforce* (Washington, DC: National Planning Association, 1989), p. 16.

commitment to a majority of their workers.[5] Employers are pursuing a work force willing to work for low wages and few, if any, benefits. Employers are also seeking a docile work force—workers who will work hard and not complain about conditions. Moreover, they want to retain workers only for that narrowly specific period of time when their labor is required.

A few analysts have begun to document these developments.[6] Barry Bluestone and Bennett Harrison provide one particularly useful framework for understanding the expansion of contingent work. In their book, *The Deindustrialization of America*, Bluestone and Harrison lay out the corporate response to the stagflation of the late 1960s and 1970s.[7] Specifically, they discuss the efforts of corporate managers to (1) find new, more profitable uses for their capital, and (2) to find new ways of cutting production costs in their operations. They cite "buying and selling entire businesses and transferring capital from one sector to another" as the most important corporate strategies for raising and protecting short-term profitability during the 1960s and the 1970s.[8] Further, they note the role of "differentially expanding and contracting facilities" as an important strategy—one that involved circumventing unions and the active pursuit of "good business climates."[9] As their work documents, corporations not only began to head south and west, away from unions, but they also challenged them directly by hiring sophisticated consulting firms to implement expensive anti-union campaigns.[10]

The connection between Bluestone and Harrison's analysis and contingent work emerges most clearly in their consideration of capital's assault on the social wage. They stress that "because so few American workers belong to unions, these managerial responses were not sufficient to make really significant, long-term dents in labor costs."[11] To achieve that objective, management set upon a deliberate campaign to make workers everywhere more "flexible." Private employers and their political allies have attempted to make the alternative to dead-end jobs unbearable, in order to make workers desperate enough to take any job under any circumstances. An important part of this campaign has been continuing attacks on the minimum wage, Social Security, public health programs, and unemployment insurance. Faced with a reduced safety net, various contingent arrangements, which were once unthinkable for many workers, become more appealing. The movement toward a contingent work force would seem both an economic as well as an ideological victory for employers as they succeed in convincing workers that any part of a job is better than none.

TYPES OF CONTINGENT WORKERS

The phrase "contingent work" does not refer to a single monolithic type of working arrangement and is not confined to any economic sector. Rather, contingent workers include employees of the temporary help industry, day laborers, migrant farm workers, guest workers, service workers, clerical workers, and part-time workers, among others.

Several important characteristics tend to be shared by contingent workers: low wages, few, if any, fringe benefits, minimal chances for occupational advancement, and virtually no opportunities to exert discretion at the work place or to utilize existing skill levels. Many contingent workers have a pervasive sense of uncertainty surrounding their work lives, but the extent to which these conditions characterize any particular contingent worker can vary considerably.

Clearly, then, the U.S. economy depends upon a large number of workers to fill a variety of jobs on a short-term, impermanent basis. Employers use temporary, part-time, and other contingent workers in an extensive number of occupational settings.

Industrial Workers in the Temporary Help Industry

Like most contingent workers, industrial workers tend to be full-time job seekers, and like involuntary part-time workers, subcontractors, and others in the contingent work force, industrial workers employed by the temporary help industry are an underemployed segment of the labor force, enduring uncertain hours, inadequate income, and a fundamental mismatch between their existing skills and the working opportunities offered by the temporary help industry. According to Steven Wasser, temporary industrial workers account for 7.4 percent of total temporary help industry revenues and 9 percent of total employment.[12]

A typical assignment for a temporary industrial worker involves working in a warehouse. Other types of assignments include laboring positions, such as construction, light assembly and manufacturing, physical plant maintenance, and inventory work. The majority of work performed by temporary industrial workers requires few, if any, skills. The only requirement is a willingness to follow directions and to perform physically demanding labor. With the exception of electronics assembly workers (who must know how to solder), most work assignments involve unskilled labor.

Industrial workers are disproportionately male. Nonwhite males in particular figure prominently in this sector of contingent employment. For example, according to BLS data for 1985, black workers made up over 20 percent of the temporary work force, although they were only 10 percent of the total labor force.[13] Further, June Lapidus's research shows that the overrepresentation among nonwhites is more pronounced for males than females, and that a black male is much more likely than a white male to work as a temporary employee.[14] Male temporary workers endure a significantly greater level of pay disparity than female workers.

Many temporary industrial workers are similar to other segments of the contingent work force in that they have salable labor market skills. A significant number of these workers have previously held full-time positions. Yet they still cannot find full-time, year-round jobs in the early 1990s, as the relationship between employers and employees in the U.S. economy grows increasingly tenuous.

Many temporary industrial workers report having had full-time working experience in areas such as construction work, maintenance, electronics assembly, transportation, sales work, and a host of other trades. Also, like other parts of the contingent army of the underemployed, most arrive at temporary work only after exhausting other, more preferable alternatives.

Day Laborers

A parallel among day laborers, part-time employees, and other elements within the contingent work force is their inability to obtain as much work as they want or require to subsist. Even in rapidly growing cities overwhelmed by construction activity, the supply of work remains inadequate for all those who are actively seeking employment. While sharing this and other features in common, day laborers are far more vulnerable to higher rates of exploitation and harsher working conditions than other sectors of the contingent work force, such as most of the employees of the temporary help industry.

In the mid-1980s, the day labor rituals of 500 homeless individuals in one rapidly growing Southwest city, Austin, Texas, were studied by Charles Grigsby.[15] Many of the homeless, more than 60 percent in this study, resorted to "labor corners" to find work. These unregulated labor corners are found in most moderate to larger sized cities. Workers congregate at specific sites looking for work for the day—mainly construction and landscaping work—and employers gravitate to such sites looking for cheap labor.

In Los Angeles, it is estimated that several thousand laborers, mostly Latino men, gather each morning at about 25 street corners scattered throughout the city seeking day work. City officials there are experimenting with programs that will likely institutionalize this type of dead-end, highly exploitative working arrangement, as day laborers are bused at city expense to designated day labor centers to get them off the streets.[16] Following Los Angeles's lead, San Francisco is resurrecting hiring halls for the city's day laborers who now populate street corners in various parts of the city.[17]

Researchers indicate that many of these contingent workers are often underpaid, and reports of workers sustaining on-the-job injuries and not receiving treatment or being dumped at a medical facility are common.

Migrant Farm Workers

The conditions faced by temporarily employed migrant farm workers are quite similar to those of day laborers. The livelihood of farm workers hinges precariously on the health of a variety of crops. Like day laborers, migrant farm workers have little control over their working conditions. Even full-time farm workers are one of the most socially disadvantaged groups in the labor force.

Whether one labors on a farm on a temporary basis or as a full-time worker has important implications. In 1990, 30 years after Edward R. Murrow's landmark documentary of migrant life in the United States, reporters for the PBS series "Frontline" retraced Murrow's journey and found that in some ways conditions were worse today than in 1960. Roughly 1,000,000 workers still follow the migrant trail eking out a subsistence existence. In 1990, the average migrant family earned less than $6,000 and had a life expectancy of just 48 years.[18] According to data compiled by Leslie Whitener, casual farm workers averaged 39 days of farm work annually, compared with 218 days for full-time year-round farm workers.[19] In the early 1980s, temporary farm laborers received just $1,071 on an annual basis, whereas full-time farm workers earned $6,080.[20] In the early 1990s, the inequality that existed a decade earlier persists. Year-round employees of South Bay Growers earn up to $24,000 annually, whereas the seasonal workers documented by "Frontline" reporters earned just over $6,000.[21]

In addition to temporary farm workers, many American corporate farmers encourage undocumented workers to migrate from Mexico, Central America, and the Caribbean to fill agricultural positions in California, Florida, and other states on a temporary or seasonal basis. In these cases, both the laborer and the employer have an incentive to keep the farm worker's employment hidden. Undocumented workers, faced with the threat of deportation if discovered, are even more likely to be victims of extreme levels of exploitation than are domestic farm workers.

Guest Workers

In addition to domestic farm workers and undocumented workers, tens of thousands of "guest workers" (under provisions of the H-2A visa program) perform agricultural work for U.S. employers on a temporary basis. The H-2A visa guest worker program allows American farmers to import workers if they cannot find American employees at the time and place of the harvest. For example, about 10,000 workers from Jamaica are allowed to migrate temporarily to the United States each year to cut Florida sugar cane.[22] When these migrants have finished their work, they are sent home. Employers of guest workers benefit from their labor in several ways. They do not have to pay for Social Security, unemployment compensation, or workman's compensation taxes. Further, if the workers complain or cause trouble, employers can quickly ship them back to their native country. For more than a decade, a steady stream of proposals has called for an expansion of the program to include as many as 500,000 guest workers.

According to an early 1980s House Labor Standards subcommittee report, U.S. farmers prefer to use guest workers even when other workers are available. For example, in the 1980s, thousands of immigrants arrived from Cuba, Haiti, and Caribbean nations. In addition, hundreds of thousands more have arrived from Central America. The majority of these immigrants are unskilled and often from rural areas; seemingly they could provide all the cheap labor farm operators could demand. Yet the House report clearly indicates that Florida farm operators have consistently requested workers from among the poorest British West Indian applicants. Clearly, employers see these workers as the most likely to work long, hard hours without complaining about conditions—a work force that is cheap, docile, and easy to control. The House report concluded that "foreign guest workers who survive the rigors of a six-day week, five month harvest season provide the growers with an elite corps of experienced sugar cane cutters that cannot strike, organize, or effectively protest."[23]

Service Workers

For several decades, service occupations have grown faster than other sectors in the U.S. labor force. In 1990, there were more than 32 million workers employed in service occupations. As with other elements of the contingent work force, these jobs are disproportionately filled by women (61 percent of the total). Also, like other industries in the U.S. economy, part-time workers make up a growing part of the service sector. Between 1979 and 1985, the percent of part-time workers within the services sector has escalated more sharply than other industries, from 17.8 percent to 31.1 percent. This gain of more than 13 percentage points in part-time work in the services industries dwarfed the growth in other industries, including transportation (+0.7), manufacturing (+2.6), wholesale trade (+4.9), construction (+2.9), and retail trade (+5.5). Further, the service industries employ 40.5 percent of all part-timers.[24]

Despite having experienced more employment growth in the 1980s than any other industry, the business services industry's impact has received little attention. The business services industry is the main provider of subcontracted labor, which in itself is a growing part of the contingent work force. Key sectors within this industry include computer and data processing services; advertising; consumer credit reporting and collection; mailing, reproduction, and stenographic services; building services; and personnel services. Workers in this industry are disassociated from the traditional employer-employee relationship. They are less likely to be unionized, have an average job tenure half that of the national median, and generally receive lower pay and fewer benefits.

Clerical Workers

Between 1940 and 1989, the number of clerical jobs in the U.S. economy increased from 4.4 to 18.6 million.[25] This burgeoning white-collar work force has become central to the emergence and expansion of the new contingent economy. For example, filling office positions is the single most frequent service the temporary help industry provides to employers. During the latter half of the 1980s, approximately 65 percent of all temporary help assignments were clerical positions.[26] Although other occupational categories within the temporary industry are growing faster (such as temporary home health care workers), clerical positions continue to provide the greatest number of employment opportunities for temporary workers. Clerk typists, secretaries, file and data-entry clerks, bookkeepers, and receptionists account for the bulk of clerical occupations. Like the involuntary part-time service workers, clerical workers express a preference for full-time work but accept whatever work they can find.

Consistent with the composition of other components of the contingent work force, the vast majority of these workers are female. Black women became an important part of the clerical work force after World War II, but entered semiskilled and unskilled low-paid positions. The racial divide in clerical work is still apparent since nonwhite workers disproportionately occupy secretarial and clerical jobs. Prior to the Civil War, most clerical workers were male, but by the early 1990s, 80 percent of clerical employees in the United States were women.[27] Furthermore, a recent National Association of Temporary Services survey showed 80 percent of all respondents were female.[28] In 1990, average hourly earnings for the recently renamed Help Supply Services Industry (more than two-thirds of whom are women) were $8.08, compared with $10.03 for all nonsupervisory and production employees.

The growing ranks of clerical workers have become a part of the contingent work force through similar backgrounds. Many, perhaps a majority of new members, are victims of U.S. corporate restructuring. As companies "rationalize" and downsize, they are creating virtually captive pools of talented labor that business services, subcontractors, temporary help companies, and other employers can exploit. Some clerical workers are recent arrivals in a city and are unable to locate permanent, full-time employment. Still others are trying to enter the labor market on a full-time basis for the first time and cannot find full-time work; finally, some are accustomed to full-time positions, but are in between jobs because of resignations, terminations, and other types of layoffs.

Part-time Workers

Another source of contingent work that has minimized employer's labor costs and enhanced profits is part-time employment. The number of part-time workers and their percentage in the labor force has been growing rapidly in the past two decades, particularly among women.[29] Part-time workers earn about 60 percent of the hourly wages that full-time workers receive. In 1990, part-time workers earned $5.06 per hour, compared with $8.09 for full-time hourly workers.

Between 1980 and 1988, the number of part-time workers in the U.S. labor force grew from 16.3 million to 19.8 million. This equates to a 21 percent increase at a time when the total labor force grew by 14 percent. Noting the rapid rise in part-time work, Susan McHenry and Linda Lee Small observe that more than 25 percent of the "much heralded 10 million jobs created during the Reagan era were part-time."[30] The expansion of part-time work has continued throughout the 1980s, such that by the end of the decade, part-time employees comprised "almost one-fifth of the U.S. work force. About 20 million people in the economy's nonagricultural sectors worked part time in 1989, making up 18.1 percent of persons at work."[31] Moreover, the increase in part-time employment would be even more profound if Labor Department and Census Bureau statisticians counted the number of part-time jobs, rather than the number of part-time workers. For example, some workers may be multiple jobholders, counted as full-time workers because they work more than 35 hours per week, but in terms of pay, benefits, and working conditions, more closely resembling involuntary part-time workers.

Involuntary part-time workers are employees who have part-time jobs out of economic necessity (they are the only jobs they can find), or their usual full-time job becomes part-time temporarily or permanently. Much of the recent increase in part-time employment is attributable to the rise in the number of involuntary part-time workers. For example, between 1970 and 1982, when the number of voluntary part-time workers rose from 9.3 million to 12.4 million (a 33 percent increase), the number of involuntary part-time workers grew by 166 percent, from 2.19 million to 5.8 million.[32] After this period of very rapid growth during the 1970s and the 1980–1982 recession, the growth rate among involuntary part-time workers slowed for much of the 1980s. Nonetheless, there were still nearly 5,000,000 involuntary part-time workers officially recorded in 1990.

The trend toward greater levels of involuntary part-time workers has resumed in the early 1990s as another recession has taken hold nationwide. Despite the slower increase in the 1980s, the involuntary part-time work force has still grown in excess of 120 percent since 1970, compared with 69 percent for voluntary part-time workers and 54 percent for all workers. In short, the involuntary part-time work force has been growing more than twice as rapidly as the civilian labor force for the past 20 years.

The examples of contingent workers presented here are suggestive of labor force trends. Most importantly, they illustrate the transformation toward a more impermanent, contingent relationship between management and labor.

DESKILLING AND CONTINGENT WORK

Harry Braverman's *Labor and Monopoly Capital* provides a provocative critique of the capitalist labor process as it evolved during the course of the twentieth century.[33] Braverman's central thesis is that, given capitalist control over the work place, there is a long-term tendency toward the mechanization, fragmentation, and rationalization of work. The result is an increasingly deskilled work force, one that steadily loses its traditional craft skills, and one that progressively witnesses worker and scientific knowledge transformed into new production technologies. Since publication, Braverman's ideas have stimulated much discussion and debate.

Perhaps the most significant criticism leveled at Braverman is his neglect of the role of working-class resistance in shaping the labor process in American capitalism. Braverman often writes as if managers had the capacity to unilaterally impose their designs on the work place. Indeed, in the preface to his book, he states that "no attempt will be made to deal with the modern working class on the level of its consciousness, organization, or activities."[34] In contrast to Braverman's position, a significant body of organizational literature demonstrates that workers vigorously resisted rationalization and that human relations approaches often had to be developed to counter this resistance.[35] A more adequate treatment of the issues involved in deskilling, then, must recognize the working class as an active force within the process of capital accumulation.

Tony Elger criticizes Braverman on several additional points. He argues, for example, that Braverman overstates the role of craft workers and craft skills as countervailing influences in the trend toward deskilling.[36] Elger points out that craft skills may be thoroughly subordinated to capital by intensification, and, by contrast, he observes that unskilled workers can substitute union membership for skills to acquire effective organization and high pay.[37] Other critics have argued that the processes of mechanization and automation do at least as much to create and upgrade skills as they do to destroy them.[38]

Braverman's ideas can be centrally linked to this essay on contingent work. The gradual deskilling process represents a fundamental social force that has permitted temporary, part-time, and other forms of contingent work to flourish. At the center of employers' efforts to remain profitable is the creation of a highly interchangeable work force. Contingent workers epitomize the interchangeability that deskilling fosters. Particularly through the processes of specialization and standardization, deskilling has laid the foundation for contingent employment. For example, temporary help firms are successful, because they can capitalize on large numbers of unskilled and semiskilled jobs in the U.S. economy. Employers using contingent workers fully understand that the average worker can fill in quickly and effectively at most positions. Indeed, as the temporary help industry likes to claim, some temporary workers may even be more skilled (because of their resourcefulness and adaptability) than the permanently employed. The fundamental point, however, is that both groups have become sufficiently deskilled so that they can be interchanged with minimal work place disruption.

Deskilling is not only essential in the creation of the preconditions for contingent employment, but it continues to serve as a catalyst once established. Despite conventional wisdom about job upgrading, many of the clerical workers that use new automated office systems are actually becoming deskilled. Much of the automated equipment significantly reduces skill requirements and decision-making ability. Automated systems also present managers with new sophisticated techniques for monitoring and controlling their workers. As suggested earlier, the impact of deskilling manifested in automation is transforming the character of clerical positions. As part of the process, it is making more clerical jobs likely candidates for part-time and temporary restructuring.

Deskilling provides both a foundation for contingent work and, through its progressive erosion of occupational skills, steadily produces new opportunities for growth in the industry. In the modern, bureaucratic, technologically advanced office of today, many traditional secretarial skills are being diminished. The proletarianization of the clerical work force documented by C. Wright Mills and Harry Braverman is evolving and entering a heightened phase. With the introduction of automated office systems, clerical workers are further hampered in their ability to exert discretion in their daily work. This deskilling of clerical work facilitates the expansion of contingent employment. Through temporary help agencies, subcontractors, and business services, employers are reaping the benefits of the decades-long deskilling process. Contingent workers are not effective in replacing workers with firm-specific skills. Contingent employees are only cost-effective for employers when workers can be easily interchanged.

To sum up, interchangeability is fostered by deskilling and intensified by the trend toward the use of electronic data processing systems. In turn, the progressive deskilling of occupations, upon which contingent work hinges heavily, has been achieved largely through the long-standing organizational principles of occupational specialization and standardization. The routinization of industrial and clerical work has made the impermanent use of cheap labor in these occupations very lucrative for employers. Further, the diversity of occupations that part-time and temporary workers now fill indicates how far deskilling has expanded.

FLEXIBILITY AND PROFIT MAXIMIZATION

Although a key factor, deskilling alone cannot account for all of the recent corporate movement toward contingent work. Deskilling has provided the foundation for a greater degree of labor exploitation, but additional factors also contribute to the expansion of contingent employment. The major contemporary factor spurring contingent labor is the widespread corporate demand for a "flexible" work place.

Employers are pursuing a multifaceted type of flexibility in their quest to maintain and expand profitability. For example, after reviewing research undertaken at the Institute of Manpower at Sussex, *The Economist* surmises that companies are looking for a mix of three kinds of flexibility: functional flexibility (so that workers can be redeployed quickly); numerical flexibility (so that the number of workers can be fluctuated at will to cope with changes in the business cycle); and financial flexibility (so that workers can be laid off quickly without extra cost).[39] Contingent workers go a long way toward addressing each of these objectives, but companies have been supplementing them with initiatives, such as offshore employment, prison labor, and wholesale capital flight. All of these schemes maximize profits by increasing the exploitation of labor.

One important aspect of employers' efforts to reduce labor costs lies in ferreting out and calculating the "hidden costs" of workers. For example, in a widely circulated study in the mid-1980s, the U.S. Chamber of Commerce calculated that an average weekly salary of $200 contains "hidden costs" of $85.64 (or an added 42 percent) in the form of mandatory taxes and insurance, hiring costs, time not worked, and company-paid benefits.[40] Actually, the fringe benefit portion of wage and salary workers' total compensation is considerably less than popularly imagined. According to the BLS's Employment Cost Index, fringe benefits accounted for 27 percent of a worker's total compensation in 1991.[41]

As intimated earlier, a central reason employers hire contingent workers is to minimize expenses associated with full-time permanent workers. Employers save because they are not required to pay either Social Security taxes or unemployment insurance premiums, and because they seldom provide (or even subsidize) fringe benefits like health insurance. Further, savings accrue because time not spent working is not compensated. Also, as financial columnist Sylvia Porter points out, through the use of impermanent employees, managers can cut down or eliminate overtime, while saving on screening costs and expenditures associated with hiring, testing, and interviewing new workers.[42]

Bluestone and Harrison's stress on the desire of managers to reduce their labor costs is consistent with the use of contingent workers today.[43] In particular, two important functions of marginal employment facilitate meeting employers' objectives. The first is a "cost-control" function. Companies that employ part-time, temporary, and subcontracted workers can rigidly control costs by avoiding all fringe benefit and related personnel expenses. The second, the so-called "planned staffing" strategy used by employers, enables management to further reduce labor costs. This use of contingent workers is designed to keep a company's payroll in synch with broader economic currents. Using this approach, managers save by maintaining the minimum number of full-time workers on their payrolls. Any fluctuations in demand for the company's products or services can be absorbed by the peripheral work force without concern for escalating unemployment insurance costs.

More important than the sheer growth are the roles part-time workers are serving. In many ways, they parallel the functions of other fragments of the contingent work force. As with subcontracting, leased employees, and temporary workers, the pivotal advantage for employers is their lower cost.

In 1990, median hourly earnings for part-time workers were $5.06, compared with $8.09 for full-time workers. Much of the pay discrepancy is owed to different types of occupations. In 1987, food service and retail sales workers comprised nearly half of all minimum-wage workers. Again, women, nonwhites, and young people are disproportionately represented among the low-wage part-time work force.[44] The expanding use of part-time workers means a reduction in benefit costs for employers as well. Few part-time workers receive sick pay, vacations, or health insurance. Further, part-time workers can undermine the struggle for job security. Part-time, temporary workers, and subcontracted workers can all be dismissed easily, unprotected as they typically are by unions and labor legislation.

Many employers regard it as axiomatic that the average contingent worker is more productive than permanent workers. National Association of Temporary Services spokesperson Sam Sacco states that "the realization that temporaries are more productive than permanent workers in many jobs has prompted management to rely more heavily on their use."[45] Some have even suggested that this alleged hyperproductivity of contingent workers may be infectious. For example, Barbara Johnson speculates that some of the "regular employees may pick up the increased work pace set by temporaries."[46] If output does increase, the heightened pace may stem instead from the anxiety permanent workers experience over the prospects of being replaced by a leased, subcontracted, part-time, or temporary worker. In short, labor cost savings as well as labor control are central motives for management in hiring contingent workers.

Paralleling capital flight in the manufacturing sector in recent decades, companies are creating offshore offices to cut costs and maximize productivity. The movement toward offshore offices has been developing over the past ten to 15 years. According to Scott Armstrong, for more than a decade, magazine publishers have shipped subscription lists to overseas plants for keypunching and computer storage.[47] In the early 1980s, an estimated 40 companies in the United States, Australia, and Japan were using offshore offices, with the number expected to rise rapidly. Some of the far-flung locations are in Ireland, Taiwan, South Korea, the Philippines, Barbados, and China, where Pacific Data Services (a Dallas-based company) has a clerical operation employing 200 workers. Armstrong says the main rationale for this innovation is the high cost of labor and, again, the high cost of office space. Moreover, he notes that in the United States, data-entry workers can earn from $5.00 to $15.00 per hour compared with Caribbean or Asian nations, where they are typically paid $1.50 or less per hour.[48] For example, in Barbados, where American Airlines set up a 200-employee office, workers earn $2.50 an hour keypunching data. Formerly, the airline had paid workers in Tulsa, Oklahoma $6.50 an hour for the same work. The move generated savings of $3.5 million in 1983, its first full year of operation.[49]

As with temporary workers, the offshore office benefits corporate employers by dividing workers and hindering organizing efforts. Further, with the offshore office, opportunities for "telescabbing" emerge. If labor strife emerges in one country, the work can be electronically transferred to one with more harmonious industrial relations. Clearly, the movement toward offshore offices potentially engenders a new age of electronic sweat shops.

The calculated, planned use of contingent workers began in earnest following the recessions of the 1970s and 1980s. The greater severity and the increasing frequency with which recessions in the past two decades occurred caused employers in many industries to become extra sensitive to all types of costs, especially labor-related ones. For many managers, the fastest and easiest way to reduce costs is to dismiss workers. With several recessions still fresh in their memories and the ongoing 1990–1992 recession continuing, employers are reluctant to hire full-time, year-round permanent workers.

Several elements within the contingent work force were widely used to provide a buffer for management against the vagaries of the business cycle. Contingent workers became a systematically planned staffing tool through their use during peak-load periods. Using seasonal, part-time, and temporary workers during peak-load periods means hiring additional workers during an employer's busiest season, whether it be retail stores in December or the IRS in April. This rationalized hiring approach, however, falls short of the full-blown planned staffing strategy. The planned staffing approach is more comprehensive, relying on the full-time, year-round use of contingent workers to serve as a continual buffer against downturns in the business cycle, fluctuations in demand resulting from seasonal differences, or any other major economic variations.

Perhaps more than its potential for providing immediate financial flexibility for management, the significance of planned staffing rests in its ability to erode the permanent full-time work force gradually. Planned staffing is critical because it encourages the continuous employment of marginal workers as a routine part of personnel policy. The savings that accrue from this method are potentially more pivotal than any of the other sources of savings. Planned staffing means having an adequate supply of workers when business is expanding and the capacity to make cuts quickly when economic conditions tighten. With many part-time, temporary, and other contingent workers already seeking full-time employment, the expansion of planned staffing would imply a growing level of underemployment among workers in the U.S. labor force.

It is difficult to predict precisely how much planned staffing may reduce the demand for full-time permanent workers. Clearly, however, some organizations are prepared to convert a large part of their work force to peripheral status. In short, the planned staffing hiring approach is an important catalyst for perpetuating and expanding the ranks of contingent workers.

Hiring contingent workers on a continuous basis is just one element of a broader drive by management to cut labor costs. Beyond shrinking the core of full-time workers through the expanded use of temporary and part-time workers, corporate employers in the early 1980s also experimented with two-tier wage structures and, as noted above, used offshore offices in pursuit of greater profitability.[50]

ENHANCING MANAGEMENT CONTROL

A seldom recognized function that contingent workers serve for employers is facilitating management control within the work place. The temporary help services industry, for example, by aggressively advertising the strategic advantages of using temporary workers, has persuaded many employers to integrate them in multiple phases of their operations. Contingent workers can help facilitate employers' control in the work place because they are not perceived as core, full-time workers. Instead, contingent workers are seen by management as just another resource in the production process.

Moreover, contingent workers represent a new division within the work place. As Richard Edwards has shown, U.S. capitalism has fractured, rather than unified, the working class.[51] Workers are divided by industrial sector, age, race, sex, and skill level. Now, with the expansion of day labor, subcontracting, part-time, and temporary employment, workers are further subdivided by their schedules and the working conditions they face. Dividing workers allows managers not only to save money, but also to limit opportunities for worker organization. Temporary workers, in particular, are effective in blunting organizing efforts, because managers often hire them one day and discharge them the next, allowing few logistical opportunities for politically oriented activity to occur at the work place.

In addition, temporary help firms, business service companies, and those involved in employee leasing enhance work place control by serving as an intermediary between workers and their true employers. Along with freeing management from what is widely viewed as burdensome paperwork, the intermediary role is significant, because managers avoid the unpleasant duty of terminating workers. Moreover, the providers of contingent labor benefit firms further because they can perform these personnel functions more expediently than the standard practices many companies allow. In most cases, for example, an employer of temporary workers can have an employee removed any time during the first working day free of charge if not satisfied.

Management control in the work place can become more finely tuned through the use of a "core and contingent" hiring arrangement. In some cases, for instance, companies use temporary help firms as a screening mechanism for potential full-time workers. Although employers are formally and legally discouraged from recruiting workers through the temporary help industry, in a recent survey, 12 percent of managers said their organizations used temporary workers for possible permanent recruitment.[52] Thus, if managers want a docile work force, they can cultivate one through the judicious selection of subcontracted, part-time, or temporary workers. This approach to human relations is doubly rewarding for managers, because it spares them expense as well as the time usually consumed by recruiting and hiring.

Marginal workers serve other stabilizing functions for employers. By filling high-turnover positions with peripheral workers, for example, frustration among permanent workers can be diverted. In particular, tiring or boring jobs, or ones that feature irregular hours, are prime positions for contingent workers to fill.

Because many contingent workers do not stay with the same employer for extended periods or because they have more than one employer, it leaves them at a disadvantage in terms of organizing and mobilizing a collective fight for their own welfare. Moreover, their presence in the work place hampers the ability of permanent full-time workers to maintain solidarity. Indeed, in the case of temporary workers, if they show any interest in aligning with permanent workers, they can be promptly removed. In short, the expanding use of all types of contingent workers helps companies avoid an organized work force.

Taken together, this set of political and economic benefits that employers derive from using contingent workers represents significant advantages. In the final analysis, the creation of a contingent work force has served to divide workers. It has erected an obstacle to communication and mobilization among workers, and pitting one group against another. Temporary workers, part-time employees, subcontractors, and others who are paid less, receive significantly fewer benefits, and have a loose affiliation with their employers serve to undermine the pay and working conditions of all workers. In this way, the use of contingent workers can be a highly effective management tool for employers—a strategy that, in the short run at least, facilitates management's control over the labor process and maximizes the potential output of every hour of paid labor.

NOTES

1. For a discussion on the parameters of the contingent work force, *see* Anne E. Polivka and Thomas Nardone, "On the Definition of Contingent Work," *Monthly Labor Review* (December 1989), pp. 9–16.

2. William Serrin, "Up to a Fifth of U.S. Workers Now Rely on Part-time Jobs," *The New York Times* (August 14, 1983), p. 1.

3. Polly Callaghan and Heidi Hartmann, *Contingent Work* (Washington, DC: Economic Policy Institute, 1991).

4. Richard Belous, *The Contingent Economy: The Growth of the Temporary, Part-time, and Subcontracted Workforce* (Washington, DC: National Planning Association, 1989), p. viii. *Also see* Lawrence Mishel and David Frankel, *The State of Working America*, 1990–1991 Edition (Armonk, NY: M. E. Sharpe, 1990).

5. *See* Jon L. Pierce et al., *Alternative Work Schedules* (Boston: Allyn and Bacon, 1989) and David Nye, *Alternative Staffing Strategies* (Washington, DC: The Bureau of National Affairs, 1988).

6. Daniel Saks, *Distressed Workers in the Eighties* (Washington, DC: National Planning Association, 1983). *See also* Teresa Sullivan, *Marginal Workers, Marginal Jobs* (Austin: University of Texas Press, 1979).

7. Barry Bluestone and Bennett Harrison, *The Deindustrialization of America: Plant Closings, Community Abandonment, and the Dismantling of Basic Industry* (New York: Basic Books, 1982).

8. Ibid., p. 164.

9. Ibid.

10. Ibid., p. 179.

11. Ibid., p. 180.

12. Steven A. Wasser, "Economics of the Temporary Help Services Industry," *Contemporary Times*, Vol. 3, No. 9 (1984), p. 14.

13. Wayne J. Howe, "Temporary Help Workers: Who They Are, What Jobs They Hold," *Monthly Labor Review* (November 1986), pp. 45–47.

14. June Lapidus, "The Temporary Help Industry and the Operation of the Labor Market" (Ph.D. dissertation, University of Massachusetts, Amherst, 1989).

15. Charles Grigsby, "Work," in Donald J. Bauman et al., *The Austin Homeless* (Mimeograph) (Austin: University of Texas at Austin, 1985).

16. Hector Tobar, "L.A. Opens Day-laborer Hiring Site to All Comers," *Los Angeles Times* (October 27, 1989), pp. A1, A28.

17. Colleen Barry, "Hiring Halls Being Revived," *Las Vegas Review Journal* (November 23, 1990), p. 4C.

18. Public Broadcasting Service, "Frontline: New Harvest, Old Shame," (April 17, 1990).

19. Leslie A. Whitener, "A Statistical Portrait of Hired Farmworkers," *Monthly Labor Review*, Vol. 107, No. 6 (1984), pp. 49–53.

20. Ibid.

21. Lori Rozsa, "Migrant Farm Workers' Lives Have Changed, but Maybe Not Enough," *Las Vegas Review Journal* (November 30, 1990), p. 12C.

22. Gil Klein, "In Florida Cane Fields, Immigration Reform Bill Is Hot Topic," *The Christian Science Monitor* (September 2, 1983), p. 13.

23. Ibid.

24. Belous, *The Contingent Economy*, pp. 22–23.

25. U.S. Bureau of Labor Statistics, "The employment situation, June 1989," News Release (July 7, 1989).

26. Louis Silverman and Susan J. Dennis, "The Temporary Help Industry: Annual Update," Reprint from *Contemporary Times* (Spring 1990), p. 1.

27. Randy Hodson and Teresa A. Sullivan, *The Social Organization of Work* (Belmont, CA: Wadsworth Publishing Company, 1990), p. 311.

28. National Association of Temporary Services, "Profile of a Typical Temporary Employee," Reprinted from *Contemporary Times* (Winter 1989), p. 2. *See also* Richard D. Leone and Donald Burke, *Women Returning to Work and Their Interaction with a Temporary Help Service* (Washington, DC: National Technical Information Service, 1976).

29. *See* Veronica Beechey and Tessa Perkins, *A Matter of Hours: Women, Part-time Work and the Labor Market* (Minneapolis, MN: University of Minnesota Press, 1987) and Hilda Kahne, *Reconceiving Part-Time Work: New Perspectives for Older Workers and Women* (Atlantic Highlands, NJ: Rowman and Allanheld Publishers, 1985).

30. Susan McHenry and Linda Lee Small, "Does Part-time Pay Off?" *Ms.* (March 1989), p. 88.

31. Chris Tilly, "Reasons for the Continuing Growth of Part-time Employment," *Monthly Labor Review* (March 1991), p. 10.

32. Serrin, "Part-time Jobs."

33. Harry Braverman, *Labor and Monopoly Capital: The Degradation of Work in the Twentieth Century* (New York: Monthly Review Press, 1974).

34. Ibid., pp. 26–27.

35. *See*, for example, Brian Palmer, "Class, Conception and Conflict: The Thrust for Efficiency, Managerial Views of Labor and the Working Class Rebellion, 1903–22," *Review of Radical Political Economics*, Vol. 7, No. 2 (1975), pp. 31–49.

36. Tony Elger, "Braverman, Capital Accumulation and Deskilling," in Stephen Wood (ed.), *The Degradation of Work?* (London: Hutchinson, 1982), pp. 23–43.

37. Ibid., p. 33.

38. Paul Adler, "Tools for Resistance: Workers Can Make Automation Their Ally," *Dollars and Sense* (October 1984), pp. 7–8.

39. *The Economist* (September 29, 1984), p. 71.

40. "Getting the Hidden Costs of People into the Open," *The Office* (September 1982), p. 40. *See also*, Samuel R. Sacco, "Temporary Help Industry: Its Impact on Business," *The Office* (September 1985), p. 38.

41. Cited in Callaghan and Hartmann, *Contingent Work*, p. 40, Table 9.

42. Sylvia Porter, "Temporary Employment Going Full Speed Ahead," *San Antonio Express News* (October 8, 1984), p. 14A.

43. Bluestone and Harrison, *The Deindustrialization of America.*

44. Sar A. Levitan and Elizabeth A. Conway "Part-timers: Living on Half-rations," *Challenge* (May–June 1988), p. 13.

45. Samuel R. Sacco, "Temporary Help Industry: Its Impact on Business," *The Office* (September 1985), p. 38.

46. Barbara Johnson, *Working Whenever You Want* (Englewood Cliffs, NJ: Prentice-Hall, 1983), p. 54.

47. Scott Armstrong, "U.S. Firms Farming Out Office Work to Places like Barbados," *The Christian Science Monitor* (June 28, 1983), p. 1.

48. Ibid.

49. "Clerical Jobs Are Moving to Countries with Cheap Labor Costs," *The Wall Street Journal* (February 26, 1985), p. 1.

50. Roy J. Harris, Jr., "More Concerns Set Two-Tier Pacts with Unions, Penalizing New Hires," *The Wall Street Journal* (December 15, 1983), p. 29.

51. Richard Edwards, *Contested Terrain: The Transformation of the Workplace in the Twentieth Century* (New York: Basic Books, 1979).

52. "Temporary Help Services—Who Uses Them and Why?" *The Office* (May 1988), p. 130.

8 Transformations in the Labor Process on a World Scale: Women in the New International Division of Labor

Julia D. Fox

Historically, capital has always attempted to achieve complete control over labor and the labor process. In fact, the intent to establish control mechanisms provided the impetus for the introduction of the factory system and the decline of the putting-out system in the early stages of industrial capitalism.[1] Similarly, in the advanced phases of monopoly capitalism, worker autonomy and solidarity may be mitigated by shifting the most labor-intensive operations to peripheral countries where the employment of a cheap and docile female labor force guarantees hegemonic control of labor on a world scale.

Throughout modern history, women have constituted one of the lowest paid segments of the population. Just as young single women were incorporated into the low-wage labor market in the earlier phases of industrial capitalism in Europe and the United States, transnational corporations have in recent decades tapped the international female labor pool.

The incorporation of women into the "new" international division of labor is the focus of this chapter. A fundamental question is posed: Why have traditionally marginal workers—women—been selectively recruited and integrated into the transnational labor force? In an attempt to explain the emergence of the international sexual division of labor, an analysis of transformations in the labor process will be undertaken. Although it will be argued that women provide a cheap source of docile labor, the analysis will transcend the profit motives of individual firms or managers. The incorporation of Third World women into the transnational labor force will be placed in the structural context of capital accumulation on a world scale.

The recruitment of low-wage women workers not only increases the international labor pool, but it concomitantly employs the most powerless segment of the population to establish total control over the labor force and thus increase the rate of exploitation. The production scheme employed to achieve this transnational objective in global capital accumulation has been export processing. The disproportionate representation of women workers in transnational export processing must therefore be placed in this context of the labor process at the global level.

To explain the gender feature of export processing, two dimensions will be analyzed. First, the genesis of export processing must be examined. If world capitalism requires a reduction in the cost of production especially in times of crisis, how do export-led models provide the structural exigencies of capital accumulation on a world scale? Second, given the demand of crises, what specific features of female labor facilitate capital accumulation?

THE NEW INTERNATIONAL DIVISION OF LABOR

With the development of export-processing industries in the Third World, the production process has become global. This investment strategy involves shifting the labor-intensive portion of the manufacturing process to peripheral countries where labor costs are lower, while the more capital-intensive portion of the process is completed in core countries. Hence, the export-processing strategy is developed for increased exploitation of labor and the maximization of profits within the framework of capitalist control of the labor process on a world scale.[2]

The international sexual division of labor can be located within the context of the new international division of labor, which operates at the level of the world capitalist system and, more concretely, at the level of particular nation states in which the specific institutional arrangements create the conditions for one of the most exploited sectors of the working class—Third World women. Thus, an analysis of global capitalist expansion can be developed that incorporates both the international division of labor driven by the exigencies of capital accumulation on a world scale and the more concrete processes of work relations at the point of production at the national level in which the social, economic, and political factors interact to create the cheapest and most repressed forms of labor.

Repressive labor policies that outlaw strikes and trade unions and the lack of laws for environmental protection, workers' health and safety, and labor conditions in general are compelling forces that attract foreign capital to the Third World.

Given these mediating conditions in Third World countries, women are selected for export-processing employment, because they are among the most exploited and most "vulnerable" sectors of the population that the transnationals feel they can most easily control. However, the internal contradictions of profit maximization and exploitation of Third World women in a given social formation foster labor militancy and resistance to repressive labor control. As export processing has rapidly created a "female proletariat," the contradictions of labor repression and female oppression have combined to produce a militant female working class that is challenging the traditional images of female docility and compliance of Third World female labor.[3]

Export Processing and Female Labor

In recent years, there has been a major shift in transnational investment policies. In the past, transnationals followed a pattern of direct investment via corporate-owned subsidiaries or joint ventures. However, in an attempt to increase the rate of profit, a new investment strategy—export processing—has been adopted. This strategy involves the division of the manufacturing process into two stages. Initially, high-skill, high-wage workers (usually in the United States or another advanced capitalist country) assemble a portion of the product. Then, this partially completed product is exported to one of the Third World countries where low-skilled, low-wage workers complete the product that is reexported to advanced capitalist markets. This process is tantamount to subcontracting on an international scale.[4]

Export Processing Zones (EPZs) are a growing worldwide phenomenon. The first EPZ was created in 1960, and by 1970, fewer than ten countries had established these zones. By 1986, however, more than "50 countries had created some 175 zones, with another 85 under construction, and over 25 more being planned"; since 1986, EPZs have grown at an even faster rate, especially in countries such as Mexico, the Philippines, Sri Lanka, Hong Kong, Singapore, Malaysia, and Taiwan.[5] Likewise, employment in EPZs has grown immensely compared to earlier periods, from 50,000 in 1970 to 1.3 million in 1986.[6]

There are three salient features of export processing. First, unlike other investment policies, labor is used as the primary resource. Second, women are disproportionately represented in export-processing industries, ranging from 90 percent of total EPZ employment in Belize, Barbados, and Jamaica to 66 percent in Mexico and Morocco; Korea and the Philippines represent the middle range of female employment in EPZs with 77 percent and 74 percent, respectively.[7] Third, technological innovations have been applied to the forces of production. The introduction of new technology not only made export processing feasible, but it provided the necessary conditions for the fragmentation and internationalization of labor.[8] That is, the new technology allowed the manufacturing operation to be subdivided into simpler components. Export processing is an investment strategy that is designed primarily for the standardization of commodity production and the division of the labor-intensive and capital-intensive operations. This is why three major industries (textiles, garment, and electronics) constitute the highest percent of investment in export-processing strategies.[9] Based on the operations of these three industries, it can be seen that export processing is a labor-intensive strategy that involves not only the increased division of labor via technological innovations, but also the international sexual division of labor.

In South Korea, for example, single young factory women are disproportionately represented in the export-processing industries. Since the emergence of these industries, young women (generally between the ages of 16 and 24) have been targeted for employment in the EPZs. Currently, women constitute 77 percent of export workers, with the highest percentage in garment, textiles, and electronics.[10]

In the Philippines, women currently comprise 74 percent of the total EPZ employment.[11] The male-female wage differentials in the EPZs indicate that female workers receive only 54 percent of male wages.[12] The pattern of hiring young Filipino females and the disproportionate representation of women in the three major industries is consistent with other export-processing strategies.

In Mexico, the *maquiladora* factories represent the export-processing industries. Although the *maquiladora* operations were first established in 1965 as an outgrowth of the Border Industrialization Program, the rapid growth of these factories occurred in the early 1980s. Between 1982 and 1988, the number of *maquiladora* plants increased from 558 to 1,500, with a correspondent increase in the number of workers from 122,500 to 390,000.[13] Historically, the multinational *maquiladora* industry has selectively targeted young single females (aged 16 to 24), and in the early stages of *maquiladora* development, women workers comprised up to 90 percent of the export-processing labor force.[14] Currently, women comprise two-thirds of the total *maquiladora* labor force.[15] Since 1982, the number of women in the *maquiladora* work force has been declining. Although there are many interpretations of this trend, the most frequently cited explanations are that the female labor force is "drying up," and there has been a shift in production from "light assembly" products to "heavy manufacturing" products (e.g., transportation equipment).[16] Despite the disagreements about why the percentage of females in the *maquiladora* industry has been declining, there is consensus that employment for women in the *maquiladora* sector is an economic necessity. Approximately 60 percent of the female workers in the Border Industrialization Program provide the sole source of family income, and in the export-processing industries in general, 30 percent of the women were the head of the household.[17]

The logic underlying the predominance of female employment in export processing is that transnationals take advantage of indigenous male-female wage differentials in Third World countries. Given the increased application of standardized technology in the world economy, the transnationals extract the highest rates of surplus value by employing the lowest paid sector of the foreign labor market. Because women are in subordinate positions, capitalists take advantage of these indigenous male-female wage differentials to increase their profit margins.[18]

Recent studies of South Korean male-female wage differentials have pointed out that there is a "bifurcated wage structure" in which women are employed in the most labor-intensive sectors, such as export processing, which pay the lowest wages.[19] The male-female wage gap is also illustrated by the disproportionate percentage of women earning wages that are less than the minimum cost of living. Overall, the majority of the South Korean working class earns less than the 507,254 Won (U.S. $638) that the government estimates to be the minimum cost of living for a family of four. In 1985, for example, 87 percent of South Korean workers earned less than this minimum. However, when these statistics are broken down by sex, there is a male-female differential for single workers' minimum cost of living. Based on the most recent data, 13.2 percent of the male workers earn wages below this minimum, whereas 63.9 percent of the females earn wages below this level.[20] Thus, conclude the authors of a recent study, "if there is any sector of the working class that approaches this condition of extreme poverty, it is single women factory workers."[21]

LABOR RELATIONS IN EXPORT-PROCESSING INDUSTRIES

Although Third World male-female wage differentials allow transnationals to generate greater surplus value by employing women workers, hence maximizing profit, the fundamental economic logic of capital accumulation only partially explains the genesis of export processing and the gender-specific nature of labor relations under this form of global accumulation. The other condition that compelled transnationals to relocate production sites in Third World countries and tap female labor reserves involves the component of control.

The labor process, in particular work relations at the point of production, should be analyzed to isolate the control mechanisms that ensure the docility of the work force. More importantly, however, we need to examine how these institutional arrangements predispose Third World women to be more easily controlled than men.

The docility of female labor should not be underestimated in addressing the feminization of Third World export processing. This can be explained by the prevalence of four interrelated components: (1) a social component (low levels of female participation in union organizations); (2) a cultural component (patriarchy); (3) an organizational component (bureaucratic managerial strategies); and (4) a political component (repressive governmental labor policies). The docility of female labor, together with its cheapness, has come to define the unique nature of the new international division of labor—the gender-specific character of Third World export-processing labor.

Control of Labor

The labor process associated with export processing leads to a highly controlled work force. More importantly, women are selectively recruited because of the potential for greater managerial control and exploitation.[22] The conjuncture of social, cultural, organizational, and political components of control bolsters the coercive labor relations of export processing, which affect, first and foremost, Third World working women.

Patriarchy and its ideological component, paternalism, have had an important impact on managerial policies and the selective recruitment of women. Those espousing the advantages of export processing argue that women are preferred because they have "nimble fingers," "small hands," "higher levels of productivity," and "a greater tolerance for tedious work."[23] Although these justifications are stereotypical notions of female labor, empirical studies of managerial strategies indicate that employers incorporate a number of such features of extant patriarchal structures to ensure female subordination.[24] The demographic profile of female workers indicates that age is an important factor as well. Managers point out that managing these young women is similar to "running a high school." In addition, managerial hegemony has been further reinforced by the establishment of dormitories in the EPZs.[25]

One of the most important features of managerial policies is the selection of novice workers. A recent U.S. Department of Labor report concludes, "EPZ employers express a clear preference for hiring women workers between the ages of 17–25—sometimes explicitly stating this preference in job advertisements."[26] Michael Van Waas in his study of the *maquiladora* program found that 60 percent of the females had never been hired before; managerial rationalizations for hiring "virgin" workers were that "they haven't picked up bad habits" and "we want to train them from the ground up in our way of thinking."[27] The significance of this policy is that novice workers lack organizational experience to counter managerial control.

Another way managerial control is achieved is through the use of Taylorist strategies. The Taylorist approach, employed as the dominant managerial strategy during the early phases of industrial capitalism, has been revitalized in Third World EPZs. Under Taylorism, the application of technological innovations promotes fragmentation, deskilling, and control of labor and the labor process.[28] However, the introduction of new technology does not inherently lead to the control of labor; rather, it is through the application of bureaucratic managerial strategies to increase exploitation that control is achieved.[29]

In the context of Third World labor policies, control is given new meaning: The labor relations of export processing have been established by government laws that translate into absolute control. The potential leverage of labor power via unionization has been eliminated by extramarket forces, such as strict labor laws.

Repression of Labor

A large number of Third World countries adopting export-processing strategies have enacted repressive labor laws. Among them, the Philippines and South Korea have employed the most draconian, militaristic measures to "discipline" their work force.[30]

In the Philippines under Marcos, a "Presidential Decree" banned all strikes in the export-processing industries. In 1982, several weeks after a general strike in Bataan, the largest EPZ in the Philippines, 200 labor organizers were arrested.[31] In an attempt to institutionalize labor conflict, the Philippine government developed a quasi-corporatist association, the Trade Union Congress of the Philippines (TUCP). The two major goals of the TUCP were to "gain greater control over the labor force" and to "purge labor unions of militant forces."[32] In addition, the Marcos government developed a labor code that allowed employers to "black list any worker who posed a serious threat," and as a result, thousands of trade unionists were placed on such lists during this period.[33]

After 14 years of dictatorship, Marcos was overthrown in 1986, and Corazon Aquino emerged as the new leader of the country. However, Aquino inherited a vastly strengthened state apparatus and a stagnant economy. The repressive apparatuses of the state have not been eliminated. Moreover, Aquino has been compelled to follow the economic policies of the Marcos administration (i.e., export-oriented development, World Bank austerity measures, and so on). Just six months after the "February Revolution," Aquino ordered a crackdown on illegal strikes and sent a directive to Augusto Sanchez, minister of labor and employment, to become more aggressive in dealing with strikes.[34] Thus, the repression of labor in the Philippines continues unabated to this day, as the government continues to provide greater incentives and a favorable investment climate for the transnational corporations in the export-processing industries.

Similarly, in South Korea, the government has taken numerous measures to suppress labor unions and strikes. After General Chun Doo Hwan took power, a "purification program" was undertaken to ban all national trade unions and make strikes illegal. The right to form unions and bargain collectively in the EPZs was restricted in South Korea until the December 1987 election of Roh Tae Woo. When these legal restrictions were eliminated in 1987, South Korea's EPZs became an active center of union organizing efforts and strikes. Thus, in 1988 and 1989, there were more than 11,000 strikes.[35] In response, the state has attempted to control this growing labor militancy. Hence by August 1989, strikes were banned in the EPZs with the directive that corporations in these zones are "public interest companies."[36]

In comparison to South Korea and the Philippines, government labor policies in Mexico are not as severe. However, the major structural barrier to worker autonomy and political power is corrupt union leadership. In the border industries, transnationals have established a "cooperative relationship" with union leaders. The type of cooperative relationship between labor leaders and managers is not comparable with the typical corporatist tripartite association of labor, business, and the state. Rather, the labor-business alliance is one in which union leadership represents business instead of rank-and-file interests. In labor grievances, for example, the arbitrator is the Conciliation and Arbitration Board (CAB), which is a business-supported labor union.[37] The official trade unions in Mexico, such as the Confederacion de Trabajadores de Mexico (CTM), "act more as a junior partner in the ruling coalition in Mexico, than an independent labor movement."[38] Moreover, these unions are "almost entirely male dominated, even where they operate in plants in which 80 percent or 90 percent of the workforce are women."[39]

Although *maquiladora* workers have the legal right to organize, only "10–20 percent belong to unions compared to 90 percent of the workers in similar non-*maquiladora* industries."[40]

Repressive labor laws in the Third World provide an incentive for transnationals to target countries that guarantee political stability and a "disciplined" labor force. Repressive legal structures in general do not tell us specifically why women have been selectively recruited. However, if we assume that repressive government policies affect a population differentially, we may have the answer as to why women workers are preferred.

Even though the bargaining power of Third World unions is severely restricted by government controls, the likelihood of organization is further reduced by employing a segment of the international pool that exhibits a pattern of nonunionization. Women workers meet this criterion. Third World women are recruited not only because they are the lowest paid segments of the population, but also because they are the most "unprotected."[41]

A concomitant factor that reinforces the low level of union membership among women is the cultural tradition of patriarchy.[42] In the Philippines, for example, "because of the traditional oppression of women, the predominant female character [of the labor force in export processing] has made union organizing—already difficult under martial law conditions—even more difficult."[43] In 1979, females comprised only 26.8 percent of the 50,000 trade union members.[44] The Mexican *machismo* cultural tradition and many corrupt, male-dominated trade unions have similarly limited the union participation of *maquiladora* women. In addition, the high unemployment rates in Mexico may further reduce the potential for collective action. Because 55 to 60 percent of all *maquiladora* female employees provide the sole source of family income, the importance of their employment places women workers in a precarious position, and hence, mitigates against strikes and walkouts.[45] Moreover, the instability of *maquiladora* employment further places women in a difficult situation, since the turnover rate is extremely high: Although the average length of employment in the electronics industry is three to four years, the average annual rate of turnover in electronics is between 25 and 33 percent of the labor force.[46]

The significance of the low levels of union participation among women export-manufacturing workers is that managerial hegemony is further intensified. In the absence of any countervailing worker power, the patriarchal, bureaucratic, and political dimensions of control are heightened, and worker autonomy under these conditions is severely limited.

Nevertheless, women workers in EPZs have put up a determined struggle against transnational capital and state repression, and are fighting back more and more.

Women Workers Fight Back

In Mexico, there have been a number of attempts by *maquiladora* workers to resist managerial control. In the mid-1970s, assembly workers in Mexicali and Nuevo Laredo went on strike against poor working conditions and "sold-out union bosses."[47] Women in the *maquiladora* industry have played a pivotal role in these labor struggles.[48] Since then, workers have attempted to improve *maquiladora* working conditions through a variety of grass-roots organizations. The patterns of "personalism" within the Mexican unions and corruption that has been endemic in the Confederacion de Trabajadores de Mexico (CTM) have been compelling forces for workers to unionize outside these corrupt organizations.[49] Rank-and-file organizing efforts have led to increased activism among a growing number of women workers in *maquiladora* industries all along the U.S.-Mexican border and to another wave of strikes in the early 1990s. In January 1992, U.S.-owned *maquiladora* plants in Matamoros, Mexico, were hit with a wave of strikes once again. Thousands of workers, many of them women, walked out in protest of low wages and poor working conditions. Workers at the Deltronicos, Grupo Nova, and Trico plants rallied in front of the shut-down factories, and waved red and black strike flags to make their demands known.

In the Philippines, too, there has been an upsurge in women's political activity culminating in the militant women's organization, General Assembly Binding Women for Reforms, Integrity, Equality, Leadership and Action (GABRIELA). Filipino working women have become increasingly aware of their exploitation, and a GABRIELA spokesperson at a recent women's rally in the Philippines concluded that "the struggle for the freedom of all women is inseparable from the struggle of the working classes and from the global struggles of peoples of the world over fighting racism and imperialism."[50]

In South Korea, women workers in the export-processing industries have been among the most militant and organized groups. In the late 1980s, during the period of militant labor insurgency, women workers at the Masan Free Export Zone organized more than 100 factories and formed the "Ma-Chang" Labor Alliance, and as male workers began to become more militant, "they found they were standing on the shoulders of women workers" who had been struggling for more than a decade.[51] Through such resistance, women workers are increasingly becoming an active part of the broader protracted working-class struggle against international capital and repressive client states throughout the Third World.

CONCLUSION

The above analysis has examined the economic and political basis of the "new" international sexual division of labor. It has been argued that the structural features of world capitalist accumulation generated a need for sources of cheap labor. The historical pattern of the flow of foreign capital in and out of countries in the quest for low-wage and unorganized labor illustrates a pattern of investments into those countries where labor is cheap and repressed. When the internal contradictions of profit maximization and the concomitant exploitation of cheap labor foster labor militancy and resistance to this exploitation, there is a shift in investment to regions where labor is cheaper and more compliant. This pattern is illustrated, for example, by the shifting of the labor-intensive operations of the microelectronics industry from the Silicon Valley in California to South Korea during periods of increasing labor repression. Also, when South Korea was beset by labor militancy that raised labor costs, the transnationals shifted investments to Mexico, where the cost of labor was lower.[52] However, given the structural constraints of world capital accumulation, the physiognomy of labor and the type of production process have taken a variable form.

Export processing was adopted as a viable temporary solution to the crisis of capitalism—a reduction in production costs to maximize profit. Because Third World wages are significantly lower than those in the advanced capitalist countries, the transnationals have shifted their production sites to Third World countries. Although foreign labor could expand the labor pool and provide greater selectivity, women are specifically preferred not only because they are cheaper, but also because of their perceived docility.

Although the genesis of export processing may be attributed to the structural exigencies of world capital accumulation, the selective recruitment of women workers involves the intentionality of capitalists within the framework of capitalist relations.

The mobility of capital not only allows transnationals to transcend national boundaries, but it permits corporations to select peripheral states that have the political machinery and institutional arrangements that would mitigate against the countervailing powers of labor organizations. Women in Mexico, the Philippines, and South Korea have been differentially affected by these repressive policies. The interaction of the political, cultural, social, and organizational dimensions of control makes them more vulnerable to exploitation.

Third World working women are in the forefront of the new international division of labor because of their subordinant position in the international labor market and in the political sphere. They will continue to be utilized as a primary resource as long as they meet the criteria of cheapness and docility. However, to counter their exploitation and repression, Third World working women are becoming more and more active, and are fighting back; they are becoming part of a global working-class struggle against transnational capital.[53]

NOTES

1. Richard Edwards et al., *Labor Market Segmentation* (New York: D. C. Heath, 1975), p. 21.

2. James Petras, *Class, State and Power in the Third World* (London: Zed Press, 1981), p. 123; Kathryn Ward (ed.), *Women Workers and Global Restructuring* (Ithaca, NY: Cornell University Press, 1990), p. 2.

3. Helen I. Safa, "Runaway Shops and Female Employment: The Search for Cheap Labor," in Eleanor Leacock and Helen I. Safa (eds.) *Women's Work* (South Headley, MA: Bergin and Garvey, 1986), p. 68; Karen J. Hossfeld, " 'Their Logic Against Them': Contradictions in Sex, Race, and Class in Silicon Valley," in Kathryn Ward (ed.), *Women Workers and Global Restructuring*, p. 152.

4. Folker Frobel, Jurgen Heinrichs, and Otto Kreye, *The New International Division of Labor* (Cambridge: Cambridge University Press, 1980), p. 29; Maria Patricia Fernandez-Kelly, "The 'Maquila' Women," *NACLA Report of the Americas*, Vol. 14, No. 5 (1980), pp. 14–19; Safa, "Runaway Shops and Female Employment"; Marlene Dixon, Suzanne Jonas, and Ed McCaughan, "Reindustrialization and the Transnational Labor Force in the United States Today," in Marlene Dixon and Suzanne Jonas (eds.), *The New Nomads: From Immigrant Labor to Transnational Working Class* (San Francisco: Synthesis, 1982), pp. 101–104; Michael Van Waas, "Multinational Corporations and the Politics of Labor Supply," *The Insurgent Sociologist*, Vol. 11, No. 3 (1982), p. 49; Robert T. Snow, "The New International Division of Labor and the U.S. Work Force: The Case of the Electronics Industry," in June Nash and Maria Patricia Fernandez-Kelly (eds.), *Women, Men and the International Division of Labor* (Albany: State University of New York Press, 1983), p. 39.

5. U.S. Department of Labor, Bureau of International Labor Affairs, "Workers Rights in Export Processing Zones," Special edition of the *Foreign Labor Trends* series (Washington, DC: Government Printing Office, 1990), p. 3.

6. United Nations Center on Transnational Corporations and the International Labour Office, *Economic and Social Effects of Multinational Enterprises in Export Processing Zones* (Geneva: ILO, 1988).

7. U.S. Dept. of Labor, "Workers Rights," p. 6; Linda Lim, *Women Workers in Multinational Enterprises in Developing Countries* (Geneva: International Labour Office, 1985).

8. Dixon, Jonas, and McCaughan, "Reindustrialization," p. 101.

9. S. Tiano, "Maquiladora Women: A New Category of Workers?" in K. Ward (ed.), *Women Workers and Global Restructuring* (Ithaca, NY: ILR Press, 1990), p. 195.

10. U.S. Dept. of Labor, "Workers Rights," p. 6; George E. Ogle, *South Korea: Dissent Within the Economic Miracle* (London: Zed Books, 1990), pp. 48–49.

11. U.S. Dept. of Labor, "Workers Rights," p. 6.

12. Mary Soledad Perpinan, "Philippine Women and Transnational Corporations," in Daniel Schirmer and Stephen R. Shalom, *The Philippines Reader: A History of Colonialism, Neocolonialism, Dictatorship, and Resistance* (Boston, MA: South End Press, 1987), pp. 234 and 240.

13. *The Economist* (September 16, 1989), p. 82.

14. Judith Ann Warner, "The Sociological Impact of the Maquiladoras," in Khosrow Fatemi (ed.), *The Maquiladora Industry: Economic Solution or Problem?* (New York: Praeger, 1990), pp. 187–88.

15. U.S. Dept. of Labor, "Worker Rights," p. 6.

16. Leslie Sklair, *Assembly for Development: The Maquila Industry in Mexico and the United States* (Boston: Unwin Hyman, 1989), p. 177.

17. Maria Patricia Fernandez-Kelly, "Mexican Border Industrialization, Female Labor Force Participation and Migration," in Nash and Fernandez-Kelly, *Women, Men, and the International Division of Labor*, p. 215; Tiano, "Maquiladora Women," p. 204.

18. Edwards et al., *Labor Market Segmentation*, p. xvi; Safa, "Runaway Shops and Female Employment."

19. *See* Alice H. Amsden, *Asia's Next Giant: South Korea and Late Industrialization* (New York: Oxford University Press, 1989), pp. 203–204.

20. Walden Bello and Stephanie Rosenfeld, *Dragons in Distress: Asia's Miracle Economies in Crisis* (San Francisco: The Institute for Food and Development Policy, 1990), p. 26.

21. Ibid.

22. Waas, "Multinational Corporations," p. 50.

23. Diane Elson and Ruth Pearson, "Nimble Fingers Make Cheap Workers: An Analysis of Workers in Employment in Third World Export Processing," *Feminist Review*, 33 (1981), p. 89; Waas, "Multinational Corporations," p. 50.

24. Waas, "Multinational Corporations,", p. 50. June Nash, "The Impact of the Changing International Division of Labor on Different Sectors of the Labor Force," in Nash and Fernandez-Kelly (eds.), *Women, Men, and the International Division of Labor*, p. x.

25. Ibid., p. 31.

26. U.S. Dept. of Labor, "Workers Rights," p. 5.

27. Waas, "Multinational Corporations," p. 50.

28. Harry Braverman, *Labor and Monopoly Capital: The Degredation of Work in the Twentieth Century* (New York: Monthly Review Press, 1974).

29. Ibid.; Dixon, Jonas, and McCaughan, "Reindustrialization," pp. 101–103.

30. Cynthia H. Enloe, "Women Textile Workers in the Militarization of Southeast Asia," in Nash and Fernandez-Kelly, *Women, Men, and the International Division of Labor*, p. 410.

31. D. Easter and M. Easter, "Women Fight Back: South Korea and the Philippines," *Multinational Monitor*, Vol. 4, No. 8 (1983), p. 12.

32. Walden Bello, David Kinley, and Elaine Elison, *Development Debacle: The World Bank and the Philippines* (San Fransico: Institute for Food and Development Policy, 1982), p. 142.

33. Ibid., p. 143.

34. *Asian Labour Review*, Vol. 3, No. 4 (November, 1986), p. 33.

35. International Labour Organization, *Yearbook of Labour Statistics* (Geneva: ILO, 1990), p. 1,027.

36. U.S. Dept. of Labor, "Workers Rights," p. 7.

37. Waas, "Multinational Corporations," p. 57.

38. Sklair, *Assembly for Development*, p. 174.

39. Ibid.

40. U.S. Dept. of Labor, "Workers Rights," p. 7.

41. Nash, "The International Division of Labor," p. 11.

42. Beverly Lindsay, *Comparative Studies of Third World Women: The Impact of Race, Sex, and Class* (New York: Praeger, 1980), pp. 39–42; I. Schuster, "Research on Women in Development," *Journal of Development Studies*, Vol. 18, No. 4 (1982), p. 513.

43. Bello, Kinley, and Elison, *Development Debacle*, p. 144.

44. Easter and Easter, "Women Fight Back," p. 13.

45. Pedro Vuskovic, "Economic Internationalism, Neoliberalism and Unemployment in Latin America," in Dixon and Jonas (eds.), *The New Nomads*, pp. 85–86; Waas, "Multinational Corporations," p. 51.

46. Waas, "Multinational Corporations," p. 50.

47. Ibid, p. 56.

48. Sklair, *Assembly for Development*, p. 175.

49. Warner, "The Sociological Impact of the Maquiladoras," p. 194.

50. Brenda J. Stoltzfus, "A Woman's Place Is in the Struggle," in Schirmer and Shalom (eds.), *The Philippines Reader*, p. 311.

51. Ogle, *South Korea*, pp. 141, 86.

52. Hossfeld, " 'Their Logic Against Them,' " p. 152; Bello and Rosenfeld, *Dragons in Distress*, p. 168.

53. *See* Ofelia Gomez de Estrada and Rhoda Reddock, "New Trends in Internationalization of Production: Implications for Female Workers," in Rosa-

lind E. Boyd, Robin Cohen, and Peter Gutkind (eds.), *International Labour and the Third World: The Making of the New Working Class* (Brookfield, VT: Gower, 1987), p. 157; Easter and Easter, "Women Fight Back."

9 Transnational Capital, the Global Labor Process, and the International Labor Movement

Cyrus Bina and Chuck Davis

The development of capitalism over the past two centuries has provided the preconditions for the collective organization of workers, and the structures of labor organizations have evolved accordingly to meet the capitalist challenge. Capitalist competition and accumulation have continuously pitted worker against worker, attempting to drive wages, conditions of work, and the quality of life to the lowest possible level. In combatting the extraction of absolute and relative surplus value, workers have always conducted an economic and, in many cases, a political, struggle to regulate and improve the terms and conditions under which they are obliged to dispose of their labor power. What is significant is that the expression of trade union unity, by transcending competition in the market for labor power, in itself potentially threatens the stability of capitalism by blocking capital's desire to minimize costs of production and, above all, to solidify the grounds for further control. This is particularly true in the present period. "Workers of the World Unite" is becoming increasingly relevant and applicable as capital transcends the boundaries of nation-states.[1]

The transnationalization of capitalist relations of production (i.e., the emergence of a global tendency to real subsumption of labor under capital—production of relative surplus value) brings the common interests of workers in different countries into sharper focus in the minds of workers themselves and elevates the potential for labor solidarity to an international level. It brings workers in different nations into a new integrated relationship. To the extent that workers can confront transnational capital with their own international organizations, they can mitigate the effects of capital mobility.

For capital to become a *de facto* global entity, there has to be a global circuit in all its forms that would, in turn, unify the spheres of production and circulation: commodity capital, money capital, and productive capital. This has been historically accomplished through the internationalization of productive capital that fulfilled the completion of the globalization of capital in all its social forms. This has resulted in the unfolding of such colossal and integrated entities as transnational corporations, which operate throughout the world. Having direct control over many different labor processes around the globe, transnational capital, in conjunction with all its circuits, exploits labor power worldwide. Here, global capital can be seen as an organic supranational socioeconomic entity that intimately corresponds to the structure of global social relations. In this context, the most appropriate unit of analysis, therefore, is none other than global capitalist relations. Thus, if capital is a global entity, so must be labor's strategy for revitalization.[2]

This chapter attempts to present a theoretical framework for the study of the labor process in contemporary capitalism and provides an analysis of the contradictions of this process at the global level. It also takes up a discussion of the nature of transnational capital, the cheapening of labor power, universal deskilling, spatial mobility, gender and the transnational labor process, and the roots of working-class unity. The chapter concludes with some observations on the current problems and the potential revitalization of the U.S. labor movement in the context of the transnational economy, and suggests that at the stage of transnational social relations (i.e., the global integration of capital), labor organizations must play a central role to enhance the capacity of the working class to transform capitalist social relations throughout the world.

CHEAPENING OF LABOR POWER: UNIVERSAL DESKILLING AND SPATIAL MOBILITY

The proliferation of capitalist relations of production and its impact on generating the labor processes that are conducive to the development of capitalism beyond the boundaries of nation-states is today a fact of life within the global economy. As a result, it becomes necessary to understand the specific mechanisms through which the unfolding of the above process takes shape. It is also imperative to investigate the consequences of such a process and its future direction in the world economy.

In order to be able to unravel the transnational character of the labor process, one has to grasp (1) the transformation of work itself in the advanced capitalist countries, and (2) the emerging global integration of capitalism, having to do directly with the spread of capitalist social relations into the former colonies, semicolonies, and less-developed countries, especially during the second half of the twentieth century. At the present stage of global capitalism, the centerpiece of global accumulation is the unifying control of the emerging transnational labor processes that would collectively represent the social character of global capital. Here, the resultant transnational labor process is, *prima facie*, a point of departure of the transnationalization of capital in general.

Since the turn of the century, there has developed a series of remarkable organizational and technological transformations that have revolutionized the very foundation of the labor process in the advanced capitalist countries, especially in the United States. These have included the application of what is known as Taylorism, which came to intensify further and regulate the real subsumption of labor under capital and which prepared the labor process for a radical transformation toward a continuous system of large-scale mass production.[3]

Based on recent advances in the field of computer technology, applications such as Robotics, Numerical Control (NC), Computer-Aided Design (CAD), and so forth, in conjunction with the telecommunications revolution, have already found their way into the present-day production processes. These technologies conferred a new meaning to the deskilling of labor and granted a new outlook to the spatial control of capital over the entire global labor process.

As Harley Shaiken, a leading authority on the application of technology, elucidates, "Once the machining knowledge is embodied in the numerical control program, it becomes possible to transfer production from a struck plant to shops that are still working, regardless of whether they are across the street or half way around the world."[4] Here, scientific management flourished through the intense application of science and technology for the sake of strengthening the control of constant capital over its variable counterpart.[5]

The consequence of these has been the continuous and progressive deskilling of labor everywhere.[6] The continuous deskilling of the labor process in the advanced capitalist countries and the development of capitalism in the Third World are, *pari passu*, the precondition of globalization of the labor process. In this manner, the process of deskilling in the advanced capitalist countries, having taken several decades to develop, finds its way into the readily transformed structure of many Third World economies. Such a deskilling is now ready to be transmitted and internalized transnationally. This, in turn, corresponds to a series of technological underpinnings that soon acquire a global character.

Universal deskilling, aside from its hegemonic appeal, allows for coexistence of the highest level of technology and the lowest possible labor cost, including the training cost of labor, especially in the case of Third World workers whose industrial training is rather slight. Thus, the intense deskilling of labor in the advanced capitalist countries over several decades suddenly finds its cumulative application within the countries of the Third World. As a result, the rising complexity of technology in the production process does not pose a physical limit to raising the exploitation of the working classes globally.

A parallel with the above historical dynamics is the advance of unfolding material conditions that surround the participation of women in the global economy. In the Third World, where abject poverty and massive unemployment are the rule, unbounded flexibility and extraordinary discipline are the *sine qua non* of the labor process. Here, the majority of the female labor force had worked in agriculture. Given the accelerated pace of transnational investment since the early 1970s, women's labor has increasingly shifted toward the manufacturing sector, especially in the so-called Newly Industrializing Countries (NICs) where the role of the export sector is significant.[7]

In addition to their role as cheap labor, it has been argued by some that employment of women by transnational capital may have also been motivated by (1) women's alleged characteristics of greater discipline in following orders and their display of work habits that generally imply "docility," (2) women's possession of "skills" that are normally attributed to their gender socialization (e.g., "nimble fingers" and ability to work with delicate objects), and (3) women's condition as a flexible source of labor supply, especially where it comes to the acceptance of temporary assignments, unstable work, and flexible hours, associated with subcontracting in most export-processing zones.[8]

THE ROOTS OF WORKING-CLASS UNITY

Today, the continuing globalization of the labor process has, in a contradictory manner, provided the material conditions for the unity of the working class across the seemingly insurmountable boundaries of nation-states. The fundamental basis of this contradictory process is the global accumulation of capital in the presence of divided global social space among nation-states and the objective conditions for working-class unity—based on local struggles that can no longer remain isolated from the global center stage. The analogue of all this is the emergence of a historical stage whose transforming capacity goes well beyond the simple export of capital or the transfer of technology from one nation to another. In fact, at the present stage of global transformation, the significance of the above symptomatic activities cannot be adequately understood except through the manifold character of transnational capital beyond the nation-state.

Given the last two decades of upheaval in the global economy, the *de facto* global character of capital has already transcended the framework of national boundaries, despite its historical origin and its early embryonic affinity. Here came the mastery of an integrated global territory for reproduction of social relations. This was also a familiar socioeconomic terrain that was long known to the pioneer of labor internationalism, the International Working Men's Association (the First International).[9] The primary issue facing labor, therefore, is how to avoid the trap of nationalism and become a formidable force in the struggle against capital transnationally.

In his inaugural address to the International Working Men's Association nearly 150 years ago, Karl Marx wondered, "If the emancipation of the working classes requires their fraternal concurrence, how are they to fulfill that great mission with a foreign policy in pursuit of criminal designs, playing upon national prejudices, and squandering in piratical wars the people's blood and treasure?"[10] Marx tried to respond to this by assigning a specific responsibility to the trade unions of his time:

> Apart from their original purpose, [the trade unions] must now learn to act deliberately as organizing centers of the working class in the broad interest of its *complete emancipation*. They must aid every social and political movement tending in that direction. . . . They must look carefully after the interests of the worst paid trade, such as agricultural laborers, rendered powerless by the exceptional circumstances . . . far from being narrow and selfish, [they must] aim at the emancipation of the downtrodden millions.[11]

The struggles between labor and capital in the Third World, in many instances, are similar to the ones waged during the early development of the advanced capitalist countries. These struggles are primarily political in nature. The workers in the Third World, even in their daily and immediate struggles, must confront the state as their ultimate adversary. For instance, the small-scale, confined appearance of an export-processing zone, or a discrete structure of an export-platform business, can hardly misdirect the attention of workers from *political* issues surrounding the work place. Thus, in such an environment, any economic issue would immediately become *political*, and any local issue would directly become a *global* one. Here, direct confrontation of workers with the state is at the same time a struggle against capital in general and, by implication, a struggle against the hegemony of transnational capital.

In the advanced capitalist countries, such as the United States, the working class (organized and unorganized alike) has already lost substantial ground during the last two decades. The economic gains of the past have disappeared through constant global restructuring, ceaseless deskilling of the work force, the exploding ranks of the working poor, the universal outbreaks of plant closings, and the growth in the size of the reserve armies of unemployed.[12] Having experienced that all these ills arise from the contradictions of the capitalist system itself, workers in the United States (and, more and more, in other advanced capitalist countries) are increasingly coming to realize that their struggle must be against capital in general, particularly transnational capital. Here, the objective conditions present in the global economy provide the basis for working-class unity throughout the world. In other words, the working classes of both the Third World and the advanced capitalist countries are in the same boat moving in the same direction. Thus, a growing number of workers, particularly in the advanced capitalist countries, are coming to realize that they must free themselves from the shackles of national chauvinism, the narrow limits of economism, and, above all, racism and sexism, in order to confront transnational capital with a powerful and unified force.

LABOR INTERNATIONALISM AND THE LABOR ARISTOCRACY

Since the nineteenth century, segments of the U.S. labor movement have supported strongly the need for international labor solidarity to confront the various stages of the internationalization of capital. From the beginning, left-wing Socialist, Communist, and anarcho-syndicalist sections of the working class have battled with the class collaborationist right wing over the control of the labor movement and the meaning of international labor solidarity. A century-long struggle continues between those elements in the U.S. labor movement that have traditionally pursued strength through increasing international working-class unity, and those who have consistently tied their future to the fortunes of national capital and have allowed themselves to be used as a tool of U.S. imperialism.[13]

Seeing itself as part of some all-embracing national interest, the American Federation of Labor (AFL) has asserted historically an identity of common global interest with U.S. capital. Recognizing the unique position of U.S. imperialism after World War II, the AFL tied labor's fate to U.S.

capital's growing global hegemony.[14] The national labor federation embraced the doctrine of *Pax Americana*. This doctrine is composed of many subdoctrines, the most significant of which is the cold war "axiom" since World War II. This axiom ramifies a complex triad of containments whose singular ambition has been to preserve U.S. global hegemony, by all means. The first two containments were intended for the Soviet Union and the Third World. This was motivated by the U.S. postwar position against Soviet ideology and the independent nationalist movements around the world.

The third containment has been a domestic one. It was designed to circumvent democratic freedoms domestically and to crush the spirit of resistance in every facet of life in the United States. McCarthyism is only one of many examples in this tragedy. This, in part, had two important social ramifications for the U.S. labor movement: (1) It broke the back of the most militant segment of organized labor and purged the movement from the best sons and daughters of the working class; and (2) it systematically submitted the workers to a complex set of legitimizing norms, imposed by the ideology of the ruling class, thus openly stigmatizing, penalizing, and, ultimately, terrorizing those who dared to depart from it.[15]

The AFL perceived American labor's well-being as part and parcel of American capital's well-being. This led the AFL (and later the AFL-CIO) to adopt a foreign policy of labor imperialism.[16] In the post–World War II era, labor imperialism has involved an explicit alliance with U.S. capital and the state. This is a specific manifestation of a labor aristocracy beyond the boundaries of an Imperialist state, since the nature of its involvement in both international labor organizations and the internal affairs of unions of other nations has been guided by the priorities of U.S. foreign policy.[17] Embracing a virulent anti-communism, which sees the world divided into East versus West, the AFL-CIO in Europe, Africa, Asia, and Latin America has, in the name of U.S. global hegemony, undermined and weakened in a variety of ways the organizational capacity of the international labor movement. It did so by establishing dual unionism—dividing labor movements along cold war lines by developing procapitalist, anti-Communist union structures sympathetic to U.S. capital and subservient to U.S. foreign policy—and by participating with the U.S. government in overt and covert political and military interventions with the purpose of overthrowing democratic, prolabor governments considered too leftist.[18] Labor's involvement in the cold war on behalf of U.S. imperialism was made possible by the purges of the Left-led unions and leftists within the labor movement. As Mike Davis notes:

By accepting the discipline of the Cold War mobilization, the unions and their liberal allies surrendered independence of action and ratified the subordination of social welfare to global anti-communism.[19]

Capital was becoming increasingly internationalized in the post–World War II period, through the control of new geoeconomic space and intensification of the realm of competition beyond the nation-state, and, by weakening international labor solidarity through its divide-and-conquer strategy, was able to prevent labor from defending itself on an international basis. The AFL-CIO compromised the organizational capacity of the working class both domestically and internationally in exchange for further material benefits.[20]

With the new phase of transnationalization of capital beginning in the early 1970s and accelerating rapidly in the 1970s and 1980s, the U.S. economy started its secular, and probably irreversible, decline in the global economy. This marked the onset of the stage of transnational global relations reflecting the global integration of capitalist production. This is tantamount to the undermining of the international system of nation-states and the status of its post–World War II hegemon, the United States.

By the early 1970s, capital accumulation had become truly global. The internationalization of capital brought on a restructuring of industrial production that shifted the concentration of basic industry from its previous centers to new locations throughout the world. Transnational corporations abandoned the United States as a principal production location, resulting in "captive imports," runaway shops, and outsourcing. The expansion of the U.S.-based transnationals was now linked to the relative decline of domestic manufacturing. This investment strategy obviously has had a negative impact on U.S. workers and has contributed significantly to the decline of their standard of living during the past two decades.[21]

The decline of U.S. global hegemony during this stage of the internationalization of capitalist relations of production has, in the meantime, led to a growing divergence between the material interests of labor and capital. The once-shared interest in the global domination of U.S. capital is now seen as a source of job loss, demands for concessions, and union busting. The economic conditions for post–World War II accommodation with capital are over. Given the absence of global labor solidarity, transnational corporations have shown their willingness to play off one group of workers against another, driving down the labor and living standards of the international working class to the lowest possible levels.

The global integration of capitalist production has undermined the material conditions that have supported AFL-CIO's traditionally nationalist, class-collaborationist posture. The discrepancy between the material foundation of the transnationalization of capitalist relations and the historical record of continuing working-class nationalism (for instance, in the United States) can be interpreted as an indicator of the contradictory balance of class forces, the backwardness of the labor movement, and anachronistic nature of nationalism at this historical juncture. More specifically, the absence of international labor solidarity can be interpreted, within our view of the internationalization of capital, as an opportunity on the part of capital to prevent what will be eventually realized—the development of the material basis and organizational capacity for working-class consciousness at the global level.

In this period of restructuring and crisis, global capital has been striving ceaselessly to extract additional surplus value by lowering the standard of living of the working class worldwide. However, this decline in living standards is forcing unions to respond to capital and the state in fundamentally new ways, thus creating a significant opportunity and sizable constituency both for revitalization of the labor movement and formation of a broad-based political movement at home and abroad. The transnationalization of capitalist relations and reorganization of global capitalism provide the material conditions for overcoming class collaboration and national chauvinism, because the labor movement can no longer survive and function without a class struggle and an internationalist perspective. This realization is being played out in a pronounced ideological struggle within the U.S. labor movement between accommodation and confrontation with transnational capital.[22] This struggle over orientation is somewhat visible in the polarized debates within the labor movement over the issues of international trade and investment, specifically, on matters of trade liberalization and regional integration.

TRADE LIBERALIZATION, REGIONAL INTEGRATION, AND THEIR IMPACT ON LABOR

The present global restructuring of capitalism through the adoption of free trade, neoliberalism, monetarism, deregulation, and privatization policies of governments throughout the capitalist world during the 1980s coincides with the global integration of capital and the transnationalization of capitalist relations of production. Given the acceleration of integration of national economies, with respect to production, finance, and trade, the adoption of the aforementioned policies has been almost a universal response both in advanced and Third World capitalist nations since the early 1970s.

Global labor has been weakened considerably because of the globalization of the labor process and the standardized deskilling of the labor force throughout the world, corresponding to the transnational character of social capital. Although individual capitals moved to restore profitability, social capital (as a whole) manifested its very fundamental characteristic through competition for global labor power. Capital has launched a series of offensives explicitly designed to weaken or destroy the barrier of the labor movement internationally, and to force its capitulation to transnational capital. For instance, an important move was to initiate a global pool of surplus labor and the corresponding reserve army of unemployed beyond national boundaries. Falling real wages, rising unemployment, increasing poverty and income inequality across the board, deteriorating living and working conditions, and increasing violations of worker, human, and civil rights are shared common problems by workers throughout both the Third World and the advanced capitalist countries. This shows that, when it comes to harm, capital is universally dispassionate.

Global social capital is also using international organizations and trade agreements, such as the General Agreement on Tariffs and Trade (GATT) and the North American Free Trade Agreement (NAFTA), to preempt democratic self-government at local, national, regional, and international levels. Global capital and its representatives follow a golden rule by which any attempt by democratic institutions to impose restrictions on transnational corporations should be outlawed by international agreements. If there is to be any regulation, it should be in the interests of global capital. This world vision is decreed through the 1989 Bilateral Free Trade Agreement (BFTA) between Canada and the United States. Canada has so far lost 150,000 manufacturing jobs because of the BFTA, and through the implementation of the BFTA, many social and environmental standards are now under attack by transnational capital.[23]

NAFTA would formalize and accelerate the process of transnationalization of capital and the global integration of production and exchange that began in Mexico and many other countries over 20 years ago. Attracted by cheap and unprotected labor and lax environmental standards, U.S.-based transnational corporations began to construct their own integrated production systems (including the Export-Processing Zones) in order to transfer much of the previously U.S.-based production activities to Mexico. The intermediate goods and final products produced in the *maquiladoras* would then flow back as imports into the United States.

By the late 1980s, limitations on foreign investment had been practically eliminated by further dismantling restrictions on foreign ownership, and reducing remaining tariffs and import barriers. This export growth strategy has proven to be an utter disaster for Mexico; it has failed to fuel national growth or to improve the overall debt situation. According to the logic of transnational capital, however, one cannot expect other than such results. For the Mexican working class, it has meant increasing poverty, declining living and working conditions, and intensified state repression of workers' rights.[24]

Trade liberalization within the stage of transnationalization of capital means further undermining of working and living conditions of labor everywhere. In the continuing global integration of the capitalist labor process, trade unions are quickly realizing that labor solidarity across borders is an essential first step for defending the most tangible interests of their members. Today, workers are discovering that defensive strategies intended for protecting the interests of local workers cannot be effective except through internationally based alliances. The globalization of working-class unity, therefore, is necessary to confront the globalization of capital. However, despite the characteristic of the epoch in which international working-class unity is tantamount to labor's material class interest, unfortunately the anachronistic ideology of national chauvinism still continues to reign high within certain sectors of the U.S. labor movement.

STRATEGIC CONSIDERATIONS FOR LABOR

Over the last 30 years, the AFL-CIO has shifted from being the most free-trade-oriented labor movement in the world to being staunchly protectionist. Fighting free trade in the name of national self-interest, the AFL-CIO embraces a strategy aimed at restoring U.S.-based capital's competitiveness in the world market through protective trade policies. Accommodating national capital industrially and pushing for protectionism politically have become the centerpiece of AFL-CIO's trade policy.

Motivated over the concern for loss of jobs and declining working and living conditions in the United States, the AFL-CIO demands fair and balanced trade, and supports the denial of benefits of specific trade privileges (and aid) to nations in which internationally recognized labor rights are not respected. Indeed, the AFL-CIO's acceptance and support of future multilateral trade agreements, such as NAFTA and GATT, are conditioned upon the inclusion of international labor standards and the democratization of trade negotiations themselves. According to the AFL-CIO, the appropriate model in terms of content, structure, and process for

NAFTA and GATT would be the European community's forthcoming Social Charter, where labor's goal is to regulate the activities of global social capital democratically and in the interests of the majority. In addition to protecting domestic jobs through tariffs and related measures, there is a call for restricting immigration, particularly Mexican labor from across the border.

Unfortunately, the AFL-CIO's analysis of international economics is limited to the level of trade. There seems to be little recognition or understanding of the global integration of production and the transnational character of capitalist social relations. Internationalization is seen primarily as nationally based capital trading with other nationally based capitals, where the solution to intranational economic problems lies in each country playing fair by adhering to the same rules of the competitive game. The logic of this response to global social capital supports and intensifies labor's subordination to corporate prerogatives. Raising the specter of "unfair competition," "opposition to free trade," and "support of fair trade" legitimizes transnational capitalist relations of production,[25] and plays into the hands of capital's divide-and-conquer strategy. Advocating competitive victory for U.S.-based capital sets workers in the United States against foreign workers and, thus, severely hampers efforts to achieve international labor solidarity.

Capitalism's success in overcoming the growing barriers to accumulation through trade liberalization and economic integration has increased the costs significantly for labor in pursuing a strategy of national autonomy. Continued reliance on nationalism will only further cripple the labor movement in the face of global capital's offensive.[26] Transnationalization of capital has gone too far for protectionism to save domestic jobs. Nationalistic confrontation with the global character of capitalist competition will only continue to demand greater concessions from U.S. workers.

Within the Canadian working class, there is an important debate on the issues of nationalism and free trade in connection with the recent Canada-U.S. free trade agreement. David McNally advances a compelling argument against nationalism of the Canadian Labor Congress (CLC) and that of the New Democratic party (NDP), both powerful institutions, one representing the main trade unions and the other an entire social democratic movement.[27]

The struggle for labor internationalism is necessary to break down the divisiveness of nationalism and build solidarity with workers' struggles throughout the world. As Primitivo Rodriquez has so eloquently stated:

> Some trade union leaders in the more developed countries seem to be opposing free trade talks out of an outmoded belief that preventing a free trade agreement will save their members' jobs. But blocking such an agreement won't erase the increasing integration among the American economies.
>
> Rather, we should look at the free trade agreement debate as an opportunity to develop a vision and an agenda which responds from a people's perspective. . . . What's promising is that today's transnational exchange may lead to the dismantling of barriers imposed by narrow and fragmented interests based on nationalistic perspectives that are increasingly ineffective in enhancing rights and a better life.[28]

Although denying free trade access to domestic markets to nations who violate internationally recognized worker rights under U.S. trade law has been inconsistently and rarely enforced and is, at the same time, protectionist, there is a growing consensus within the labor movement that recognition and struggle for international labor standards, as a condition of trade, are a political act that has the potential to enhance the organizational capacity of the working class internationally and, thereby, provide legitimacy for an international solidarity.

The concern for internationally recognized labor rights goes beneath the level of trade and calls attention to the very global relations of capital. Global integration of the capitalist labor process is, at the same time, integration of the social relations of capital worldwide, which is providing workers with the opportunity to build international solidarity. Workers worldwide are increasingly recognizing and acting on the notion that "an injury to one [anywhere in the world] is an injury to all." Thus, as William Tabb points out, "making the linkage between labor repression in the developing nations . . . and the decline of U.S. labor standards represents growth in class awareness and is a major milestone in the decline of U.S. exceptionalism."[29]

Labor unions in the Americas are finding trade union unity essential in their efforts to defend the interests of their members. U.S., Mexican, Central, and South American unions are jointly demanding the enforcement of international labor standards under U.S. trade laws. Ending violations of worker rights is increasingly being seen as mutually beneficial and as a direct challenge to the prerogatives of U.S. imperialism.

Although enforcement under current law and inclusion of such labor standards in future multilateral trade agreements are highly unlikely, their importance for U.S. labor lies in using them along with other measures as a focus for domestic and international political actions in the process of developing international labor solidarity and working-class consciousness. Although in the struggle to protect their wages and working and living conditions the workers are building new, and using preexisting, transnational structures to confront global capital, the task of establishing effective international activity is an extremely difficult one, which often seems impossible given the maze of contradictions between and within national labor movements. A central divisive issue in building international labor solidarity is, without a doubt, how the labor movement relates to U.S. foreign policy.[30]

The goal of international labor solidarity has been poorly served by the nationalist, class-collaborationist and anti-Communist approach to U.S. foreign policy adopted by the AFL-CIO during the cold war period in the 1950s and 1960s. However, since the late 1970s and early 1980s, opposition to the AFL-CIO's blind support of U.S. foreign policy has been growing within the labor movement. Open conflict has developed within the house of labor over Central America and U.S. foreign policy in general. For example, over half the affiliates of the national federation have actively engaged in efforts to oppose the federation's position on Central America.

The AFL-CIO's views of the world are being challenged by a new generation of trade union leadership and activists both here and abroad who advocate class struggle and labor internationalism regardless of the unions' political affiliation.[31] This opposition is taking shape within and outside the national labor federation. Some state federations of labor have passed resolutions in opposition to the national AFL-CIO's position on U.S. foreign policy and its long-standing practice of "shunning" unions affiliated with the World Federation of Trade Unions (WFTU) and other Socialist- and Communist-influenced trade union federations.

The objective conditions for international working-class solidarity are stronger today than ever before. Plans for international cooperation and mutual aid in support of organizing the unorganized, collective bargaining, strikes, and so forth, in both the Third World and the advanced capitalist countries, reflect the increasingly transnational character of capitalist relations of production. Economic integration has led to international solidarity networks of workers within the same corporations, industries, and geographic region. By working for the same transnational corporation, workers are recognizing that "they have more in common with each other than with their respective national capitals."[32] Rather than just lamenting job loss to Mexico as a result of trade liberalization, unions are making united working class action a living reality. For example, the United Auto Workers (UAW) Council of Ford Workers, which represents Canadian, U.S., and Mexican workers, has proclaimed "the time has come to prevent Ford from pitting worker against worker, plant against plant, nation against nation."[33] Also, the Cuautitlan Ford workers' democratic union movement in Mexico has pledged to resist Canadian and U.S. transferred work if Canadian and U.S. workers assist them in gaining wage and benefit increases and democratic unions.

In late 1991, trade union leaders from the Americas met to assess the economic and social effects of free trade in the Western Hemisphere. Shirley Carr, president of the CLC, has summed up the situation as follows:

> Either we sit back and let capital divide us one against the other or we try and find ways to cooperate and develop common strategies to tackle the challenges. There is no question that international capital is on the march in this hemisphere and these forces are driving the restructuring of our societies.[34]

A new strategy for labor is emerging in response to the transnationalization of capital. This strategy is to establish a "new popular internationalism" that can combine the strengths of class politics and popular social movements—a new kind of international working-class solidarity that incorporates many forms of struggle and organization. The growing response to such development is transnational cooperation and coalition building among labor, political, environmental, women's, human rights, social justice, and other groups. The goal is to wrestle political and economic control from transnational capital at both the domestic and international levels.

CONCLUDING REMARKS

Considering capital as a social relation, not a fetishized object of exchange, we have argued that essentially any contemporary labor process would exhibit two broadly recognized historical tendencies: (1) a progressive deskilling of labor power through the everlasting subjugation of living labor by machinery, thus raising the rate of exploitation, and (2) a global victory of capital over the remaining vestiges of old and disintegrating modes of production, beyond the boundaries of the nation-state.

Hand in hand with the above processes is the spatial mobility of capital based on the global victory of the capitalist mode of production. The result has been the formation of an integrated network of transnationalized labor processes that are conducive to added deskilling of labor globally. This global process of socialization of production, in turn, demands an all-embracing and unified action on the part of international labor. The concept of international solidarity is indeed a minimal platform upon which labor can stand, especially in view of today's world in which the very existence of labor is threatened, both in the advanced capitalist nations and their counterparts in the Third World.

The issue of trade liberalization and its formalization in free trade agreements within the context of the transnationalization of capitalist relations of production has accelerated the development of global trade unionism and has begun to legitimate a popular progressive internationalism. Many labor unions in the Third World and in advanced capitalist countries are beginning to view themselves as part of a broader process of economic and political transformation. They see their problems as rooted in the nature of world capitalism and are struggling to find fundamental solutions.

A new labor movement is emerging internationally where unions are becoming more autonomous in relation to their respective nation-states, are becoming increasingly committed to organizing the unorganized (including the traditionally underrepresented), are encouraging rather than impeding rank-and-file involvement in their organizations, are reaching out and building alliances with other groups, are more committed to global agendas, and through a more class-oriented politics are fully pledged to democratizing societies.

The final act is yet to be written. The new labor movement worldwide is divided between social democratic reformism, which desires to obtain the best deal possible for workers from a regulated transnational capital, and a revolutionary socialism, which seeks that remedies go beyond the *status quo* throughout the world. The outcome of the process now unfolding on a global scale will be in good part determined by the struggle over leadership of the labor movement itself.

NOTES

1. The theoretical arguments advanced in this chapter are adapted from our "Global Competition and the Proliferation of the Labor Movement: Wage Labor and Capital Beyond the Nation-State" (forthcoming). The literature on the globalization of capital is vast. At the same time, there are several strands within this literature, from viewing the global transformation along the neo-Smithian division of labor, to the Monthly Review School of Monopoly Capitalism, to the classical Marxian Social Relation School, having to do with deskilling of the labor process and global competition. This chapter follows Marx's lead, in the latter framework, to explain the emergence of global labor processes that are presently proliferating, albeit unevenly, beyond the boundaries of nation-states. *See* Cyrus Bina and Behzad Yaghmaian, "Post-War Global Accumulation and the Transnationalization of Capital," *Capital & Class*, No. 43 (Spring 1991), pp. 107–130; Sol Picciotto, "The Internationalization of the State," *Capital & Class*,

No. 43 (Spring 1991), pp. 43–63; Berch Berberoglu, *The Internationalization of Capital* (New York: Praeger Publishers, 1987); Jerry Lembcke, *Capitalist Development and Class Capacities: Marxist Theory and Union Organization* (Westport, CT: Greenwood Press, 1988); James Cypher, "The Internationalization of Capital and the Transformation of Social Formations: A Critique of the Monthly Review School," *Review of Radical Political Economics*, Vol. 11, No. 4 (1979); Rhys Jenkins, *Transnational Corporations and Uneven Development* (New York: Methuen, 1987); William K. Tabb, "Capital Mobility, the Restructuring of Production, and the Politics of Labor," in Arthur MacEwan and William K. Tabb (eds.), *Instability and Change in the World Economy* (New York: Monthly Review Press, 1989); John Willoughby, *Capitalist Imperialism, Crisis and State* (New York: Harwood Press, 1986); Robert Brenner, "The Origins of Capitalist Development: A Critique of Neo-Smithian Marxism," *New Left Review*, No. 104 (July–August 1977), pp. 25–92; Cyrus Bina and Chuck Davis, "The Transnationalization of Capital and the Decline of the U.S. Labor Movement." Paper presented at the Annual Meeting of the Allied Social Science Associations in Washington, DC (December 28–30, 1990). For a systematic treatment of the issue of international trade, *see* Anwar Shaikh, "Foreign Trade and the Law of Value I-II," *Science and Society* (Fall 1979 and Spring 1980).

2. *See* Tabb, "Capital Mobility, the Restructuring of Production, and the Politics of Labor," pp. 259–78. Here in this essay, the author's position is one of international solidarity. Unfortunately, he offers no specific theoretical framework concerning the transnationalization of the labor process.

3. *See* Frederick W. Taylor, *Scientific Management* (New York: Harper, 1947).

4. Harley Shaiken, *Work Transformed: Automation and Labor in the Computer Age* (Lexington, MA: Lexington Books, 1986), p. 260.

5. As Marx maintains, "The principle of developed capital is precisely to make special skills superfluous, and to make manual work, [that is to say] directly physical labor, generally superfluous both as skill and as muscular exertion; to transfer skill, rather, into the dead forces of nature." Karl Marx, *Grundrisse* (New York: Vintage, 1973), p. 587. The most basic law of developed capitalism is not the usage of readily available cheap labor, but rather the *cheapening* of labor power through constant improvements in the means of production, and thereby the universal deskilling of labor. A by-product of this is a massive surplus population at the global level. The outcome will be the downgrading of working-class living standards everywhere.

6. Harry Braverman, *Labor and Monopoly Capital: The Degradation of Work in the Twentieth Century* (New York: Monthly Review Press, 1974). Here, Braverman defines deskilling in terms of (1) the disassociation of the labor process from the skills of the workers, (2) the separation of conception from execution, and (3) monopoly over knowledge to control each step of the labor process and its mode of execution. Although these and many other points in the above volume present new insights in the analysis of the labor process, we

believe that Braverman's failure to incorporate the historical importance of class struggle diminishes his work.

7. Lourdes Beneria, "Gender and the Global Economy," in MacEwan and Tabb, *Instability and Change in the World Economy*, pp. 246–47.

8. Ibid., pp. 250–51. *Also see* Diane Elson and Ruth Pearson, "Nimble Fingers Make Cheap Workers: An Analysis of Workers in Employment in Third World Export Processing," *Feminist Review*, Vol. 33 (1981).

9. *See* L. E. Mins (ed.), *Founding of the First International: A Documentary Record* (New York: International Publishers, 1937).

10. Ibid., p. 38.

11. Karl Marx, "Trades' Unions, Their Past, Present and Future," in Simeon Larson and Bruce Nissen (eds.), *Theories of the Labor Movement* (Detroit, MI: Wayne State University Press, 1987), pp. 36–37 (emphasis in original).

12. For extensive data and analysis of these and other related domestic consequences of the globalization process, *see* Berch Berberoglu, *The Legacy of Empire: Economic Decline and Class Polarization in the United States* (New York: Praeger, 1992), Chaps. 4 and 5.

13. *See* Lembcke, *Capitalist Development and Class Capacities*.

14. Stanley Aronowitz, *Working Class Hero: A New Strategy for Labor* (New York: Adama Books, 1983).

15. *See* Noam Chomsky, *Necessary Illusions: Thought Control in Democratic Societies* (Boston: South End Press, 1989).

16. Jack Scott, *Yankee Unions, Go Home! How the AFL Helped the U.S. Build an Empire in Latin America* (Vancouver: New Star Books, 1978), pp. 9–14, 201–38.

17. Kim Moody, *An Injury to All: The Decline of American Unionism* (London: Verso, 1988). *See also* Sheila Cohr's review of Moody's book, titled: "Us and Them: Business Unionism in America and Some Implications for the U.K.," *Capital and Class*, No. 45 (Autumn 1991), pp. 95–127.

18. Scott, *Yankee Unions, Go Home!*, Chaps. 15–19.

19. Mike Davis, *Prisoners of the American Dream: Politics and Economy in the History of the U.S. Working Class* (London: Verso, 1986), p. 96.

20. Carolyn Howe, "The Politics of Class Compromise in an International Context: Considerations for a New Strategy for Labor," *Review of Radical Political Economics*, Vol. 18, No. 3 (1986), pp. 1–22.

21. *See* Berberoglu, *The Legacy of Empire*, Chaps. 4 and 5.

22. Ibid.; Tabb, "Capital Mobility, the Restructuring of Production, and the Politics of Labor."

23. Jeremy Brecher and Tim Costello, *Global Village vs. Global Pillage: A One-World Strategy for Labor* (Washington, DC: International Labor Rights Education and Research Fund, 1991).

24. Jack Sheinkman, "Preface: Worker Rights in Central America," in *Worker Rights in the New World Order* (New York: The National Labor Committee in Support of Democracy and Human Rights in El Salvador, 1991).

25. John Willoughby, "The Promise and Pitfalls of Protectionist Politics," in Robert Cherry et al. (eds.), *The Imperiled Economy*, Book I (New York: Union for Radical Political Economics, 1987), pp. 215–23.

26. David McNally, "Beyond Nationalism, Beyond Protectionism: Labor and the Canada-U.S. Free Trade Agreement," *Capital & Class*, No. 43 (Spring 1991), pp. 233–52.

27. Ibid.

28. Quoted in Brecher and Costello, *Global Village vs. Global Pillage*, pp. 33–34.

29. Tabb, "Capital Mobility, the Restructuring of Production, and the Politics of Labor," p. 268.

30. *See* "Solidarity Across Borders: U.S. Labor in a Global Economy," *Labor Research Review*, Vol. 8, No. 1 (Spring 1989).

31. Moody, *An Injury to All*, p. 247.

32. Howe, "The Politics of Class Compromise in an International Context," p. 18.

33. Elaine Burns, "Free Trade Era Looms over Mexico," *Guardian* (January 8, 1991), p. 16.

34. Quoted in *The Union Advocate* (August 5, 1991).

10 The Labor Process and Class Struggle: Political Responses to the Control and Exploitation of Labor

Walda Katz-Fishman and Jerome Scott

Machine-based factory production, which has historically enhanced the productivity of human labor, a characteristic of the epoch of capitalist production, is rapidly coming to a close.[1] It is being replaced by computer-automated high-tech production—computer-run machines, robotics, and all forms of automation in the production process. This type of production, although it may at first appear as a quantitative advance within the era of machine-based production, is in fact a qualitatively new type of productive force.[2] Computer-automated production does not simply augment the productive capacity of human labor power; rather, it increasingly displaces human labor from the production process. Thus, the production process itself is increasingly a process with less and less human labor power embodied in it.[3] Hence, under advanced capitalism, the growth in technology is creating the very conditions for the increasing elimination of industrial labor power from the production process and is setting the stage for the struggle for social transformation.

This essay provides a brief analysis of the changing role of labor in the production process, and the nature and forms of the class struggle on the shop floor and in the larger society.

THE CHANGING ROLE OF LABOR IN CAPITALIST PRODUCTION

The growth of technology challenges the very foundations of capitalist social relations. The development of capitalist society demanded the ever-expanding application of machine technology to the production process, with its simultaneous enhancement of labor productivity and increasing degradation of the human labor process. The key to capitalist development was the production and sale of commodities for profit in a once expanding market. This process transformed millions of human beings worldwide into wage laborers. Their labor power thus became a commodity that had to be sold for a wage, so that they could use their wages to purchase other commodities necessary for their survival.[4]

Today, wage laborers, as consumers, constitute two-thirds of the market for the sale of all commodities in the United States. The market for the circulation of commodities, essential to the capitalist economy, is today contracting. It is the decline in consumption by workers—resulting from unemployment, underemployment, and low wages—that is fueling the economic crisis.

Throughout the era of capitalist development, the capitalists sought to maximize their profits by driving down the cost of production. They accomplished this in large measure by driving down wages, the largest component of the cost of production.

Keeping down the wage component of the cost of production has depended, in part, on the capitalists' ability to stifle union development, and to deny to the workers the weapon of organization in their fight for higher wages and safer work places. This process can best be understood within the historical context of slave labor in the southern plantation economy, and the political and economic struggles of the Civil War and Reconstruction. With the defeat of Reconstruction, the political and economic system in the South, as with the earlier slave system, undercut the position of labor throughout the country (and increasingly throughout the world).[5]

The southern states, through "states' rights" and the enactment of Jim Crow constitutions in the 1890s and early 1900s, followed by passage of "right-to-work" laws in the 1940s and 1950s, blocked aggressive unionization of labor on a national basis. An ample supply of nonunion, cheaper priced labor was used time and again as a threat, and as a reality to break strikes and to break the unity of workers in their struggle for organization and higher wages. Even in the North and in Appalachia, the bosses employed the Pinkerton guards, the national guard, state troopers, and other forms of state harassment to fight the unions.

The development of a distinct northern and southern labor market, breaking the unity of labor nationwide, was further fragmented by significant internal divisions within labor in the North. Immigrant labor from Europe and later black labor from the South were used to drive down the value of labor throughout the country. Cheaper priced women workers, "drafted" into the labor force during and after World War II also acted as a drag on labor.[6]

By the turn of the century and the advent of modern imperialism, the superexploitation of colonial and later neocolonial labor set the material basis for the bribe of a skilled section of the U.S. working class.

From the air traffic controllers' strike in the early 1980s to the lockout of the paper workers' union in the late 1980s to the continual refusal of southern employers to negotiate contracts with workers who have voted in unions (e.g., the catfish workers in the Mississippi Delta and the textile workers in the Blackbelt of Georgia), the state has openly attacked unions or used its power in support of capital over labor.

Today in the United States, wage labor in the South, of all colors and nationalities and both women and men, is paid less than its counterparts in the rest of the country. Throughout the United States, African American workers are paid less and have higher unemployment rates than other workers. All workers of color, generally, are paid less and are more often unemployed than white workers. Among workers of all colors, regions, and nationalities, women workers are paid less than their male counterparts and black women workers in the South are the most superexploited workers in the United States.[7]

Today, transnational capital, through its worldwide expansion and restructuring of the international division of labor, has elevated the superexploitation of wage labor to the world level.[8] Increasingly in the postwar period, transnational capital moved manufacturing production to low-wage areas of the Third World where cheaper labor, and especially women workers, are superexploited. Significant Export-Processing Zones (EPZs) were created, particularly in the Pacific Rim and in Central and South America. The fast track for the North American Free Trade Agreement (NAFTA) has accelerated this process along the U.S.-Mexican border. Here the *maquiladoras* are paid a fraction of U.S. wages to produce the same commodities at much lower cost than if higher priced U.S. labor were used.

This transfer of the manufacturing process to cheap labor areas in the hemisphere and overseas has resulted in a shift in the U.S. labor force structure from manufacturing to the service sector where wages are much lower.[9] With the accompanying rise in overall unemployment and underemployment, the growing glut of labor has served to erode further the position of labor in its struggles for wages and benefits. Workers, now an abundant commodity, are paid less, with the lowest paid workers acting as a drag on the price of higher priced labor. Full-time workers are replaced by temporary and part-time workers who have few, if any, benefits.

The superexploitation of large sectors of the U.S. working class and of workers in the Third World has not only been a significant source of profits for the capitalists; it has also been the key to the relatively higher wages of unionized workers during the postwar economic expansion, which came to a close in the early 1970s.[10]

The process of superexploitation of a growing segment of the working class in the United States and internationally has developed and continues to expand as a separate but parallel process to the growth in technology—the other significant process at work that drives down wages.

Throughout the era of capitalist development, from the invention of the steam engine to the present, the continuous introduction of advanced technology was labor-enhancing. It rendered human labor power more and more productive. Workers were needed to run the machines, which made them more productive. Despite their falling wages, they were still able to afford the necessities of life and thus maintain the market. The labor-enhancing technology of the past period, however, is more and more being replaced by the labor-eliminating technology of the present period. The fluctuations in poverty and cyclical unemployment of the earlier period are increasingly giving way to the polarization of wealth and poverty, and growing permanent unemployment of the present period.[11] Thus, the expansion and maintenance of the market of the previous period have turned into the contraction and decline of the market of the present period.

THE LABOR PROCESS AND THE CAPITALIST CRISIS

The technological revolution (automation) in the labor process (leading to the elimination of manufacturing jobs) *and* the internationalization of capital (leading to the relocation of production in low-wage areas of the Third World) are the *dual causes of the restructuring of the division of labor and of the labor process itself.* Both contribute to the growing domestic economic crisis. With automation, labor is increasingly superfluous; unemployment increases and the value of employed labor is driven down; purchasing power declines and capital cannot sell the glut of commodities being produced.

Restructuring and declining real wages have been a reality in the manufacturing sector and among blue-collar workers in general; they are now a fact of life in the service sector and among white-collar workers, as well.[12]

Today's economic crisis is devastating for the working class. Millions of workers are unemployed, and millions more are working part-time because full-time jobs are not available. Many workers who are still employed are paid lower and lower wages, and have lost benefits once taken for granted.[13] Workers' standard of living is rapidly declining, and their children are now the age group most threatened by poverty.[14] Education, housing, food, health care, the environment, and the services and infrastructure of working-class communities are deteriorating daily—all this in a world that has developed the capacity to produce enough goods and services so that no human being needs to be in want.[15] Ironically, there is not only an abundance of goods, but there is a *glut* that is unsold, unused, and often destroyed while millions of working people are unable to afford the basic necessities of life.

This overproduction of commodities and the blockage in their circulation mean that even the capitalists are experiencing the effects of the crisis. As the economic expansion of the postwar period came to a close by the mid-1970s, the contraction of the past two decades evolved into a full-blown crisis of immense proportions.

A third of the nation's savings and loan institutions have gone under, with an estimated cost to the taxpayers of $500 billion. Now the banking industry is following suit. Over 1,200 banks have failed since 1984, placing the Federal Deposit Insurance Corporation (FDIC) in jeopardy. The number of banks that failed outright in 1991 totaled 127, at a cost of $64 billion; another 168 banks were seized by regulators or merged.[16]

The financial crisis is now spilling over into the insurance industry, which had invested much of its capital in ailing real estate mortgages, junk bonds, and other assets that have declined in value or gone into default. As more become insolvent, they are dipping into their own guarantee funds to settle their claims. The Pension Benefit Guaranty Corporation (PBGC), the federal agency that insures the pensions of 40 million workers, is also in the red by $2 billion. It is estimated, however, that the pension shortfall is as high as $40 billion because of underfunding by companies and the increasing failure of major corporations. Huge shortfalls also exist even among still viable major corporations, like Chrysler for $3.3 billion, Bethlehem Steel for $1.3 billion, and General Motors for $7.2 billion.[17]

Debt and bankruptcies, personal and corporate, are soaring. A record 810,000 Americans filed for bankruptcy in 1991 alone. Household debt now stands at $3.9 trillion, or $41,000 per household, and Dun & Bradstreet Corporation reported a 54 percent increase in businesses filing for bankruptcy between 1990 and 1991; failures were up in every region of the country and in every major industry sector except mining, and the size of failed businesses is growing larger.[18]

The accumulated debt of the federal government is nearly $4 trillion in 1992. With each annual budget deficit and military expenditure, costing

$200 billion and $300 billion a year, respectively, in the early 1990s, the federal debt is rapidly increasing. A growing number of states—30 as of early 1991—were "in the red" by over $10 billion, while hundreds of cities face a similar predicament. Cities, states, and the federal government have decided to cut needed social services, and to raise taxes to continue to fund a bloated military budget and to bail out the corporations and the banks. Increasingly this also means furloughs and layoffs of employees, such as IBM and GM's layoff of some 20,000 and 74,000 workers, respectively, as announced in late 1991.

In early 1992, the official unemployment rate was over 7 percent, with nearly 10,000,000 workers out of work; for African Americans, the rate was double at 14 percent. Moreover, another million workers were listed as "discouraged," that is, unemployed but not counted as such because they had stopped looking for work. Also more than 7,000,000 workers were working part-time and wanted full-time work, but were unable to find it.[19]

In 1990, only 37 percent of jobless workers received unemployment insurance, a record low for any recession year since World War II. Between June and November 1991, each month over 300,000 workers exhausted their unemployment benefits, and it was estimated that 3.4 million workers will exhaust their unemployment benefits in 1992.[20]

The actual number of jobs is also in decline. In 1991, between 2,000 and 3,000 workers lost their jobs *every day*. Blue-collar workers in manufacturing, typically hard-hit in a recession, have lost 786,000 jobs (or 4.1 percent of all jobs) between July 1990 and October 1991.[21] White-collar unemployment among managers and professionals, as well as technical, sales, and administrative personnel, is also on the rise. In October 1991, it ranged from 900,000 (or 2.9 percent) among managers and professionals to 2,000,000 (or 5.1 percent) among technical, sales, and administrative personnel.[22] It is very likely that this trend, unknown in previous downturns, will continue and accelerate as restructuring and high technology are increasingly applied to the service sector.

Given the rising unemployment rate, fewer and fewer workers are producing an increasing number of goods and services. Thus, fewer have the money to buy the growing volume of goods that are produced. Food is grown and harvested that cannot be sold, while millions go hungry. Houses and apartments are built that remain empty, because the workers lack rent and mortgage payments, while millions are in the streets or near homelessness. Hospitals and doctors' offices close or turn away those who are ill, because they cannot pay. Thus, although the gross national product continues to increase, the unsold goods and services translate into a glut—an overproduction—of things that cannot be sold in the market because the workers who are unemployed, in poverty, or paid less and less cannot afford to buy them.

Such are the consequences of the process of capitalist development, as the fundamental contradiction between advances in the productive forces and capitalist social relations within which they develop intensifies on a world scale. Thus, the stage is set for the political struggle necessary to resolve this contradiction.

CLASS STRUGGLE AND SOCIAL TRANSFORMATION

The dire conditions that labor faces in the United States today call forth and make possible the potential for social transformation. Throughout human history, every society has been organized around its tools, labor power, and production process. Today, technological expansion in the productive forces is the material foundation of the economic, social, and political changes that are taking place in society around the world. Capitalist organization of society based on the traditional production process, private ownership of the productive forces, and distribution of the necessities of life based on capitalist relations of production and exchange is no longer viable. These relations have, as a result, moved from contradiction to antagonism in an open political way. Social transformation is the process of the developing class struggle that will and must bring the social relations of production and organization of society into line with the very advanced productive forces.[23]

Class Struggle at the Point of Production

There is increasing evidence of renewed working-class struggles in the United States. Organizing efforts are expanding across the country, and rank-and-file workers' movements are springing up in a number of major industries.[24]

During the course of the past two decades, workers across the United States have engaged in numerous strikes, walkouts, and other forms of protest. The period from the late 1970s onward saw intensified rank-and-file struggles in confronting the power of capital at the point of production. An increasing number of workers at the grass-roots level have taken the initiative to exert their collective strength and fight back to protect their hard-won rights.

In 1978, more than 160,000 coal miners went on strike, which lasted several months; the strike ended only when the government intervened with the full force of the Taft-Hartley Act. In 1979, over 35,000 International Harvester workers walked out of their jobs, striking the company for five and a half months. In early 1980, more than 60,000 oil and petrochemical workers went on strike against Gulf, Texaco, Cities Service, and other big oil companies. In March 1981, 170,000 miners belonging to the United Mine Workers of America (UMWA) went on strike once again and, in September, nearly 400,000 workers gathered in Washington, DC on Solidarity Day, one of the largest protest demonstrations in U.S. history.

With the onset of the recession in 1982, early in the year, more than 30,000 demonstrators, including many trade unionists and unemployed workers, marched in New York City against Reagan administration policies. In August 1983, more than 700,000 workers went out on strike against American Telephone & Telegraph (AT&T) and paralyzed the phone system nationwide. Just one week after the AT&T strike, 40,000 Western Electric workers walked out in support of the striking AT&T workers on the picket lines.

In April 1985, over 150,000 people, including a large contingent of workers, marched nationwide for jobs, peace, and justice. In October 1986, some 30,000 longshoremen went on strike in ports from Maine to Virginia along the eastern coastline of the United States. In April 1987, over 45,000 workers took part in an anti-war march of 150,000 in Washington, DC, protesting against U.S. intervention in Central America and demanding that plant closings and layoffs, as well as the rollback in wages and benefits, be stopped. In May, thousands of meat-packing workers went on strike at the John Morrell plant in Sioux Falls, South Dakota. Later, in August, several thousand union members and their supporters from neighboring states converged on the city in a militant demonstration of support for the striking meat packers.

In January 1988, all commercial shipping in every port in Oregon and Washington came to a standstill as thousands of Northwest longshore workers went out on strike on the West Coast. In March 1989, more than 8,000 machinists went on strike against Eastern Airlines, which turned into one of the longest strikes in U.S. history; in April, thousands of Pittston miners in Virginia went on strike and stood firm in their stand against the coal companies. Also, Solidarity Day II on Labor Day 1991, brought thousands of workers from organized labor, joined by the unemployed, the homeless, students, environmentalists, and others, to Washington DC to express their dissatisfaction with current government and corporate policies.

In the early 1990s, striking workers in the coal mines, at Caterpillar, General Motors, and other plants, as well as in a variety of other workplaces, have kept alive labor struggles during these difficult times.

Finally, the anti-concessions struggle, centered in the auto industry in the early 1990s, was the most prominent shop-floor struggle in recent years. This fight was directed against concessionary contracts that took back benefits and reduced workers' wages. Similar struggles to protect hard-won benefits of workers in various other industries in the United States have led to greater mobilization of labor to effect positive change.

Throughout the United States, workers who have been displaced at the point of production and are becoming part of the growing army of the permanently unemployed, and working-class women employed at low-wage jobs struggling to support their families are also organizing in large numbers. As their struggles mature, the unemployed workers, as well as those fighting on the shop floor and in the public sector, are more and more confronting the repressive arm of the capitalist state. Thus, their struggles are increasingly taking on a political character. This is an important aspect of the development of class consciousness that is leading the working class to take political action to protect and advance its class interests.

Class Struggle and Political Action Beyond the Shop Floor

The social and political changes that are developing in the United States today are a historical outcome of the process of transformation that American society is undergoing as capitalism further evolves along its contradictory path.

Today, although the social struggle is scattered, disorganized, and isolated, a class-conscious working class is emerging across the country. The development of class consciousness among a growing number of workers and their organizations is setting the stage for the emergence of an independent political party of the working class that would play an active role in political battles that are part and parcel of the continuing class struggle between labor and capital at various levels of life under capitalism.

As the objective conditions for the transformation of capitalism ripen over time, and as the subjective factors facilitating the development of class consciousness take root among an increasing number of workers in the United States, the articulation of the interests of the working class through its own independent organizations will become more and more a reality. With this, the objectives of the working-class struggle thus will become clarified—control over the labor process, transformation of work relations, restructuring of relations of production at the societal level, and the abolition of private ownership of the major means of production—hence the abolition of the control and exploitation of labor—all of which depend on the outcome of the struggle between labor and capital in holding on to or capturing the reigns of state power, a struggle that at root is a *political* struggle. Thus, as its protection of property rights over workers' rights increasingly reveals the class nature of the capitalist state, these struggles will more and more take on a *political* character—one that will point to the revolutionary transformation of capitalist society by the working class.

CONCLUSION

We have argued in this chapter that there has occurred a major change in the labor force structure in the United States over the past several decades such that traditional machine-based factory production, which constituted the basis of the U.S. manufacturing industry for more than a century, is giving way to computer-automated mass production. This development, coupled with the internationalization of U.S. capital since World War II in search of cheap labor and a more favorable investment climate overseas, has effected a shift toward low-paid service occupations and has led to increased unemployment among a growing segment of the working class—a situation that has become a permanent fixture of contemporary U.S. capitalism.

The resulting decline in purchasing power and standard of living of workers who are now consuming less and less of the goods produced in a shrinking market has plunged the U.S. economy into a structural crisis that has ushered in a period of decline and decay, such that it has pushed the country to the edge of depression in many sectors of the economy, including real estate, banking, insurance, auto, and the manufacturing sector in general. The S&L and banking crisis, the depressed housing market, personal and corporate bankruptcies, mushrooming public and private debt now in the trillions of dollars, and a general loss of confidence among millions of Americans in the future of the U.S. political economy are all signs of the growing instability and crisis that are gravely affecting the great majority of the American people, who are increasingly becoming conscious of their class interests and are beginning to take political action to reverse the current situation.

Class consciousness and class struggles are beginning to develop and are becoming widespread at the shop-floor level and beyond in an increasing number of industries and communities across the United States. Also, as the economy sinks further into crisis and disintegrates, causing many more human casualties, an emerging class-conscious leadership of the working class will come to play a pivotal role in leading the workers out of this crisis and toward a system and society that benefit all working people, where the control and exploitation of labor for private profit will become a thing of the past!

NOTES

1. Barry Bluestone and Bennett Harrison, *The Deindustrialization of America: Plant Closings, Community Abandonment, and the Dismantling of Basic Industry* (New York: Basic Books, 1982).

2. J. Francis Reintjes, *Numerical Control: Making a New Technology* (New York: Oxford University Press, 1991).

3. David E. Noble, *Forces of Production: A Social History of Industrial Automation* (New York: Oxford University Press, 1984).

4. David Harvey, *The Limits to Capital* (Chicago: University of Chicago Press, 1982).

5. *See*, for example, John Keller, *Power in America: The Southern Question and the Control of Labor* (Chicago: Vanguard Press, 1983).

6. James Geschwender, "Race, Ethnicity, and Class," in R. Levine and J. Lembcke (eds.), *Recapturing Marxism* (New York: Praeger, 1987), pp. 136–60.

7. U.S. Bureau of the Census, *Statistical Abstract of the United States, 1991* (Washington, DC: Government Printing Office, 1991), p. 415.

8. *See* Howard M. Wachtel, *The Money Mandarins: The Making of a Supranational Economic Order* (New York: Pantheon Books, 1986).

9. In *The Great American Job Machine*, Barry Bluestone and Bennett Harrison reported that in the late 1970s and early 1980s when jobs were eliminated in manufacturing, workers—mostly white men in unionized jobs—who found jobs in the service sector were paid about one-fourth of their previous wages. *See* Barry Bluestone and Bennett Harrison, *The Great American Job Machine: The Proliferation of Low Wage Employment in the U.S. Economy* (Washington, DC: Joint Economic Committee, U.S. Congress, 1986), pp. 1–7.

10. Berch Berberoglu, *The Legacy of Empire: Economic Decline and Class Polarization in the United States* (New York: Praeger, 1992), Chap. 4 and 5.

11. Walda Katz-Fishman and Ralph C. Gomes, "A Critique of *The Truly Disadvantaged*," *Journal of Sociology and Social Welfare*, Vol. XVI, No. 4 (December 1989), pp. 77–98.

12. The most recent permanent layoffs announced by corporate America in late 1991 reveal the extent of the current economic crisis. According to *The Wall Street Journal*, in the fourth quarter of 1991, U.S. business called for an average of 2,600 layoffs per day, "the highest we've ever seen." General Motors announced the elimination of 74,000 jobs, including a substantial number of white-collar jobs, and the closing of 21 plants. Other cutbacks include 20,000 at IBM; 5,000 at Allied-Signal; 4,000 at Tenneco; 2,500 at Xerox; 10,000 at TRW; 1,800 to 3,800 at McDonnel Douglas; and 10,000 at Digital Equipment. *See*

Alan Murray and David Wessel,"Torrents of Layoffs Show Human Toll of Recession," *The Wall Street Journal* (December 12, 1991), pp. A1, A9.

13. Frances Fox Piven and Richard Cloward, *The New Class War* (New York: Pantheon Books, 1982).

14. Children's Defense Fund, *The State of America's Children* (Washington, DC: CDF, 1991); U.S. Bureau of the Census, *Statistical Abstract of the United States, 1991* (Washington, DC: Government Printing Office, 1991), p. 463, Table 747.

15. F. Block, R. Cloward, B. Ehrenreich, and F. Piven, *The Mean Season: The Attack on the Welfare State* (New York: Pantheon Books, 1987).

16. David Skidmore, "Bank, S&L Failures Declined in '91, but Analysts Expect a New Upswing," *The Washington Post* (January 2, 1992), p. D13.

17. Marc Levinson, "Retire or Bust," *Newsweek* (November 25, 1991), pp. 50, 52.

18. John Berry, "Recession Deeper in First Quarter," *Washington Post* (April 27, 1991), p. A1.

19. Bureau of Labor Statistics, *Employment and Earnings* (January 1992), p. 12, Table A-1.

20. Center on Budget and Policy Priorities, *Unemployment Insurance Runs Out* (Washington, DC: CBPP, 1991); A. Swardson and S. Mufson, "A Tightening Grip on Jobs," *The Washington Post* (November 3, 1991), pp. H1, H4–H5.

21. A. Swardson and S. Mufson, "A Tightening Grip on Jobs," p. H4.

22. Ibid., p. H5.

23. Walda Katz-Fishman, R. Gomes, N. Peery, and J. Scott, "African American Politics in an Era of Capitalist Economic Contraction," in R. Gomes and L. Williams (eds.), *From Exclusion to Inclusion* (New York: Greenwood Press, 1992), pp. 85–96.

24. This section of the chapter on working-class struggles draws heavily from the information provided in B. Berberoglu, *The Legacy of Empire: Economic Decline and Class Polarization in the United States*, Chap. 7.

Selected Bibliography

Adler, Paul. 1984. "Tools for Resistance: Workers Can Make Automation Their Ally," *Dollars and Sense* (October).

Aronowitz, Stanley. 1973. *False Promises: The Shaping of American Working Class Consciousness*. New York: McGraw-Hill Co.

———. 1983. *Working Class Hero: A New Strategy for Labor*. New York: Adama Books.

Baker, Elizabeth Faulkner. 1964. *Technology and Women's Work*. New York: Columbia University Press.

Baran, Paul and Paul M. Sweezy. 1966. *Monopoly Capital*. New York: Monthly Review Press.

Baron, James N. and William T. Bielby. 1984. "The Organization of Work in a Segmented Economy," *American Sociological Review* 49.

Beechey, Veronica and Tessa Perkins. 1987. *A Matter of Hours: Women, Part-time Work, and the Labor Market*. Minneapolis: University of Minnesota Press.

Belous, Richard. 1989. *The Contingent Economy: The Growth of the Temporary, Part-Time, and Subcontracted Workforce*. Washington, DC: National Planning Association.

Beneria, Lourdes. 1989. "Gender and the Global Economy," in Arthur MacEwan and William K. Tabb (eds.), *Instability and Change in the World Economy*. New York: Monthly Review Press.

Bensman, David and R. Lynch. 1987. *Rusted Dreams: Hard Times in a Steel Community*. New York: McGraw-Hill.

Berberoglu, Berch. 1987. *The Internationalization of Capital*. New York: Praeger.

———. 1992. *The Legacy of Empire: Economic Decline and Class Polarization in the United States*. New York: Praeger.

Berman, Daniel M. 1978. *Death on the Job: Occupational Health and Safety Struggles in the United States*. New York: Monthly Review Press.

Bernardi, Gigi M. and Charles M. Geisler. 1984. *The Social Consequences and Challenges of New Agricultural Technologies*. Boulder, CO: Westview Press.

Bina, Cyrus and Chuck Davis. 1990. "The Transnationalization of Capital and the Decline of the U.S. Labor Movement." Paper presented at the 1990 Annual Meeting of the Allied Social Science Associations in Washington, DC (December 28–30).

Bina, Cyrus and Behzad Yaghmaian. 1991. "Post-War Global Accumulation and the Transnationalization of Capital," *Capital & Class*, No. 43 (Spring).

Blau, Francine D. 1984. "Women in the Labor Force: An Overview," in Joe Freeman (ed.), *Women: A Feminist Perspective*. Palo Alto, CA: Mayfield.

Bluestone, Barry and Bennett Harrison. 1982. *The Deindustrialization of America: Plant Closings, Community Abandonment, and the Dismantling of Basic Industry*. New York: Basic Books.

Bowles, Gladys K. 1967. "The Current Situation of the Hired Farm Labor Force," in E. E. Bishop (ed.), *Farm Labor in the United States*. New York: Columbia University Press.

Bowles, Samuel and Richard Edwards. 1985. *Understanding Capitalism*. New York: Harper & Row.

Braverman, Harry. 1974. *Labor and Monopoly Capital: The Degradation of Work in the Twentieth Century*. New York: Monthly Review Press.

Brecher, Jeremy. 1972. *Strike!* Greenwich: Fawcet.

Brecher, Jeremy and Tim Costello. 1991. *Global Village vs. Global Pillage: A One-World Strategy for Labor*. Washington, DC: International Labor Rights Education and Research Fund.

Brenner, Robert. 1977. "The Origins of Capitalist Development: A Critique of Neo-Smithian Marxism," *New Left Review*, No. 104 (July–August).

Bridges, William P. 1982. "The Sexual Segregation of Occupations: Theories of Labor Stratification in Industry," *American Journal of Sociology*, 88.

Brock, Gerald W. 1975. *The U.S. Computer Industry*. Cambridge, MA: Bollinger Publishing Company.

Burawoy, Michael. 1979. "Toward a Marxist Theory of the Labor Process: Braverman and Beyond," *Politics and Society* 8, Nos. 3–4.

———. 1979. *Manufacturing Consent: Changes in the Labor Process under Monopoly Capitalism*. Chicago: University of Chicago Press.

———. 1983. "Between the Labor Process and the State: The Changing Face of Factory Regimes under Advanced Capitalism," *American Sociological Review*, Vol. 48, No. 3.

Chan, Sucheng. 1989. *This Bittersweet Soil: The Chinese in California Agriculture, 1860–1910*. Berkeley: University of California Press.

Clawson, Dan. 1980. *Bureaucracy and the Labor Process: The Transformation of U.S. Industry, 1860–1920*. New York: Monthly Review Press.

Clement, Andrew. 1988. "Office Automation and the Technical Control of Information Workers," in Vincent Mosco and Janet Wasko (eds.), *The Political Economy of Information*. Madison: University of Wisconsin Press.

Cockcroft, James D. 1986. *Outlaws in the Promised Land: Mexican Immigrant Workers and America's Future*. New York: Grove Press.

Cohr, Sheila. 1991. "Us and Them: Business Unionism in America and Some Implications for the U.K.," *Capital and Class*, No. 45 (Autumn).

Copley, Frank B. 1923. *Frederick W. Taylor: Father of Scientific Management*. 2 vols. New York: Harper and Brothers.

Coriat, B. 1980. "The Restructuring of the Assembly Line: A New Economy of Time and Control," *Capital and Class* 11.

Cypher, James. 1979. "The Internationalization of Capital and the Transformation of Social Formations: A Critique of the Monthly Review School," *Review of Radical Political Economics*, Vol. 11, No. 4.

Davis, Mike. 1986. *Prisoners of the American Dream: Politics and Economy in the History of the U.S. Working Class*. London: Verso.

DeLamarter, Richard T. 1986. *Big Blue: IBM's Use and Abuse of Power*. New York: Dodd, Mead Publisher.

Dixon, Marlene, et al. 1982. "Reindustrialization and the Transnational Labor Force in the United States Today," in Marlene Dixon and Suzanne Jonas (eds.), *The New Nomads: From Immigrant Labor to Transnational Working Class*. San Francisco: Synthesis.

Dohse, K., U. Jurgens, and T. Malsch. 1985. "From Fordism to Toyotism? The Social Organization of the Labor Process in the Japanese Automobile Industry," *Politics and Society*, Vol. 14, No. 2.

Dunne, John G. 1967. *Delano, The Story of the California Grape Strike*. New York: Farrar, Straus & Giroux.

Edwards, Richard. 1978. "Social Relations of Production at the Point of Production," *Insurgent Sociologist*, Vol. 8, Nos. 2–3.

———. 1979. *Contested Terrain: The Transformation of the Workplace in the Twentieth Century*. New York: Basic Books.

Edwards, Richard, et al. 1975. *Labor Market Segmentation*. New York: D. C. Heath.

Elger, Tony. 1982. "Braverman, Capital Accumulation and Deskilling," in Stephen Wood (ed.), *The Degradation of Work?* London: Hutchinson.

Elson, Diane and Ruth Pearson. 1981. "Nimble Fingers Make Cheap Workers: An Analysis of Workers in Employment in Third World Export Processing," *Feminist Review*, Vol. 33.

Fantasia, Rick. 1988. *Cultures of Solidarity: Consciousness, Action, and Contemporary American Workers*. Berkeley: University of California Press.

Fishman, Katherine Davis. 1981. *The Computer Establishment*. New York: Harper & Row.

Flamm, Kenneth. 1988. *Creating the Computer*. Washington, DC: Brookings Institution.

Ford, Henry. 1923. *My Life and My Work*. London: Heinemann.

Foster, John. 1974. *Class Struggle and the Industrial Revolution*. New York: St. Martin's Press.

Foster, John Bellamy and Henryk Szlajfer (eds.). 1984. *The Faltering Economy: The Problem of Accumulation under Monopoly Capitalism*. New York: Monthly Review Press.

Foster, J. and C. Woolfson. 1989. "Post-Fordism and Business Unionism," *New Left Review*, No. 174.

Friedland, William and Dorothy Nelkin. 1971. *Migrant Workers in America's Northeast*. New York: Holt, Rinehart and Winston.

Friedland, William, Amy Barton, and Robert Thomas. 1981. *Manufacturing Green Gold: Capital, Labor, and Technology in the Lettuce Industry*. Cambridge: Cambridge University Press.

Friedman, Andrew L. 1977. *Industry and Labor: Class Struggle at Work and Monopoly Capitalism*. London: Macmillan.

Frobel, Folker, Jurgen Heinrichs, and Otto Kreye. 1980. *The New International Division of Labor*. Cambridge: Cambridge University Press.

Fuentes, Annette and Barbara Ehrenreich. 1983. *Women in the Global Factory*. Boston: South End Press.

———. 1983. "New Factory Girls," *Multinational Monitor*, Vol. 4, No. 8.

Garlarza, Ernesto. 1964. *Merchants of Labor: The Mexican Bracero Story, an Account of the Managed Migration of Mexican Farm Workers in California*. Santa Barbara, CA: McNally and Lofton.

Garson, Barbara. 1975. *All the Livelong Day: The Meaning and Demeaning of Routine Work*. New York: Penguin Books.

Gartman, David. 1982. "Basic and Surplus Control in Capitalist Machinery," *Research in Political Economy*, Vol. 5.

———. 1986. *Auto Slavery: The Labor Process in the American Automobile Industry*. New Brunswick, NJ: Rutgers University Press.

Georgakas, Dan, and Marvin Surkin. 1975. *Detroit: I Do Mind Dying*. New York: St. Martin's Press.

Geschwender, James. 1977. *Class, Race, and Worker Insurgency*. Cambridge: Cambridge University Press.

Glenn, Evelyn Nakano and Roslyn L. Feldberg. 1977. "Degraded and Deskilled: The Proletarianization of Clerical Work," *Social Problems* 25.

Gordon, David, R. Edwards, and M. Reich. 1982. *Segmented Work, Divided Workers*. Cambridge: Cambridge University Press.

Green, J. 1980. *The World of the Worker: Labor in Twentieth Century America*. New York: Hill and Wang.

Greenbaum, Joan. 1976. "Division of Labor in the Computer Field," *Monthly Review* (July–August).

———. 1979. *In the Name of Efficiency: Management Theory and Shop Floor Practice in Data-Processing Work*. Philadelphia: Temple University Press.

Gregory, James. 1989. *American Exodus: The Dust Bowl Migrations and Okie Culture in California*. New York: Oxford University Press.

Guarasci, R. and G. Peck. 1987. "Work, Class, and Society: Recent Developments and New Directions in Labor Process Theory," *Review of Radical Political Economics.*

Gutman, Herbert. 1976. *Work, Culture, and Society in Industrializing America.* New York: Knopf.

Hakken, David. 1988. "Studying New Technology after Braverman: An Anthropological Review," *Anthropology of Work Newsletter*, Vol. 1, No. 1.

Halperin, Martin. 1988. *UAW Politics in the Cold War Era.* Albany: State University of New York Press.

Hartman, Heidi. 1976. "Capitalism, Patriarchy and Job Segregation by Sex," *Signs* 1.

Hayes, Dennis. 1989. *Behind the Silicon Curtain.* Boston: South End Press.

Heckscher, C. 1980. "Worker Participation and Management Control," *Journal of Social Reconstruction*, Vol. 3, No. 1.

Herman, A. 1982. "Conceptualizing Control: Domination and Hegemony in the Capitalist Labor Process," *The Insurgent Sociologist*, Vol. 11, No. 3.

Hill, Stephen. 1981. *Competition and Control at Work: The New Industrial Sociology.* Cambridge, MA: MIT Press.

Hodson, Randy and Teresa A. Sullivan. 1990. *The Social Organization of Work.* Belmont, CA: Wadsworth Publishing Company.

Hossfeld, Karen J. 1990. " 'Their Logic Against Them': Contradictions in Sex, Race, and Class in Silicon Valley," in Kathryn Ward (ed.), *Women Workers and Global Restructuring.* Ithaca, NY: Cornell University Press.

Howe, Carolyn. 1986. "The Politics of Class Compromise in an International Context: Considerations for a New Strategy for Labor," *Review of Radical Political Economics*, Vol. 18, No. 3.

Hunnius, Gerry, et al. (eds.). 1973. *Workers' Control: A Reader on Labor and Social Change.* New York: Vintage Books.

Jenkins, Rhys. 1987. *Transnational Corporations and Uneven Development.* New York: Methuen.

Johnson, Barbara. 1983. *Working Whenever You Want.* Englewood Cliffs, NJ: Prentice-Hall.

Kahne, Hilda. 1985. *Reconceiving Part-time Work: New Perspectives for Older Workers and Women.* Atlantic Highlands, NJ: Rowman and Allanheld Publishers.

Kalleberg, Arne L. and Ivar Berg. 1987. *Work and Industry: Structures, Markets and Processes.* New York: Plenum Press.

Kanter, Rosabeth Moss. 1977. *Men and Women of the Corporation.* New York: Basic Books.

Katz-Fishman, Walda, et al. 1992. "African American Politics in an Era of Capitalist Economic Contraction," in R. Gomes and L. Williams (eds.), *From Exclusion to Inclusion.* New York: Greenwood Press.

Keeran, Roger. 1980. *The Communist Party and the Auto Workers' Unions.* Bloomington, IN: Indiana University Press.

Keller, John. 1983. *Power in America: The Southern Question and the Control of Labor*. Chicago: Vanguard Press.

Kennedy, Martin and Richard Florida. 1988. "Beyond Mass Production: Production and the Labor Process in Japan," *Politics and Society* 16.

Kimeldorf, Howard. 1988. *Reds or Rackets? The Making of Radical and Conservative Unions on the Waterfront*. Berkeley: University of California Press.

Kitano, Harry and Roger Daniels. 1988. *Asian Americans: Emerging Minorities*. Engelwood Cliffs, NJ: Prentice Hall.

Kraft, Phil. 1977. *Programmers and Managers. The Routinization of Computer Programming in the United States*. New York: Springer-Verlag.

Leggett, John C. 1991. *Mining the Fields: Farm Workers Fight Back*. Highland Park, NJ: The Raritan Institute.

Lembcke, Jerry and W. Tattam. 1984. *One Union in Wood: A Political History of the International Woodworkers of America*. New York: International Publishers.

Lembcke, Jerry. 1988. *Capitalist Development and Class Capacities: Marxist Theory and Union Organization*. Westport, CT: Greenwood Press.

Levenstein, Harvey. 1981. *Communism, Anticommunism, and the CIO*. Westport, CT: Greenwood Press.

Levine, Rhonda. 1988. *Class Struggle and the New Deal: Industrial Labor, Industrial Capital, and the State*. Lawrence, KS: University Press of Kansas.

Lingenfelter, Richard E. 1974. *The Hardrock Miners: A History of the Mining Labor Movement in the American West, 1863–1893*. Berkeley: University of California Press.

Littler, Craig R. 1982. *The Development of the Labour Process in Capitalist Societies*. London: Heinemann Educational.

Lynd, Alice and Staughton Lynd. 1973. *Rank and File*. Boston: Beacon Press.

Lynd, Staughton. 1976. "Workers' Control in a Time of Diminished Workers' Rights," *Radical America*, Vol. 10, No. 5 (September–October).

Mandel, Ernest. 1975. *Late Capitalism*. London: Verso.

Marglin, Stephen. 1974. "What Do Bosses Do? The Origins and Functions of Hierarchy in Capitalist Production," *Review of Radical Political Economics* 6 (Summer).

Marx, Karl. 1967. *Capital*. 3 vols. New York: International Publishers.

———. 1973. *Grundrisse*. New York: Vintage.

———. 1987. "Trades' Unions, Their Past, Present and Future," in Simeon Larson and Bruce Nissen (eds.), *Theories of the Labor Movement*. Detroit, MI: Wayne State University Press.

McClellan, Stephen T. 1984. *The Coming Computer Industry Shakeout*. New York: John Wiley and Sons.

McNally, David. 1991. "Beyond Nationalism, Beyond Protectionism: Labor and the Canada-U.S. Free Trade Agreement," *Capital & Class*, No. 43 (Spring).

McWilliams, Carey. 1971. *Factories in the Field*. Santa Barbara and Salt Lake City: Peregrine Publishers.

Meier, August and Elliot Rudwick. 1979. *Black Detroit and the Rise of the UAW*. New York: Oxford University Press.

Meyer III, Stephen. 1981. *The Five Dollar Day: Labor Management and Social Control in the Ford Motor Company, 1908–1921*. Albany: State University of New York Press.

Miles, Marina. 1990. *Patriarchy and Accumulation on a World Scale: Women in the International Division of Labor*. London: Zed Books.

Milkman, Ruth. 1987. *Gender at Work*. Urbana: University of Illinois Press.

Mines, Richard and Philip L. Martin. 1986. *A Profile of California Farm Workers*. Berkeley, CA: The Giannini Foundation of Agricultural Economics, University of California, Berkeley.

Mins, L. E. (ed.). 1937. *Founding of the First International: A Documentary Record*. New York: International Publishers.

Montgomery, David. 1976. "Workers' Control of Machine Production in the Nineteenth Century," *Labor History*, Vol. 17, No. 4.

Moody, Kim. 1988. *An Injury to All: The Decline of American Unionism*. London: Verso.

Moore, Truman. 1965. *The Slaves We Rent*. New York: Random House.

———. 1979. *Workers' Control in America*. Cambridge: Cambridge University Press.

———. 1987. *The Fall of the House of Labor*. Cambridge: Cambridge University Press.

Nash, June. 1983. "The Impact of the Changing International Division of Labor on Different Sectors of the Labor Force," in June Nash and Maria Patricia Fernandez-Kelly (eds.), *Women, Men, and the International Division of Labor*. Albany: State University of New York.

Nelkin, Dorothy. 1970. *On the Season: Aspects of the Migrant Labor System*. Ithaca, NY: New York School of Industrial and Labor Relations.

Nevins, Allan and Frank Hill. 1954. *Ford: The Times, the Man, the Company*. New York: Scribner's.

Nichols, Theo and Huw Beynon. 1977. *Living with Capitalism: Class Relations and the Modern Factory*. London: Routledge and Kegan Paul.

Noble, David F. 1984. *Forces of Production: A Social History of Industrial Automation*. New York: Oxford University Press.

O'Connor, James. 1975. "Productive vs. Unproductive Labor," *Politics and Society*, Vol. 5, No. 3.

Padfield, Harland and William E. Martin. 1965. *Farmers, Workers and Machines*. Tucson, AZ: University of Arizona Press.

Palmer, Brian. 1975. "Class, Conception and Conflict: The Thrust for Efficiency, Managerial Views of Labor and the Working Class Rebellion, 1903–22," *Review of Radical Political Economics*, Vol. 7, No. 2.

Peet, Richard (ed.). 1987. *International Capitalism and Industrial Restructuring*. Boston: Allen & Unwin.

Peterson, Joyce Shaw. 1987. *American Automobile Workers, 1900–1933*. Albany: State University of New York Press.

Pfeffer, Richard M. 1979. *Working for Capitalism.* New York: Columbia University Press.

Picciotto, Sol. 1991. "The Internationalization of the State," *Capital & Class*, No. 43 (Spring).

Piven, Frances Fox and Richard Cloward. 1982. *The New Class War.* New York: Pantheon Books.

Prechel, Harland. 1990. "Steel and the State: Industry Politics and Business Policy Formation, 1940–1989," *American Sociological Review*, Vol. 55, No. 5 (October).

Reintjes, J. Francis. 1991. *Numerical Control: Making a New Technology.* New York: Oxford University Press.

Remy, Dorothy and Larry Sawers. 1984. "Women's Power in the Workplace," in Liesa Stamm and Carol D. Ryff (eds.), *Social Power and Influence of Women.* Boulder, CO: Westview Press.

Roobeek, Annemieke. 1987. "The Crisis of Fordism and the Rise of a New Technological Paradigm," *Futures* 19 (April).

Roos, Patricia. 1981. "Sexual Stratification in the Workplace: Male-Female Differences in Economic Returns to Occupation," *Social Science Research* 10.

Sabel, Charles. 1982. *Work and Politics: The Division of Labor in Industry.* Cambridge: Cambridge University Press.

Safa, Helen I. 1986. "Runaway Shops and Female Employment: The Search for Cheap Labor," in Eleanor Leacock and Helen I. Safa (eds.), *Women's Work.* South Headley, MA: Bergin and Garvey.

Sattel, Jack. 1978. "The Degradation of Labor in the 20th Century: Harry Braverman's Sociology of Work," *The Insurgent Sociologist*, Vol. 8, No. 1 (Winter).

Sayer, A. 1985. "New Developments in Manufacturing: The Just in Time System," *Capital and Class* 30.

Shaiken, Harley. 1986. *Work Transformed: Automation and Labor in the Computer Age.* Lexington, MA: Lexington Books.

Sheinkman, Jack. 1991. "Preface: Worker Rights in Central America," in *Worker Rights in the New World Order.* New York: The National Labor Committee in Support of Democracy and Human Rights in El Salvador.

Sirianni, C. 1982. *Workers' Control and Socialist Democracy: The Soviet Experience.* London: Verso Books.

Sklair, Leslie. 1989. *Assembly for Development: The Maquila Industry in Mexico and the United States.* Boston: Unwin Hyman.

Snow, Robert T. 1983. "The New International Division of Labor and the U.S. Work Force: The Case of the Electronics Industry," in June Nash and Maria Patricia Fernandez-Kelly (eds.), *Women, Men and the International Division of Labor.* Albany: State University of New York Press.

Soma, John T. 1975. *The Computer Industry.* Lexington, MA: D. C. Heath.

Stein, Walter J. 1973. *California and the Dust Bowl Migration.* Westport, CT: Greenwood Press.

Stone, Katherine. 1974. "The Origins of Job Structures in the Steel Industry," *Review of Radical Political Economics*, Vol. 6, No. 2.

Storper, Michael and R. Walker. 1989. *The Capitalist Imperative: Territory, Technology, and Industrial Growth*. New York: Basil Blackwell.

Sullivan, Teresa. 1979. *Marginal Workers, Marginal Jobs*. Austin: University of Texas Press.

Sweezy, Paul M. 1942. *The Theory of Capitalist Development*. New York: Monthly Review Press.

Szymanski, Albert. 1978. "Braverman as a Neo-Luddite?" *The Insurgent Sociologist*, Vol. 8, No. 1 (Winter).

———. 1983. *Class Structure*. New York: Praeger.

Tabb, William K. 1989. "Capital Mobility, the Restructuring of Production, and the Politics of Labor," in Arthur MacEwan and William K. Tabb (eds.), *Instability and Change in the World Economy*. New York: Monthly Review Press.

Taylor, Frederick W. 1947. *Scientific Management*. New York: Harper.

———. 1967. *The Principles of Scientific Management*. New York: W. W. Norton & Co.

Terkel, Studs. 1972. *Working*. New York: Random House.

Thomas, Robert J. 1981. "The Social Organization of Industrial Agriculture," *The Insurgent Sociologist* (Winter).

———. 1982. "Citizenship and Gender in Work Organization: Some Considerations for Theories of the Labor Process," *American Journal of Sociology* (Supplement) 88.

Thompson, E. P. 1963. *The Making of the English Working Class*. New York: Pantheon Books.

———. 1967. "Time, Work Discipline, and Industrial Capitalism," *Past and Present* 38.

Twiss, Brian C. (ed.). 1981. *The Managerial Implication of Microelectronics*. London: Macmillan.

Waas, Michael Van. 1982. "Multinational Corporations and the Politics of Labor Supply," *The Insurgent Sociologist*, Vol. 11, No. 3.

Wachtel, Howard M. 1986. *The Money Mandarins: The Making of a Supranational Economic Order*. New York: Pantheon Books.

Ward, Kathryn (ed.). 1990. *Women Workers and Global Restructuring*. Ithaca, NY: ILR Press.

Wasser, Steven A. 1984. "Economics of the Temporary Help Services Industry," *Contemporary Times*, Vol. 3, No. 9.

Weinstein, Harry. 1985. "The Health Threat in the Fields," *The Nation*, Vol. 240 (May 11).

Wilk, V. and D. M. Hancock. 1991. "Farmworker Occupational Health and Safety in the 1990's," *New Solutions*, Vol. 1 (Spring).

Wilkinson, Alec. 1989. *Big Sugar: Seasons in the Cane Fields of Florida*. New York: Vintage Books.

Willoughby, John. 1986. *Capitalist Imperialism, Crisis and State*. New York: Harwood Press.

———. 1987. "The Promise and Pitfalls of Protectionist Politics," in Robert Cherry et al. (eds.), *The Imperiled Economy*, Book I. New York: Union for Radical Political Economics.

Wolf, Wendy C. and Neil D. Fligstein. 1979. "Sex and Authority in the Work Place: The Causes of Sexual Inequality," *American Sociological Review* 44.

Wood, Stephen (ed.). 1982. *The Degradation of Work? Skill, Deskilling, and the Labor Process*. London: Hutchinson and Company.

———. 1989. *The Transformation of Work?* London: Unwin Hyman.

Wright, Dale. 1965. *They Harvest Despair: The Migrant Farm Workers*. Boston: Beacon Press.

Zimbalist, Andrew. 1975. "The Limits of Work Humanization," *Review of Radical Political Economics*, Vol. 7, No. 2 (Summer).

———. 1979. *Case Studies on the Labor Process*. New York: Monthly Review Press.

Index

Accumulation: capital, 44–46, 47, 49, 50, 54, 55, 56, 137, 141, 152, 154, 159, 163, 167; crisis, 44, 45, 46, 47, 50
AFL-CIO, 158, 159, 160, 162, 163, 165
African Americans, 173, 176. *See also* Blacks
Agriculture: division of labor in, 97–113; farm workers in, 97–113, 121, 122
Alienation, 80–81, 82, 92; dimensions of, 80–81; and power at work, 80–83
Allied-Signal, 181
American Federation of Labor (AFL), 12, 157
Anarcho-syndicalism, 2, 3
Anti-communism, 3, 6, 158, 159, 165
Apple computer, 62
Aronowitz, Stanley, 6
Assembly work, 22–23, 26, 35
AT&T, 177
Authority, 45, 46, 48, 49, 51, 52, 54–56, 78, 82, 85, 86, 87
Automation, xi, 127, 171, 174
Automobile industry, 21–40

Babbage principle, 28
Barton, Amy, 102
Benenson, Harold, 9
Blacks, 31, 36–37, 38, 100, 172, 176
Blauner, Robert, 80
Bluestone, Barry, 11, 118, 181
Braverman, Harry, 4, 9, 22, 28, 67, 68, 82, 126, 168
Bureaucracy, 82

Cadillac Motors, 33
Canada, 161, 163, 166
Cannery and Agricultural Workers Industrial Union, 110
Capital: accumulation, 44–46, 47, 49, 50, 54, 55, 56, 137, 141, 152, 154, 159, 163, 167; concentration of, 101–2; internationalization of, xi, xii, 64, 157, 160, 166, 174, 180; overaccumulation of, 64, 65; struggles between labor and, 156, 157, 179; transnational, 152–67, 173; on a world scale, 137–38, 141
Capitalism, 22; development of, 152, 154, 167, 174; patriarchy and, 91, 92; revolutionary transformation of, 180

Capitalist production, 81, 93
Centralization, 44, 45, 47, 48, 52–56
Capitalist production, 81, 93
Chavez, Cesar, 104, 111
Chemicals, in the fields, 112–13
Chicanos. *See* Mexicans
Child labor, 109
Chinese, 98–100
Cities Service, 178
Class, 6, 8, 9–15, 78; analysis, 79, 80, 81; capacity, 4, 8, 9–15, 18; categories, 80; collaboration, 160, 165; dimensions of, 8, 13; formation, 5, 13; and gender, 78–80; position, 79, 84; relations, 25, 29, 38, 40, 81; structure, 79, 92; struggle, xii, 14, 22, 24, 25, 36, 37, 38, 177–80; working, 78, 81–83, 87
Clegg, Stewart, 84
Cockcroft, James, 107
Cold War, 158, 159, 165
Collective bargaining, 37, 38
Communist Party, 2, 7, 14
Communists, 110, 111
Comparable worth, 86
Computer industry, 59–77; development of, 59–64; women workers in, 71–74; working conditions in, 72–73
Computers, 59–77; diversification of, 61, 62, 63; generations of, 61, 66, 69, 70, 71; history of, 60, 62; personal or mini, 62, 63; software, 62–63; and standardization, 69, 70
Confederacion de Trabajadores de Mexico (CTM), 144, 146
Congress of Industrial Organizations (CIO), 3, 7, 8, 12, 14
Contingent work, 116, 117, 129, 132–33, 173; definition of, 116; growth of, 117
Control, xi-xii, 11, 23–24, 26, 29–36, 44, 45, 46–56, 66–73, 78, 79, 81–83, 84, 87, 89, 90, 92, 101–2, 132–33, 137, 142, 143, 179, 180; budgetary, 49, 50, 52, 53, 54; bureaucratic, 48, 49, 51–53; bureaucratic managerial strategies for, 142, 143; centralization of in farming, 101–2; conceptual, 82, 83, 84; of the creative process, 66–70, 73; economic, 79; of the labor process, 23–24, 26, 29–36, 137, 142, 143; of labor and the production process, 78, 81–83, 87, 92; of labor by management, 11, 89, 132–33, 137, 179, 180; managerial, 44, 53, 55; new forms of, 69–70; over the work environment, 81, 84, 87, 90; at the point of production, 70–73; technical, 52, 53; top managerial, 51, 53, 55
Craft labor, 22–26
Creative process, 65, 66–70, 73, 74; contradictions in, 65, 68; control of, 66–70, 73; vs. labor process, 67–69, 74
Creative workers, 64, 65, 69, 70, 74
Creativity, 59, 64–70, 80, 84; autonomization of, 65; commodification of, 59, 64–65, 66, 73; creative work, 81, 93
Crew leader, 105

Davis, Mike, 158
Debt: corporate, 175; federal government, 175, 176; personal, 175
Debt peonage, 106–7
Deficit, budget, 175
Deindustrialization, 14
Delano, California, 111
Deskilling, 3, 4, 9–11, 12, 22, 26–27, 29–33, 67, 82–84, 126–28, 153, 154, 155, 161, 166, 167, 168
DiGiorgio Corporation, 98

Digital Equipment Corporation (DEC), 62
Division of labor: in agriculture, 101–4, 108–10; division of household labor, 93; by gender, 78, 79, 85, 86, 91; international, 173; in manufacturing, 138, 140, 141, 143; restructuring of, 174
Dunkerly, David, 84

Earnings, 78–79, 80, 85–88, 90, 92; gender gap in, 86–87, 92. *See also* Wages
Eastern Airlines, 177
Eckert, John, 60
Economic crisis, xi, 174, 175, 180, 181
Edwards, Richard, 132
Employers, 82, 83
Employers' Association of Detroit (EAD), 24–25, 30
Exploitation of labor, 81, 84, 85, 138, 142, 143, 173, 174
Export Processing Zones (EPZs), 138–39, 140, 141, 155, 156, 161, 173; employment in, 139, 140; female labor in, 139–41; in Mexico, 139, 140–41; in South Korea, 139, 140; in Taiwan, 139
Export processing industries, 140, 141–42, 147; labor relations in, 141–47

Family, 9–11, 79, 84, 85, 86, 87, 92, 93
Fantasia, Rick, 6
Farming: concentration of capital in, 101–2; centralization of control in, 101–2; commercial, 98: tenant based, 99
Farm labor, 97–113; contractor, 104–7; migration, 97; mobility of, 109–10; nationality of, 97, 98, 105, 111; wages and earnings of, 98, 103–4, 109, 111
Farm Labor Organizing Committee, 111
Federal Deposit Insurance Corporation (FDIC), 175
Female labor, 137–38, 139, 140, 141, 142–43, 146; low wage, 138–39, 141; selective recruitment of in the Third World, 137–38, 142. *See also* Women
Field crews, 102–4
Filipinos, 100, 110, 111
Flexible work, 39, 119, 128–32
Forces of production, 140, 177
Ford, Henry, 21, 26, 27, 29, 70
Fordism, 44–46, 47, 49, 50, 53–56, 59, 64, 69
Ford Motor Company, 25, 26, 28, 32, 33, 34, 35
Foremen, 23, 25, 32, 33
Fresno Valley, 99
Friedland, William, 102

Gender, 78–93; and class, 78–80; and control over the labor process, 78–96; differences in income, 87; discrimination, 87; division of labor, 78, 79, 85, 86, 91; inequality, 79, 84, 86; occupational gender segregation and power at work, 84–87; relations, 92. *See also* Women
General Motors, 21, 28, 39, 40, 176, 181
General Agreement on Tariffs and Trade (GATT), 161, 162, 163, 164, 167
Great Plains migrants, 100, 110
Great Depression, 14, 15, 110–11
Griffin, Larry, 80
Growers, 104, 107
Gulf Oil, 178

Harrison, Bennett, 11, 118, 181
Hierarchy, 54, 55
Hiring halls, 121

IBM, 60–63, 74, 176, 181
Ideas, 64, 68–69, 70
Imperial Valley, 99, 106, 110, 111
Income. *See* Earnings; Wages
Indians, 98, 101
Industrial Workers of the World (IWW), 3, 34, 36
Inequality, 79, 80; economic, 82, 92; gender, 79, 84, 86; of power, 79
Innovations, 61, 63, 64, 71, 73, 74; technological, 64
Intel, 61
Interchangeable work force, 127–28
International Harvester strike, 177–78
International Brotherhood of Teamsters, 111–12
Internationalization of capital, xi, xii, 64, 157, 160, 166, 174, 180

Jaffe, David, 14
Japanese, 99–100
Job, autonomy, 78, 81, 82, 84, 90; definition of, 83; discretion and self-direction, 83–84; hierarchies, 36; part- time and full-time, 173, 174
John Morrell strike, 177

Kalleberg, Arne, 80
Kanter, Rosabeth, 80, 87
Keeran, Roger, 7
Kimeldorf, Howard, 7
Knowledge workers. *See* Creative workers
Kraft, Philip, 67, 68

Labor: aristocracy of, 157–60, 173; black, 172; blue collar, 174, 176; changing role of in production, 171–74; cheapening of, 153, 154, 167, 168; contingent, 116–33; contractor, 104–8; control of, xi-xii, 11, 23–24, 26, 29–36, 44, 45, 46–56, 66–73, 78, 79, 81–83, 84, 87, 89, 90, 92, 101–2, 132–33, 137, 142, 143, 179, 180; crisis of, 13–15; division of, 26, 27–33, 37–40, 78, 79, 85, 86, 91, 138, 140, 141, 143, 173, 174; exploitation of, xi-xii, 155, 156, 173, 174, 179, 180; in export-processing zones, 139–42; farm, 121–22; female, 137–38, 139, 140, 141, 142–43, 146, 155, 172–73; intensity of, 23, 24, 32, 33-36; internationalism, 157-60; in machine shops, 26–27; in manufacturing, 26, 138, 140, 141, 143; in *maquiladora* industries, 140, 144, 145; mental and manual, 68, 82, 83–84; militancy of, 144; new international sexual division of labor, 137, 146; potential for international solidarity of, 152, 156, 157, 162, 163, 164, 165, 166, 167; productivity of, 27–28, 39; repression of, 138, 143–46, 162; skilled, 173; strikes, 144, 146; struggles, 147, 179; studies, 6–9; in the Third World, 156; transnational, 137; turnover, 25, 36; unions, 164, 166, 167; white collar, 174, 176. *See also* Workers; Working class
Labor force, 78, 84, 173; shift in the structure of U.S., 173
Labor market, 25, 28–31, 79, 82, 92; women's participation in, 78, 79, 85, 87
Labor movement: international, 152–67; U.S., 153, 157, 158, 159, 160, 162, 164, 165

Labor process: and capitalist crisis, 174–77; fragmentation of, 140, 143; gender and, 78–93; global, 137–38, 152–67; rationalization of, 82; transnational character of, 152, 153, 154, 155, 161, 168; women in global, 153, 155
Lapidus, June, 120
League of Revolutionary Black Workers, 38
Levenstein, Harvey, 7
Lipset, Seymour Martin, 4, 6
Lordstown (Ohio) plant of General Motors, 38, 43

Machine tools, 23, 26–27
Machinists, 23
Management, 44–56; lower, 55; middle, 46, 47, 50, 54; top, 44, 5, 47–52, 54–56. *See also* Scientific management
Management control, of workers, 132–33
Managers, 83, 87, 90
Mandel, Ernest, 64
Manufacturing: division of labor in, 138, 140, 141, 143; production, 173, 174
Maquiladora industry, 140, 141, 143, 144, 145, 146, 161, 173; labor force in, 140, 144, 145
Marglin, Stephen, 28
Martin, Philip, 105
Marx, Karl, 4, 16, 27, 28, 156, 167, 168
Marxism, 4, 5, 80, 92
Mass production, 24, 69, 70
Mauchly, John, 60
McCarthyism, 7, 158
McDonnel Douglas, 181
McWilliams, Carey, 99, 110
Mechanization, 103
Mexicans, 100–101, 104, 105, 107, 108, 110, 111
Mexico, 100, 107, 139, 140, 141, 144, 147, 161, 162, 165, 166
Microprocessor, 61
Migrant farmworkers, 121–22
Mills, C. Wright, 6, 127
Mines, Richard, 105
Mobility: capital, 10, 11; labor 10, 11
Monopoly capitalism, 64, 65, 69, 73
Montgomery, David, 11, 24
Mueller, Charles, 86, 87

New Left, 2, 6, 7
New products, 61, 69, 71, 73. *See also* Ideas; Innovations
North American Free Trade Agreement (NAFTA), 161, 162, 163, 164, 167, 173

Occupations, 78, 79, 85–88, 92; blue collar, 82, 87; clerical, 82, 92; craft, 82, 84, 85; gender segregation in, 78, 82, 84, 86, 87–92; professional and managerial, 82, 84, 85, 90, 92; structure of, 92; traditional female, 78, 79, 80, 85, 87, 90–92, 93; white collar, 78, 82, 85, 87, 92
Offe, Claus, 8
Olds, Ransom, 26
Oldsmobile Motor Works, 24
Overproduction, of commodities, 175, 176

Panitch, Leo, 15
Parcel, Toby, 86, 87
Part-time workers, 117, 123, 125–26, 129, 173; growth of 125–26; wages of, 129
Patriarchy, 79, 142, 145; capitalism and, 91, 92
Peet, Richard, 11, 14
Pension Benefit Guaranty Corporation (PBGC), 175

Philippines, 139, 140, 143, 146
Pilcher, William, 9
Pittston strike, 177
Plant closings, 157
Post-Fordism, 44, 45, 46, 53, 55–56, 59, 68, 69, 74
Production: capitalist, 81, 82, 92, 93, 171; computer automated, 171; machine-based factory, 171, 180; means of, 81; relations of, 78, 79, 81, 82
Production process. *See* Labor process
Productivity, measurement of, 67
Profits, 82, 85, 86, 141, 172, 174
Proletarianization, 4, 7, 12, 13, 81, 82, 83

Quality control circles, 21
Quality of work-life programs, 21, 38, 39, 40

Race, 86, 98
Relations of production: capitalist, 171, 177; transnationalization of capitalist, 152, 154, 156, 159, 161
Research and development, 65–69, 74
Resources, 80; access to, 83; organizational, 83; resource efficacy, 86; scarce, 79
Restructuring, 160, 174; global, 160
Right-to-work laws, 172
Robotics, 171

Saab-Scania, 39
Sacramento Valley, 99
Salinas Valley, 102, 111
San Joaquin Valley, 99, 106, 110, 111
Scientific management, 44, 45, 47, 48, 154; Fordism, 44–46, 47, 48, 49, 50, 53–56; post-Fordism, 44, 45, 46, 53, 55, 56; Taylorism, 44, 45, 47, 49, 56
Service sector, 82, 85, 123, 173, 174, 176
Sexism, 71–72. *See also* Gender; Women
Shaiken, Harley, 154
Silicon Valley, 71, 73, 147
Skill: levels of, 80, 82, 83, 86; training and education, 82, 85, 86. *See also* Deskilling
Slave labor: in farming, 98, 100; in the southern plantation economy, 172
Smith, Adam, 21, 27
Socialism, 167
Solidarity Day, 178
South Korea, 139, 140, 141, 144, 147
Standardization, 52–55, 140, 141
Steel industry, 44–58
Stein, Walter J., 110, 111
Strikes, 177–78
Studebaker Corporation, 36
Subcontracting, 139
Supervisors, 78, 83, 85, 89, 90
Surplus value, 141, 160

Tabb, William, 164
Taft-Hartley Act, 177
Taylor, Frederick, 42
Taylorism, 44, 45, 47, 49, 56, 64, 65, 67, 68, 69, 73, 143, 154
Team work, 69
Technology: expansion of, 177; growth of, 154, 174
Temporary help industry, 117, 120, 124
Temporary workers, 116–33, 173; clerical, 124; industrial, 120; wages of, 124
Tenneco, 181
Texaco, 178
Therborn, Goran, 8

Thernstrom, Stephen, 13
Third World, 71–72, 173, 174; exploitation of workers in, 174; low wages in, 174
Thomas, Robert J., 102
Thompson, E. P., 2
Time-and-motion studies, 34, 42, 44
Toxins, at work sites, 107, 112–13
Trade Union Unity League, 110
Transnational: capital, 152–67, 173; corporations, 153, 159, 161; labor force, 137

Undocumented workers, 122
Unemployment, 174, 176
Unions, 12–13, 24–25, 36, 85, 110–12, 144, 166, 167; unionization, 81, 109, 110; women workers and, 142, 145
United Auto Workers (UAW), 7, 37, 165
United Automobile, Aircraft, and Vehicle Workers, 36
United Farm Workers (UFW), 104, 106, 107, 110, 111, 112
United Mine Workers of America (UMWA), 178
UNIVAC, 60

Wages, 28, 98, 103–4, 109, 111, 173, 174; decline in real, 174; of farm workers, 98, 103–4, 109, 111
Watson, Jr., Thomas J., 60
Western Electric, 177
Williams, William Appleman, 2
Women, 31, 36–37, 78–93, 137–38; and class struggle, 146–48; disadvantaged position of, 78, 83, 85, 92; empowerment of, 83, 93; exploitation of Third World working women 137, 138, 139, 155; in export processing zones, 139–41; labor force participation of, 78, 79, 85, 87; and the new international division of labor, 137–48; women's power as wage earners, 78–93; women's work, 80, 85, 96; workers, 71–74, 78–93, 139–41, 172–73. *See also* Gender
Work: activities and tasks, 80, 81, 82, 83, 86; clerical, 82; contingent, 116–33; crews, 108–10; degradation of, 1–6; deskilling of, 22, 26–27, 29–33; and family, 79; force, 79; progressive layout of, 32, 26–27, 33–36; relations, 138; routinization of, 81, 82, 84; supervision of 23, 24, 30, 32, 33; women's, 80 85, 96. *See also* Labor; Occupations
Workers: agricultural, 97–113; black, 172, 173; blue collar, 174, 176; contingent, 116–33; control of labor process by, 23–24, 29; clerical, 124; craft, 22–26; creative, 64, 65, 69, 70, 74; decline in standard of living of, 174, 175, 180; exploitation of, 155, 173, 174, 179, 180; farmworkers, 121–22; female, 155; guest, 122; international solidarity of, 152, 156, 157, 162, 163, 164, 165, 166, 167; part-time, 117, 123, 125–26, 129, 173; repression of, 143–46; service, 123; skilled, 22–26; temporary, 116–33; textile, 173; Third World, 156; traditions of, 24, 29, 32; training of, 27, 30; unskilled, 29–32, 36; white collar, 174, 176; women, 71–74, 78–93, 146–47, 172–73
Work group teams, 99–100, 108
Working class: capacity, 4, 6; class consciousness of, 179, 180; exploitation of, 155, 166, 173, 174, 179, 180; impact of economic crisis on, 174; repression of, 162; struggles, 179; unity, 152, 153,

155–57, 162, 164, 165. *See also* Labor
Work power, 78, 80, 81, 82, 92; definition of, 83–84; and gender, 78–96
Work site toxins, 107, 112–13
World economy, 153, 157, 159
World Federation of Trade Unions (WFTU), 165
Wright, Erik Olin, 8, 83, 84

About the Editor and Contributors

MARINA A. ADLER is Assistant Professor of Sociology at the University of Maryland, Baltimore County. She received her Ph.D. from the University of Maryland, College Park in 1990. She has published articles in *The Sociological Quarterly*, *Mid-American Review of Sociology*, *Teaching Sociology*, and other journals. A member of Sociologists for Women in Society (SWS), her areas of specialization include social stratification, inequality, race relations, and women's studies.

BERCH BERBEROGLU is Professor of Sociology at the University of Nevada, Reno. He received his Ph.D. from the University of Oregon in 1977. Dr. Berberoglu is the author of six books, including *The Internationalization of Capital*, *Political Sociology*, *The Legacy of Empire: Economic Decline and Class Polarization in the United States*, and *The Political Economy of Development*. He has also published several edited volumes and numerous articles in *Development and Change*, *Nature, Society, and Thought*, *Humanity and Society*, and other scholarly journals throughout the world. His areas of specialization include political economy, class analysis, international development, industrial sociology, and labor studies.

CYRUS BINA is an economist and a Research Associate at the Center for Middle Eastern Studies, Harvard University. He received his Ph.D. in economics from The American University in Washington, DC in 1982. Dr. Bina is the author of *The Economics of the Oil Crisis* and is co-editor of *Labor Confronts the 1990s*. He has also published numerous articles in *Capital & Class*, *Review of Radical Political Economics*, *American Jour-*

nal of Economics and Sociology, and other journals. A member of the editorial board of the *Journal of Economic Democracy*, his areas of specialization include international political economy, crisis theory, and labor studies.

CHUCK DAVIS is a member of the Graduate Faculty of the Labor Education Service, Industrial Relations Center, University of Minnesota. He received his Ph.D. in economics from The American University in Washington, DC in 1986. Dr. Davis is co-editor of *Labor Confronts the 1990s,* and has published numerous articles in the *Labor Studies Journal*, *Atlantic Economic Journal*, and other scholarly publications. Currently Vice-President of the University and College Labor Education Association, his areas of specialization include political economy and labor studies.

JULIA D. FOX teaches sociology at the University of Oregon. She is a candidate for the Ph.D. in sociology at the University of Oregon, and is writing a doctoral dissertation on the corporate power structures of South Korea, Japan, and the United States. Her areas of specialization include political sociology, class analysis, and comparative political economy.

DAVID GARTMAN is Associate Professor of Sociology at the University of South Alabama. He received his Ph.D. from the University of California, San Diego in 1980. Dr. Gartman is the author of *Auto Slavery: The Labor Process in the American Automobile Industry*. He has also published articles in *Theory and Society*, *Critical Sociology*, and *Case Studies on the Labor Process*. His areas of specialization include social theory, industrial sociology, and labor studies.

WALDA KATZ-FISHMAN is Associate Professor and Director of Graduate Studies in Sociology at Howard University in Washington, DC. She received her Ph.D. from Wayne State University in Detroit in 1978. A past president of the Association for Humanist Sociology, Dr. Katz-Fishman is co-editor of *Readings in Humanist Sociology*. She has also published numerous articles in *Humanity and Society*, *Critical Sociology*, *Social Research,* and other journals. Her areas of specialization include sociological theory and race, class, and gender inequality.

JOHN C. LEGGETT is Professor of Sociology at Rutgers University. He received his Ph.D. from the University of Michigan in 1962. Dr. Leggett is the author of a number of books, including *Class, Race, and Labor,*

Race, Class, and Political Consciousness, and *Mining the Fields: Farm Workers Fight Back*. He is also a co-editor of *The American Working Class* and has published many articles in scholarly journals, such as the *American Sociological Review*, *Social Forces*, *American Journal of Sociology*, and *Humanity and Society*. His areas of specialization include political sociology, social stratification, race and ethnic relations, and labor studies.

JERRY LEMBCKE is Assistant Professor of Sociology at Holy Cross College in Worcester, Massachusetts. He received his Ph.D. from the University of Oregon in 1978. Dr. Lembcke is the author of several books, including *One Union in Wood: A Political History of the International Woodworkers of America*, *Capitalist Development and Class Capacities: Marxist Theory and Union Organization* (Greenwood Press, 1988) and *Race, Class and Urban Change*. He has also published articles in numerous journals, including *Critical Sociology*. His areas of specialization include industrial sociology, labor studies, class analysis, and urban sociology.

NAVID MOHSENI is Assistant Professor of Sociology at Hamline University in St. Paul, Minnesota. He received his Ph.D. from the University of Kentucky in 1990. Dr. Mohseni is the author of a forthcoming book, *The Creative Process and Monopoly Capitalism*. His areas of specialization include political economy, social theory, and the sociology of science.

ROBERT E. PARKER is Assistant Professor of Sociology at the University of Nevada, Las Vegas. He received his Ph.D. from the University of Texas at Austin in 1986. Dr. Parker is the co-author of *Building American Cities*. He has also published numerous articles in *Research in the Sociology of Work*, *Urban Affairs Annual*, and *Research in Politics and Society*. His areas of specialization include the sociology of work, urban sociology, and race and ethnic relations.

HARLAND PRECHEL is Assistant Professor of Sociology at Texas A & M University. He received his Ph.D. from the University of Kansas in 1986. Dr. Prechel has published numerous articles in *Sociological Quarterly*, *American Sociological Review*, *Political Power and Social Theory*, and other journals. His areas of specialization include political sociology, complex organizations, and industrial sociology.

JEROME SCOTT is Director of Project South at the Institute for Community Research and Education in Atlanta, Georgia. A labor and community organizer, he was also a founding member of the League of Revolutionary

Black Workers in Detroit in the late 1960s. He has contributed articles to *Race, Class, and Urban Social Change*, *Humanity and Society*, and other publications. Currently he is affiliated with Fund for Southern Communities, Southern Rainbow Education Project, and other organizations in the South.